An Experiential Introduction to Principles of Programming Languages

An Experiential Introduction to Principles of Programming Languages: For Java Programmers

Hridesh Rajan

The MIT Press
Cambridge, Massachusetts
London, England

The MIT Press would like to thank the anonymous peer reviewers who provided comments on drafts of this book. The generous work of academic experts is essential for establishing the authority and quality of our publications. We acknowledge with gratitude the contributions of these otherwise uncredited readers.

This book was set in Times New Roman by Westchester Publishing Services. Printed and bound in the United States of America.

Library of Congress Cataloging-in-Publication Data

Names: Rajan, Hridesh, author.
Title: An experiential introduction to principles of programming languages : for Java
    programmers / Hridesh Rajan.
Description: First edition. | Cambridge, Massachusetts : The MIT Press, [2022] | Includes
    bibliographical references and index.
Identifiers: LCCN 2021037263 | ISBN 9780262045452 (hardcover)
Subjects: LCSH: Java (Computer program language)—Programmed instruction. |
    Computer programming—Programmed instruction.
Classification: LCC QA76.73.J38 R347 2022 | DDC 005.13/3—dc23/eng/20211130
LC record available at https://lccn.loc.gov/2021037263

10   9   8   7   6   5   4   3   2   1

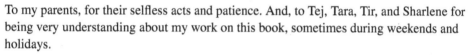

To my parents, for their selfless acts and patience. And, to Tej, Tara, Tir, and Sharlene for being very understanding about my work on this book, sometimes during weekends and holidays.
— Hridesh Rajan

For the things we have to learn before we can do them, we learn by doing them.
—Aristotle, *The Nicomachean Ethics*

I hear and I forget. I see and I remember. I do and I understand.
—Confucius

Contents

List of Figures   xiii
List of Tables   xvii
Preface   xix
Road Map   xxiii

I   **PRELIMINARIES**   1

1   **Introduction**   3
1.1   Kinds of Programming Languages   3
1.2   Our Goals   5
1.3   Parts of a Programming Language   6
1.4   Mathematical Concepts and Notations   7
1.5   Java: A Brief Review   8

2   **Inductive Sets and Functions**   15
2.1   Definitions of Inductive Sets   15
2.2   Examples: Inductive Sets   17
2.3   Functions over Inductive Sets   19
2.4   Functions over Inductively Specified Lists   23
2.5   Recipe for Recursion   23

II   **BUILDING A PROGRAMMING LANGUAGE**   33

3   **Getting Started**   35
3.1   Arithlang: An Arithmetic Language   35
3.2   Legal Programs   38
3.3   Syntax Derivation   40
3.4   Two Possibilities for Implementation   44
3.5   Reading Programs   45
3.6   Storing Programs   48
3.7   Analyzing Programs   52
3.8   Legal Values   59
3.9   Evaluating Programs to Values   60
3.10   Read-Eval-Print Loop   65

4   Varlang: A Language with Variables   71
    4.1   Variables as Means of Abstraction   71
    4.2   Variable Definition and Usage   72
    4.3   Variable Scoping   75
    4.4   Reading Let and Var Expressions   79
    4.5   AST Nodes for Let and Var   81
    4.6   Lexically Scoped Variable Definitions   82
    4.7   Environment Abstraction   85
    4.8   Environment-Passing Interpreters   87
    4.9   Value of a Var Expression   90
    4.10 Value of a Let Expression   90

5   Definelang: A Language with Global Variables   95
    5.1   Local versus Global Definitions   95
    5.2   Define, Define   97
    5.3   Semantics and Interpretation of Programs with Define Declarations   98

6   Funclang: A Language with Functions   105
    6.1   Function as Abstraction   105
    6.2   Function Definitions and Calls   106
    6.3   Functions for Pairs and Lists   108
    6.4   Higher-Order Functions   115
    6.5   Functional Data Structures   121
    6.6   Currying   123
    6.7   Syntax of Lambda and Call Expressions   125
    6.8   Value of a Lambda Expression   126
    6.9   Value of a Call Expression   128
    6.10 Call-by-Name Evaluation   134
    6.11 Semantics of Conditional Expressions   138
    6.12 Semantics of Pairs and Lists   140

III   REFERENCES AND CONCURRENCY   145

7   Reflang: A Language with References   147
    7.1   Heap and References   147
    7.2   Memory-Related Operations in Reflang   151
    7.3   Parsing Reference-Related Expressions   152
    7.4   RefVal: A New Kind of Value   153
    7.5   Heap Abstraction   154
    7.6   Semantics of Reflang Expressions   154
    7.7   Realizing Heap   157
    7.8   Evaluator with References   159
    7.9   Problems with Manual Memory Management   160

8   Forklang: A Language with Concurrency and Parallelism   169
    8.1   Explicit versus Implicit Concurrency   170

8.2   Explicit Concurrency Features   170
8.3   Semantic Variations of Fork   171
8.4   Semantic Variations of Lock Expressions   172
8.5   New Expressions for Concurrency   173
8.6   Semantics of a Fork Expression   174
8.7   Semantics of a Lock-Related Expression   175
8.8   Data Races in Forklang Programs   177
8.9   Deadlocks in Forklang Programs   178

IV   TYPES AND SPECIFICATIONS   185

9   Typelang: A Language with Types   187
9.1   Why Types?   187
9.2   Kinds of Specifications   188
9.3   Types   190
9.4   Adding Type Annotations   190
9.5   Checking Types   193
9.6   Typechecking Rules for Constants   194
9.7   Typechecking Rules for Atomic Expressions   194
9.8   Typechecking Rules for Compound Expressions   195
9.9   Types for Variables   196
9.10   Types for Functions and Calls   200
9.11   Types for Reference Expressions   206

10   Speclang: A Language with Specifications   209
10.1   Motivation   209
10.2   Language Features for Specifications   210
10.3   Example Specifications for List Functions   213
10.4   Syntax of New Features for Writing Specifications   216
10.5   Checking Specifications: Static versus Dynamic   217
10.6   Typechecking Specifications   219
10.7   Side-Effect Freedom   219
10.8   Runtime Specification Checking   223

V   ADVANCED FEATURES   229

11   Msglang: A Language with Message-Passing Concurrency   231
11.1   Examples   232
11.2   New Expressions   238
11.3   ProcessVal: A New Kind of Value   239
11.4   Receiving a Message   241
11.5   Semantics of Msglang Expressions   243

12   Eventlang: A Language with Events   251
12.1   Event-Driven Programming   251
12.2   Syntax of New Features for Event-Driven Programming   255

12.3 Semantics of Events and Event Creation   256
12.4 Semantics of Subjects and Event Announcements   258
12.5 Semantics of Handlers and the When Expression   259

Appendix   ANTLR: A Brief Review   265

Bibliography   269
Index   271

List of Figures

0.1 A road map and alternative paths through this textbook   xxiv

1.1 A Java class `Apple` and its class declaration   9

1.2 A Java class `Fruit` and its class declaration   9

1.3 A Java class `Apple` inheriting from the Java class `Fruit`   10

1.4 A Java class `Apple` inheriting from the Java class `Fruit` and initializing `edible`   10

1.5 A Java class `Wahoo` inheriting from the Java class `Fruit` and initializing `edible`   10

1.6 A Java class `Orange` inheriting from the Java class `Fruit` and initializing `edible`   11

1.7 An abstract Java class `Fruit` with abstract behavior `isSweet`   11

1.8 Java classes `Apple` and `Orange` inheriting from the Java class `Fruit` and providing concrete behaviors for the `isSweet` abstract method   12

1.9 Java classes `Person` and `Boy` inheriting from the Java class `Person`   12

1.10 Java class `FruitProgram` that is the client of all the declared classes so far   13

1.11 A Java interface `Food`   13

1.12 A Java class `Fruit` implementing the Java interface `Food`   14

1.13 A more general implementation of the class `Person` using interface `Food`   14

2.1 The inductive set `digit`   16

2.2 The inductive set `boolean`   16

2.3 The inductive set `natural`   17

2.4 The inductive set `list of natural numbers`   18

2.5 Examples of inductive set `list of natural numbers`, defined using two rules   18

2.6 The inductive set `tree of natural numbers`   19

2.7 A simple mechanical tally counter   20

2.8 The `nextdigit` function   21

2.9 The `evendigit` function   21

2.10 The predecessor function   22

2.11 The `even` function   22

2.12 The `null` function   23

2.13 The `cdr` function   23

2.14 A recipe for recursion   24

2.15 Outline of the length function   25

2.16 Outline of the `listequal` function   26

2.17 Outline of the `equal` function   28

3.1 A simple calculator   36

3.2 Some Arithlang programs and their results   36

3.3 Grammar for the Arithlang language   39

3.4 A leftmost syntax derivation of the program "(+ 0 0 0)"   42

3.5 A leftmost syntax derivation of the program "(+ 1 2)"   43

3.6 A rightmost syntax derivation of the program "(+ 1 2)"   43

3.7 A parse tree for the Arithlang program "(+ 3 4)"   46

3.8 An abstract syntax tree for the Arithlang program "(+ 3 4)"   47

3.9 An entity relationship (ER) diagram for the Arithlang grammar in figure A.1   49

3.10 A UML diagram for the AST hierarchy designed to store Arithlang programs as defined by the grammar in figure A.1   50

3.11 Concrete implementation of `ASTNode`, `Program`, `Exp`, and `NumExp` in Java   51

3.12 Concrete implementation of `CompoundArithExp` and `AddExp`   52

3.13 The `Visitor` interface   54

3.14 A code formatter: An example of `visitor`   54

3.15 A sequence diagram showing the control flow of the `prog.accept(f)` call   55

3.16 A sequence diagram showing the control flow of the `prog.accept(f)` call   58

3.17 The set of legal values for the Arithlang language   59

3.18 Values in Arithlang   60

4.1 Grammar for the Varlang language   80

4.2 A leftmost syntax derivation for the program `(let ((x 1)) x)`   81

4.3 A UML diagram for the AST hierarchy designed to store Varlang programs as defined by the grammar in figure 4.1   82

4.4 New AST nodes for the Varlang language   83

4.5 The `visitor` interface for the Varlang language   83

4.6 Illustrating substitution-based semantics of the `let` expression   84

4.7 Illustrating substitution-based semantics of the `let` expression   84

4.8 Illustrating environment for the Varlang language   85

4.9 Environment data type for the Varlang language 85

4.10 Empty environment for the Varlang language 86

4.11 Extended environment for the Varlang language 86

4.12 Evaluating a program to value in the Varlang language 88

5.1 Grammar for the Definelang language 97

5.2 The set of legal values for the Definelang language 100

6.1 Grammar for the Funclang Language 125

6.2 New AST nodes for the Funclang language 126

6.3 The set of legal values for the Funclang language 127

6.4 FunVal: A new kind of value for functions 127

6.5 The set of legal values for the Funclang language with new dynamic error values 129

6.6 Extended grammar for the Funclang language 138

6.7 The set of legal values for the Funclang language with new **Boolean value** 139

6.8 Extended grammar for the Funclang language 141

6.9 The set of legal values for the Funclang language with new **pair and null values** 142

7.1 Grammar for the Reflang language 153

7.2 The heap abstraction in the Reflang language 154

7.3 An implementation of the heap abstraction in Reflang 158

7.4 An implementation of the `RefVal` abstraction 159

7.5 Evaluator with reference expressions 160

7.6 Evaluator with reference expressions 161

8.1 New expressions for explicit concurrency 173

9.1 Grammar for the Typelang language 191

9.2 Basic types in Typelang 191

9.3 Syntax of the `let` expression in Typelang 199

9.4 Syntax of the lambda expression in Typelang 201

9.5 Syntax of the `ref` expression in Typelang 206

10.1 Grammar for the Speclang language 217

11.1 Grammar for the Msglang language 238

11.2 Implementation of `ProcessVal` in the Msglang language 240

11.3 The `sendhelper` method within `ProcessVal` in the Msglang language 242

11.4 The run procedure of `ProcessVal` in the Msglang language 243

11.5 Semantics of `ProcessExp` in the Msglang language 243

11.6 Semantics of `SendExp` in the Msglang language 244

11.7 Semantics of `ReceiveExp` in the Msglang language   245

11.8 Semantics of `SelfExp` in the Msglang language   246

11.9 Semantics of `StopExp` in the Msglang language   247

12.1 Grammar for the Eventlang language   256

A.1 Grammar for the Arithlang language (without actions)   266

List of Tables

3.1   Some Arithlang programs and their infix forms   36

4.1   Some Varlang programs and their results   72

Preface

Perhaps the most important goal of computer science is the study and application of computers to the representation of processes, both natural and artificial, as computational processes so that we can improve upon them for the betterment of society. Programming languages play a crucial role in reaching this goal. A suitable programming language can enable and aid the representation of computational processes, their efficiency, and their correctness. The selected programming language can also have a significant impact on the productivity of developers.

The goal of this book is to help you understand the key principles of programming languages—ideas that form the core of most programming languages used in practice. Our intention is to focus on principles instead of on a specific programming language. Programming languages come and go, but these key principles are long lasting.

Styles of Learning Programming Languages

There are two styles for learning the principles of computer programming languages: survey-based and experiential.

- In a *survey-based learning style*, students typically

  - read about a set of programming languages,
  - compare and contrast these languages, and
  - study their variations, strengths, and weaknesses by analysis.

- In an *experiential learning style*, students would

  - implement a set of programming language features,
  - write programs using this programming language implementation, and
  - study their variations, strengths, and weaknesses by experience.

This book follows the experiential learning style. The four differences between the approach taken by this book and other experiential approaches for teaching principles of programming languages are using Java as a first, defining language, covering emerging trends in programming languages, discussing semantic variations and trade-offs, and listing the minimal prerequisites.

Choice of the Defining Language

In an experiential learning style, each concept discussed in the book is implemented in a prototype interpreter that is gradually developed. An *interpreter* is a computer program that consumes another computer program and produces its values. The programming language used to implement the interpreter is called the *defining language*, and the programming language that is being implemented is called the *defined language*.

This book uses the programming language Java as the defining language; that is, all the interpreters in this book are written in Java. Students using this book build several defined languages over the course of the chapters, starting with a functional, core language.

The choice of defining language is intentional, to enable students to focus most of their efforts on realizing the concepts and to take advantage of the prevalence of Java as an introductory programming language in computing curricula.

The choice of the defined language is also intentional, to enable students to become familiar with functional programming concepts, an extremely important tool for modern multiparadigm programmers, along with other concepts such as reactive programming and logic programming.

Other Differences

We cover a broader spectrum of emerging trends in programming languages (e.g., concurrency, Big Data, and reactive programming) than what has been done in similarly themed material in the past. While students are certainly exposed to some of these topics in other courses, our belief is that discussing them in programming languages courses and textbooks can further reinforce and emphasize language-specific issues that frequently arise.

We also discuss semantic variations and trade-offs, as appropriate. These variations are also prototyped in our interpreter. Our motivation behind discussing these variations is to allow readers to see the trade-offs that are typically made in programming-language design and implementation.

We assume that readers will have very little background in this area, which allows this book to be used in courses with fewer prerequisites.

This book can be used in both undergraduate and graduate courses. Since we assume very little background, it can be used in a course taught as early as the junior year in an undergraduate curriculum.

This book is organized as follows. In the formative chapters, we develop the basic concepts of languages, including means of computation using primitive values, means of combination such as variable definition and functions, and means of abstraction such as functions and recursive functions. We then look at imperative features such as references, concurrency features such as fork, and reactive features such as event handling. Next, we explore language features that cover important and often different perspectives of thinking about computation, such as that in logic programming and flow-based programming. The first six chapters should be read in sequence. Afterward, a course can adopt one or more later chapters as they are developed in a fairly independent manner.

Comments can be sent to the author at his e-mail, hridesh@iastate.edu. We welcome any feedback that you may have on this material.

Book code: A language implementation for each chapter is available as part of the book code. We invite you to try out examples and look over concrete implementation as you read through the material.

Contributors

Samantha Khairunnessa
Department of Computer Science
Iowa State University
Ames, IA, USA

Wei Le
Department of Computer Science

Iowa State University
Ames, IA, USA

Jia Tao
Department of Computer Science
Lafayette College
Easton, PA, USA

Road Map

This book requires students to have adequate programming background in the Java programming language. Typically, this would mean having taken at least two full-semester courses on introduction to computer programming and data structures using Java. A good understanding of object-oriented classes, inheritance, polymorphism, and static classes is assumed. A short primer is provided in chapter 1, but that is not meant to replace prior background; rather, it is just a refresher on the key ideas.

There are three possible pathways through this book, as shown in figure 0.1. For a short (half-semester) course at the undergraduate level or a short lower-level graduate course, it would suffice to cover chapters 1 through 6. These chapters have tight forward dependencies and may not be used out of order. This will provide students with a good introduction to a typical front end of a programming language compiler or tool. An introduction to concrete syntax trees and abstract syntax trees (ASTs), visitor design patterns, and traversing abstract trees will prepare students for an upper-level course on a topic such as program verification or program analysis. The coverage of variables in chapters 4 and 5 will prepare students for concepts such as symbol tables, def-use analysis, and other more advanced concepts. Finally, the introduction to functional programming concepts in chapter 6 will provide students with another tool in their programming methodology toolbox.

For a full-semester course, chapters 1 through 10 could be covered, and chapters 11 and 12 could be assigned for additional reading for students interested in exploring these topics further. Those students who may be interested in exploring parallelism and concurrency-related topics could benefit from the preparation in chapters 11 and 12.

For programming language courses that are focusing on implementation aspects of programming languages, chapters 9 and 10 might be skipped.

For courses focusing on programming language design and program verification issues, chapters 9 and 10 could be covered instead of implementation. Chapter 9 presents an introduction to type-based program verification concepts, and chapter 10 delves deeper into richer properties that could be expressed as specifications. Chapter 9 has some minor dependencies on chapter 7, especially basic understanding of program expressions for memory allocation, free, and others. These concepts could be explained by drawing comparisons with similar notions in the Java programming language. Alternatively, one can also include chapter 7 in this pathway, which will ensure sufficient coverage of dependencies.

In computer science or similarly named computing programs that incorporate software engineering courses, coverage of chapters 9 and 10 is recommended, as students will relate

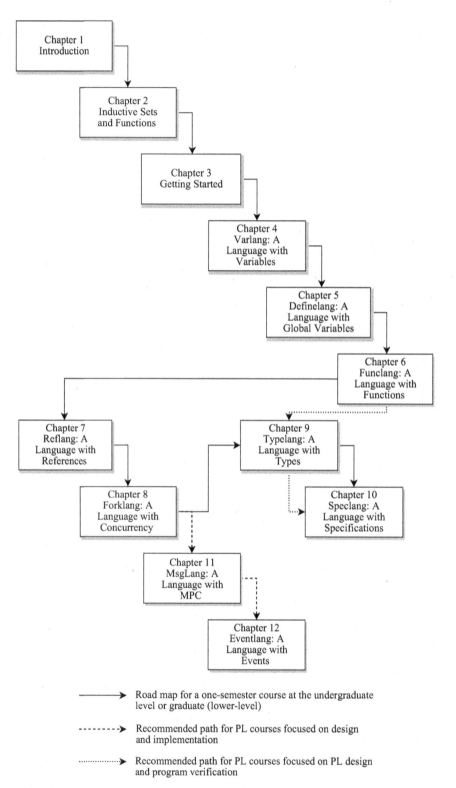

Figure 0.1
A road map and alternative paths through this textbook

well to other software engineering courses, such as those on requirements engineering, software design, or software testing. It may also be helpful to draw attention to concepts such as object-oriented design patterns that are typically covered in courses on software design, object-oriented design, or similarly named courses. In addition, the material in this book could be used as a concrete case study to explain the visitor pattern that is typically covered in object-oriented software design courses.

I PRELIMINARIES

1 Introduction

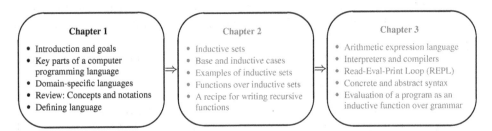

Chapter 1	Chapter 2	Chapter 3
• Introduction and goals • Key parts of a computer programming language • Domain-specific languages • Review: Concepts and notations • Defining language	• Inductive sets • Base and inductive cases • Examples of inductive sets • Functions over inductive sets • A recipe for writing recursive functions	• Arithmetic expression language • Interpreters and compilers • Read-Eval-Print Loop (REPL) • Concrete and abstract syntax • Evaluation of a program as an inductive function over grammar

This book provides an introduction to key concepts in design, semantics, and implementation of computer programming languages, here onward referred to as "programming languages" or just "languages" (if that use does not cause any ambiguity). It has three goals. The first is to significantly improve your programming skills by reviewing a variety of programming patterns and by providing a deeper understanding of common (and rare) programming language features. The second is to prepare you to design your own programming language. The last is to prepare you to select an appropriate programming language for software development tasks out of hundreds of programming languages available today.

The material discussed in this book can be best learned via active participation. Each chapter is associated with a working implementation of a small programming language, and readers are encouraged to obtain the code corresponding to the chapters and follow along. Just reading the book or reading the code separately may not be as fruitful.

1.1 Kinds of Programming Languages

There are two kinds of computer programming languages: general-purpose and domain-specific.

The goal of a domain-specific programming language is to provide specialized support for concepts in the target application area (domain). These concepts could be data types, relations, operations, or other elements. For example, the Dot language for Graphviz, a software for graph visualization,[1] offers support for nodes and edges that are basic graph concepts. Similarly, the Hypertext Markup Language (HTML), a domain-specific

---

1. Graphviz is a software for graph visualization. More information available at http://www.graphviz.org/doc/info/lang.html.

language for representing web pages, gives support for markup-related concepts.[2] A related domain-specific language, Cascading Style Sheets (CSS),[3] has specialized features for describing the format and layout of web pages. Structured Query Language (SQL), a domain-specific language for querying databases, has support for data-related features such as query and join. Julia[4] is a domain-specific language for numerical computing.

The goal of a general-purpose computer programming language is to be able to express all computations. Languages such as C,[5] Fortran,[6] LISP, Ada, Scheme, C++, Java, C#, Haskell,[7] Scala,[8] Swift,[9] Clojure,[10] Lua,[11] and Objective-C,[12] are examples of general-purpose languages, and so are Smalltalk,[13] Perl,[14] Python,[15] Ruby,[16] JavaScript,[17] Dart,[18] Go,[19] and Rust.[20]

In general, domain-specific languages (because they are specifically designed for the task) are an excellent choice when representing computational problems in their target

2. Hypertext Markup Language (HTML) is an example of domain-specific language. See http://www.w3 .org/html/.

3. Cascading Style Sheets (CSS) is a domain-specific language for describing the presentation aspects of a document. See http://www.w3.org/Style/CSS/.

4. Julia is a domain-specific programming language for numerical computing. See https://julialang.org/.

5. C, designed by Dennis Ritchie around 1973, is a general-purpose programming language designed for providing high-level abstractions, as well as low-level access to memory operations. See https://www.iso.org/standard /standard/74528.html.

6. Fortran is a general-purpose programming language primarily used for scientific computing. See https://fortran -lang.org.

7. Haskell (https://www.haskell.org/) is a general-purpose programming language that is best known for being statically typed and purely functional. It also provides type inference and lazy evaluation.

8. Scala (https://www.scala-lang.org) is a multiparadigm general-purpose programming language that combines functional and object-oriented features.

9. Swift is a general-purpose programming language developed by Apple in collaboration with others primarily for programming Apple devices. See https://developer.apple.com/swift/.

10. Clojure is a variant of the LISP programming language. It provides LISP-like features on the Java platform. See https://clojure.org.

11. Lua is a cross-platform programming language that is primarily designed for writing applications that are embedded inside software written in other languages. See https://www.lua.org.

12. Objective-C is an extension of the C programming language that adds message-passing features to the language. See https://developer.apple.com/library/archive/documentation/Cocoa/Conceptual/Programming WithObjectiveC/Introduction/Introduction.html.

13. Smalltalk is a general-purpose programming language and one of the first object-oriented languages. See https://smalltalk.org/.

14. Perl is a general-purpose scripting language that was originally designed to make report processing easier. See https://www.perl.org.

15. Python is a general-purpose programming language that emphasizes code readability; it is also one of the few languages that uses indentation for semantic purposes. See https://www.python.org.

16. Ruby is a general-purpose, object-oriented scripting language. It is a multiparadigm language combining object-oriented and functional features, while providing dynamic typing and garbage collection. See https://www .ruby-lang.org.

17. JavaScript is a general-purpose language originally designed for World Wide Web applications. It supports event-driven, functional, and imperative programming paradigms. JavaScript is defined by the ECMAScript Language Specification, available at https://tc39.es/ecma262/.

18. Dart is a general-purpose programming language designed by Google primarily for developing web and mobile applications. See https://www.dartlang.org.

19. Go is a general-purpose programming language designed by Google primarily for writing concurrent applications. See https://golang.org.

20. Rust is a general-purpose programming languages designed primarily to balance performance and safety for concurrent applications. See https://www.rust-lang.org/.

application area, but computational problems in other domains could be harder or at least awkward to represent using such languages. Also, implementations of domain-specific languages are able to exploit deeper semantic properties of the domain when performing program optimization. On the other hand, while a general-purpose language can theoretically represent all computational problems, the representation might not be as elegant or succinct as a domain-specific language. There is often also a larger software development cost because the developer has to build up the scaffolding for the domain before getting to representing the actual problem.

1.2 Our Goals

In this book, we will study fundamental building blocks that form the basis of both domain-specific and general-purpose languages. Our goal will be to prepare you to design, implement, analyze, and understand both kinds of languages.

Now, it is true that many readers will not go on to design their own general-purpose programming language, but knowing about the principles of programming language design, semantics, and implementation is important for several reasons, described next.

1.2.1 Language Learning

As you can perhaps imagine from the list of programming languages given here, new computer programming languages are continuously introduced to address new needs. In fact, several new computer programming languages have been introduced in the last decade. For example, Apple introduced the Swift programming language, a general-purpose language, for programming its devices. Google has introduced two new programming languages, Go and Dart. Go is a general-purpose programming language for distributed message-passing applications, and Dart is a general-purpose programming language aimed at building web applications. Dart programs are compiled to JavaScript, another general-purpose programming language. The usage of Clojure and Scala is on the rise as well, and TypeScript and F# are coming out of Microsoft.

It is common for computing professionals to learn several programming languages during their careers. So, knowing about the principles of languages and core ideas will enable the reader to more easily pick up a new language and be productive. Readers will be able to determine the concepts that transfer over and those that are unique to the new language (and focus on mastering those new concepts).

1.2.2 Productive Programming

Perhaps related to the first point, knowing about computer programming languages, perhaps more deeply than others who do not have similar training, gives you the necessary skills to be a more productive programmer. The benefits and the limits of the language are clearer.

Knowing about programming language features and their trade-offs will also help readers select the appropriate computer programming language for the software development task at hand.

1.2.3 Designing in DSL and API

The most important benefit may come from the usefulness of these skills toward a future domain-specific language (DSL) design and implementation that the reader might undertake. We believe that each reader will design a DSL in their lifetime to enhance their own productivity, as well as of fellow workers in their organization. The knowledge of language design and implementation will greatly aid such DSL design and implementation efforts.

The design of programming languages, data types, and application programming interfaces (APIs) are related. Therefore, skills acquired while studying principles of programming languages will benefit readers during these other activities.

1.3 Parts of a Programming Language

According to Sussman and Abelson (1979), programming language features can be broadly classified into three categories: means of computation, means of combination, and means of abstraction. An effective language should provide each of these.

1.3.1 Means of Computation

These programming language features enable basic computation (e.g., addition, subtraction, multiplication, division, string concat). In a nutshell, these features are atomic, indivisible instructions defined by the language in question.

1.3.2 Means of Combination

These programming language `features` enable us to take two or more computations and combine them to form a larger piece of computation. Such a combination may introduce an order—for instance, instruction A happens before instruction B—or it may introduce a deterministic or nondeterministic choice, among other things. An example of means of combination is a sequence often written as ";" in C, C++, and Java-like languages. A sequence combines computation to the left and the right into one larger computation. Another example is the conditional expression often written as "x > 0 ? y : z." A conditional combines three expressions; based on the result of the first expression, either the first or the second expression is evaluated.

1.3.3 Means of Abstraction

These programming language `features` enable us to create a proxy, a name that can then be used to refer to a complex piece of computation. An example of means of abstraction is a function in mathematics, such as $f(x) = x^2$, which gives us a name, f, that we can then use to refer to the computation that happens inside the function body. This function abstraction is also adopted in most computer programming languages.

In the next few chapters, we will gradually build a general-purpose programming language. We will begin this work by discussing some means of computation, supporting a number of them in our language. We will then gradually add means of combination and abstraction to arrive at a complete core by the end of chapter 5. This core can then be used to build your own domain-specific programming language or to enrich it with more expressive extensions. At each step, we provide a number of problems that we hope will be helpful in solidifying your understanding of the material.

Exercises

1.3.1. Write down the names of programming languages that you have used or heard about. Try to identify key design goals for each of these languages.

1.3.2. Identify an application domain that is of interest to you. Search and list one or more domain-specific programming languages that are designed to make software development for that domain easier.

1.3.3. In section 1.1, a comparative analysis of domain-specific programming language and general-purpose programming language is presented. Think of, and write down, an additional argument in favor of adopting a domain-specific programming language and one in favor of adopting a general-purpose programming language.

1.3.4. For your favorite programming language, identify means of computation, means of combination, and means of abstraction.

1.3.5. For a recently released programming language, make a list of all the features that the language makes available. Then, categorize these features into means of computation, means of combination, and means of abstraction.

1.4 Mathematical Concepts and Notations

Now, we introduce some concepts and notations that we will use throughout this book. Readers familiar with these concepts may also want to skim through this section to refresh their memory and to make a note of notational differences, if any.

1.4.1 Functions
We will write functions as follows, where f is the name of the function, D is the *domain* of the function, and R is the *range* of the function:

$$f \; : \; D \; \text{->} \; R$$

1.4.2 Sets and Operations on Sets
We will use explicit enumeration to define a set. For instance, $\{a, b\}$ defines a set containing two elements, a and b.

We may also use comprehension to define a set. For instance, $\{a \mid a \in B\}$ defines a set that contains all elements a that are also in the set B.

The notation $a \in B$ will be used to mean that a is a member of (or an element of) B.

We will use the notation $\emptyset$ to refer to the set containing no elements.

We will use the notation $A \subseteq B$ to mean that A is a subset of B.

We will use the notation $A \setminus B$ to denote the difference of set A and B, meaning a set that has elements from A that are not in B.

1.4.3 Logical Rules

In describing the intended semantics of programming languages, we will often need to make statements like "B is true when A is true." We will state this relation as follows:

$$\text{RELATION BIFA}$$
$$\frac{A}{B}$$

In the relation here, A is called the *premise* and B is called the *conclusion* of the rule. Similarly, the relation "C is true when both A and B are true" is stated as follows:

$$\text{RELATION CIFAANDB}$$
$$\frac{A \quad B}{C}$$

We take the conjunction of the conditions above the line.

A relation "A is unconditionally true" is stated as follows:

$$\text{RELATION AUNCONDITIONALLY}$$
$$A$$

1.5 Java: A Brief Review

The rest of this book assumes that you have a familiarity with the Java programming language. If you haven't programmed in Java before, we encourage you to refer to several excellent textbooks and tutorial materials on this programming language. Next, we provide a short review of the programming language. Readers familiar with Java may also want to skim this section to refresh their memory about the object-oriented terminology.

Java is an object-oriented programming language: that is, basic elements of a Java program are called "objects." For example, a program may have objects such as an apple, a second apple, an orange, a boy, a girl, or a bicycle. An object can have certain properties. Apples and oranges could have weight, color, or other characteristics. Boys and girls could have properties such as age, name, and height. An object may also be capable of performing certain operations. For example, boys and girls may be able to eat an apple or ride a bicycle. There could be several objects in a program that are similar in nature, in that they have the same set of properties, but they are not the same. For example, two apple objects could both have weight and color as properties, but with different values, such as "0.15 lb" and "0.17 lb" and "red" and "green." An object-oriented programmer uses a "class" as a template for objects that have the same set of properties. For example, one would write a class `Apple` in Java, as shown in figure 1.1.

The form in figure 1.1 is called a *class declaration*. The act of writing the code for a class is referred to as *declaring a class*. In the class declaration in the figure, notice two statements about `weight` and `edible`. The statements at lines 2 and 3 says that

```
1  class Apple {
2    double weight;
3    boolean edible = true;
4    boolean isEdible() {
5      return edible;
6    }
7  }
```

Figure 1.1
A Java class `Apple` and its class declaration

all "Apple" objects will have a property "weight" and a property "edible." These two statements are called *field declarations*. The two forms of field declarations are shown at lines 2 and 3. Both start by declaring that this field's legal values will be limited to those that can be taken by a `double` and a `boolean`. A `boolean` can only take two legal values: `true` and `false`. So, by stating `boolean edible`, this field declaration says that this field `edible` must be either true or false. The rest of the field declaration at line 3 gives an initial value to the field; it says that each apple will start with the field (property) `edible` as true. A class declaration can also include a *method declaration*, which represents actions that can be performed on an object of that class. For example, in the class declaration for `Apple` at lines 4–6, there is a method declaration `isEdible`. A method declaration has several parts: return value (what the operation produces when it is done), name (what is it called), and arguments (what it consumes). The declaration of the method `isEdible` says that it produces a value that is limited by a `boolean`, its name is "isEdible," and it does not consume anything (denoted by "()"). We will soon see examples of method declaration that consume values as well.

Given the class declaration of `Apple`, we can create apple objects. The following example creates two objects `apple1` and `apple2`:

```
1  Apple apple1 = new Apple();
2  Apple apple2 = new Apple();
```

To allow programmers to reuse code, object-oriented languages also allows a class to inherit all the functionalities from some other class. For example, we could choose to write a more general class `Fruit`, as shown in figure 1.2.

```
1  class Fruit {
2    double weight;
3    boolean edible;
4    boolean isEdible() {
5      return edible;
6    }
7  }
```

Figure 1.2
A Java class `Fruit` and its class declaration

Notice that this class doesn't give an initial value to the field `edible` so that it can support both edible and inedible fruits.

Then, the `Apple` class can inherit all the functionalities from the `Fruit` class, as shown in figure 1.3.

```
1  class Apple extends Fruit {
2  }
```

Figure 1.3
A Java class `Apple` inheriting from the Java class `Fruit`

This version of the `Apple` class also has two fields, `weight` and `edible`, and the method `isEdible`—even though it doesn't explicitly declare them—because it inherits those properties from the `Fruit` class. In object-oriented terminology, `Apple` is called a *subclass*, and `Fruit` a *superclass*. A class in Java can have exactly one superclass.

This definition of `Apple` is not sufficient, though: it doesn't define apples to be edible. We can fix that by defining a *constructor*, which gives an initial value to the edible field, as shown in figure 1.4.

```
1  class Apple extends Fruit {
2    Apple () {
3      edible = true;
4    }
5  }
```

Figure 1.4
A Java class `Apple` inheriting from the Java class `Fruit` and initializing `edible`

A constructor is a special kind of operation. It runs exactly once, when objects are being created. In Java, constructors are operations that do not produce any value. In this case, the constructor for `Apple` changes the field `edible` so that apples are considered edible.

The listing in figure 1.5 defines another class to represent objects of `Wahoo`, which are not edible.

```
1  class Wahoo extends Fruit {
2    Wahoo () {
3      edible = false;
4    }
5  }
```

Figure 1.5
A Java class `Wahoo` inheriting from the Java class `Fruit` and initializing `edible`

We can also create an `Orange` class as a template for creating all oranges in our program as shown in figure 1.6. This class can also inherit `weight` and `edible` fields from its parent class, `Fruit`.

```
1  class Orange extends Fruit {
2    boolean peeled = false;
3    Orange () {
4      edible = true;
5    }
6  }
```

Figure 1.6
A Java class `Orange` inheriting from the Java class `Fruit` and initializing `edible`

The `Orange` class, declared in the listing in figure 1.6, also declares a new field `peeled`, in addition to all the fields that it inherited from the class `Fruit`. It also provides a constructor.

A superclass such as `Fruit` need not declare all the functionalities. It may just leave the precise meaning of some operations undefined. Such a class is referred to as an *abstract superclass*. For example, figure 1.7 redefines the class `Fruit`; at line 1, the keyword `abstract` says this class is not fully defined.

```
1  abstract class Fruit {
2    double weight;
3    boolean edible;
4    boolean isEdible() {
5      return edible;
6    }
7    abstract boolean isSweet();
8  }
```

Figure 1.7
An abstract Java class `Fruit` with abstract behavior `isSweet`

In the class declaration at line 7, the method declaration `isSweet` is not fully defined. A subclass will provide an adequate definition of this method. The new definition of the class `Apple` in figure 1.8 now provides a method declaration at lines 2–4 that provides a concrete definition of the method `isSweet`.

The class `Orange` in figure 1.8 also provides a concrete definition of the method `isSweet`, which is different from `Apple`'s definition.

We can similarly create a `Person` class and a `Boy` class and have `Boy` inherit all the functionality from the `Person` class, as shown in figure 1.9.

The declaration of the `Person` class has a method declaration for an operation `willYouEat`. This method produces a value that is limited by values that `boolean` can take, and it consumes a value `f`, which is a `Fruit`. By default, a person always eats fruit.

The subclass `Boy` inherits the functionality from the superclass `Person`, but it also has the method declaration `willYouEat` at lines 9–14. Notice that this method declaration has the same name and same arguments (`Fruit f`) as the corresponding method in the superclass. Such methods are said to *override* corresponding methods in the superclass. The statements at lines 10–13 define the logic of this *overriding method*. They say that,

```
1   class Apple extends Fruit {
2     Apple () {
3       edible = true;
4     }
5     boolean isSweet() {
6       return true;
7     }
8   }
9   class Orange extends Fruit {
10    boolean peeled = false;
11    Orange () {
12      edible = true;
13    }
14    boolean isSweet() {
15      return false;
16    }
17  }
```

Figure 1.8
Java classes `Apple` and `Orange` inheriting from the Java class `Fruit` and providing concrete behaviors for the `isSweet` abstract method

```
1   class Person {
2     int age;
3     String name;
4     boolean willYouEat (Fruit f) {
5       return true;
6     }
7   }
8   class Boy extends Person {
9     boolean willYouEat (Fruit f) {
10      if (f.isEdible ())
11        return true;
12      else
13        return false;
14    }
15  }
```

Figure 1.9
Java classes `Person` and `Boy` inheriting from the Java class `Person`

unlike a person who unconditionally eats a fruit, a boy will eat a fruit only if it is edible. The statement at line 10, `f.isEdible()`, is called a *method call*. It should be thought of as asking object f to complete operation `isEdible` and provide the result of that operation. A method call is the primary mean of requesting an object to perform an operation. In a method call, the object that is being requested is referred to as the *receiver* object.

When a method (e.g., `willYouEat`) is called, the body of some method declaration (e.g., line 5 in class `Person` or lines 10–13 in class `Boy`) runs. The process of determining which method declaration runs is called *dispatch*. In the Java language, the most specific method declaration is run. To illustrate all this, consider a new class `FruitProgram`, shown in figure 1.10, which combines all the classes that we have discussed so far.

```
1  class FruitProgram {
2    static void main (String[] args) {
3      Person p = new Boy();
4      Fruit  f = new Apple();
5      p.willYouEat(f);
6    }
7  }
```

Figure 1.10
Java class `FruitProgram` that is the client of all the declared classes so far

In Java, by convention, a full program must have a class that provides a method with the signature matching line 2 in the code in the figure. When you run this Java program, it runs the statement at line 3 that creates a `Boy` object p and an `Apple` object f and then calls the method `willYouEat` on the receiver object p at line 5. This will cause the method declaration `willYouEat` in the class `Boy` to run (see previous page), which in turn will cause the method declaration `isEdible` in the class `Apple` to run.

Object-oriented languages often distinguish between "what" an object does and "how" it does it. This allows "how" to be changed, provided that the object continues to do the same kinds of things. The programming language feature *interfaces* allows a Java programmer to express "what." This example shown in figure 1.11 defines an interface `Food`.

```
1  interface Food {
2    boolean isEdible ();
3  }
```

Figure 1.11
A Java interface `Food`

An interface defines what it means for the object to be "Food": it must provide the operation `isEdible`. We can rewrite the class `Fruit` as shown in figure 1.12.

The change at line 1 now says that a fruit is a kind of `Food`. It allows the class `Person` to become more general, as shown in figure 1.13.

At lines 4 and 9, the two method declarations now declare `Food` as an argument, which means that we can apply them to objects of other kinds than `Fruit` (provided that those objects are of the kind `Food`).

```
1  abstract class Fruit  implements Food {
2    double weight;
3    boolean edible;
4    boolean isEdible() {
5      return edible;
6    }
7    abstract boolean isSweet();
8  }
```

Figure 1.12
A Java class Fruit implementing the Java interface Food

```
1   class Person {
2     int  age;
3     String  name;
4     boolean willYouEat (Food f) {
5       return true;
6     }
7   }
8   class Boy extends Person {
9     boolean willYouEat (Food f) {
10      if  (f.isEdible ())
11        return true;
12      else
13        return false;
14    }
15  }
```

Figure 1.13
A more general implementation of the class Person using interface Food

Summary

Object-oriented programs in Java are a collection of objects. The properties of an object are defined by its class declarations. A class declaration can define properties as field declarations, operations as method declarations, and initializing operations as constructor declarations. A class can inherit functionality from a superclass, which allows code to be reused. The functionality of a program can be divided into "what" (interfaces) and "how" (class declarations). This division makes programs more extensible.

2 Inductive Sets and Functions

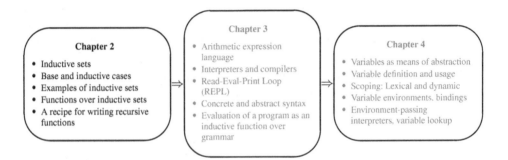

inductive (adjective): characterized by the inference of general laws from particular instances

Before we start discussing programming languages, their design, and their implementation, it would be useful to understand the notion of inductive sets. Inductive sets are a particular kind of set that, as the definition suggests, are characterized by a set of rules that define them. This is unlike a regular set, which can be defined by explicitly enumerating all elements and do not necessarily have to follow any rules. Inductive sets are very handy when we need to define a possibly infinite set using a finite set of rules. You could imagine that there is an infinite number of programs that are defined by a finite set of rules of the programming language, an infinite number of types that are defined by a finite set of rules for defining types, an infinite number of classes that are defined by a finite set of rules for defining classes, and so on. The idea of inductive sets is prevalent in the study of programming languages.

2.1 Definitions of Inductive Sets

An *inductive set* is a set that is characterized by defining the rules for the set of base elements that belong to the set (*base case*), zero or more inductive rules that define memberships of new elements in terms of existing elements (*inductive case*), and a *closure rule*, which specifies that the inductive set doesn't contain any other elements besides those defined by the base case and the inductive case.

The simplest examples of inductive sets are those that just have base elements. For example, Boolean is an inductive set defined by two rules for base elements: true is a member of the set Boolean, and false is a member of the set Boolean. An English alphabet is an inductive set defined by 26 rules for base elements: *a* is a member of the English alphabet, *b* is a member of the English alphabet, . . . , ending with *z* is a member of the English alphabet. We will start writing these inductive sets more precisely, but for the moment, let us just focus on the concept. Similarly, `digit` is an inductive set defined by 10 rules for base elements: 0 is a member of the set `digit`, 1 is a member of the set `digit`, 2 is a member of the set `digit`, 3 is a member of the set `digit`, 4 is a member of the set `digit`, 5 is a member of the set `digit`, 6 is a member of the set `digit`, 7 is a member of the set `digit`, 8 is a member of the set `digit`, and 9 is a member of the set `digit`. Similarly, `hexadecimal digit` is an inductive set defined by 16 rules for base elements: 0–9 are members of the set `hexadecimal digit`, A is a member of the set `hexadecimal digit`, B is a member of the set `hexadecimal digit`, C is a member of the set `hexadecimal digit`, D is a member of the set `hexadecimal digit`, E is a member of the set `hexadecimal digit`, and F is a member of the set `hexadecimal digit`.

We can write the definition of inductive sets more systematically. For instance, see figure 2.1 for a more precise definition of the set `digit`.

```
digit  ::=                                              Digit
               0                                         Zero
             | 1                                          One
             | 2                                          Two
             | 3                                        Three
             | 4                                         Four
             | 5                                         Five
             | 6                                          Six
             | 7                                        Seven
             | 8                                        Eight
             | 9                                         Nine
```

Figure 2.1
The inductive set `digit`

The definition in figure 2.1 defines the set `digit` and elaborates 10 possible members of that set. In later chapters, we will see much shorter definitions. The form a ::= b can be read as that b is a kind of a. Similarly, the form a ::= b | c can be read as both b and c being kinds of a. The definition in figure 2.1 effectively says digit ::= 0 | 1 | 2 | 3 | 4 | 5 | 6 | 7 | 8 | 9. In other words, 0, 1, 2, 3, 4, 5, 6, 7, 8, and 9 are kinds of digit. In section 1.4, we learned about set notation. In that alternative notation, this would be written as digit = {0, 1, 2, 3, 4, 5, 6, 7, 8, 9}. Both notations are equivalent.

Figure 2.2 defines the inductive set `Boolean`.

The inductive sets that just have base elements are incredibly useful, and we have seen several useful examples of such sets already in this chapter. Another kind of inductive set is

```
bool  ::=                                              Boolean
               true                                       True
             | false                                     False
```

Figure 2.2
The inductive set `Boolean`

one that is defined by some rules for base elements and some rules for inductive elements. In the next section, we will look at several examples of inductive sets.

2.2 Examples: Inductive Sets

2.2.1 Natural Numbers

As another example, consider the set of natural numbers, `natural`. Recall that the natural numbers are 0, and all are positive integers. For inductive sets such as the English alphabet, digit, hexadecimal digit, and Boolean, we can write all the members for the sets. We cannot do that for the set of natural numbers. Inductive rules help us solve this problem by allowing us to define a set using a combination of rules for base elements and inductive elements. We define a small number of rules for describing all base elements in the set, and then define a small number of inductive rules to come up with new elements using existing elements in the set.

The set of natural numbers is defined by two rules, shown in figure 2.3. The first rule is for base elements, and it says that 0 is a natural number. The second inductive rule says that if *n* is a member of `natural`, then the successor of *n* is a member of `natural`. Using just these two rules, the entire set of natural numbers could be defined.

`natural` ::=		*Natural Numbers*
	0	*Zero*
	| succ n **where n is a** natural	*Successor*

Figure 2.3
The inductive set `natural`

Unlike previous definitions of sets such as the English alphabet, Boolean, and digit, where the definition of the inductive set describes membership of the respective sets, the rules for defining the set of natural numbers give a *membership test* to check whether a particular element is a member of that set. For instance, to check whether 2 is a member of the set `natural`, we can argue that 0 is a member of `natural`, and so the successor of 0 that is 1 is a member of `natural`, and so the successor of 1 that is 2 is a member of `natural`. The following table shows the inductive representation of several natural numbers:

Inductive representation	Arabic representation
0	0
succ 0	1
succ succ 0	2
succ succ succ 0	3
succ succ succ succ 0	4
succ succ succ succ succ 0	5
succ succ succ succ succ succ 0	6
succ succ succ succ succ succ succ 0	7
succ succ succ succ succ succ succ succ 0	8
succ succ succ succ succ succ succ succ succ 0	9
succ succ succ succ succ succ succ succ succ succ 0	10

This representation is also often called *unary notation* because it is possible to encode it using a (possibly empty) sequence of single bits.

Unlike previous definitions of sets such as the English alphabet, Boolean, and digit, where the definition of the inductive set describes membership of the respective sets, the rules for defining the set of natural numbers give a check whether a particular element is a member of that set. For instance, to check whether 2 is a member of the set `natural`, we can argue that 0 is a member of `natural`, and the successor of 0 that is 1 is also a member of `natural`, and the successor of 1 that is 2 is also a member of `natural`.

2.2.2 Lists

As another example, consider the set of lists. A *list* is a sequence of elements. For the sake of simplicity, let us first consider the list of natural numbers. Similar to natural numbers, we cannot write out all the members of this set. Inductive rules once again help us solve this problem. We can define a small number of two rules for describing all possible elements in the set, as shown in figure 2.4. The first rule describes the single base element in the set, and the second rule provides a strategy for constructing new elements using existing elements in the set.

```
list-of-naturals  ::=                                    List of Naturals
                       ()                                          Empty
                  | n . lon                                         Cons
                  where n is a natural, lon a
                  list-of-naturals
```

Figure 2.4
The inductive set `list of natural numbers`, defined using two rules

In the first rule, we are using the notation `()` to denote an empty list. This rule says that an empty list is a kind of list, or an empty list is a list.

The second rule says that appending a natural number in front of an existing list of natural numbers also gives us a list of natural numbers. In the second rule, the notation `.` represents an append operation. See figure 2.5 for several examples of `list of natural numbers`.

An empty list	`()`
A list containing 5	`5.()`
A list containing 4 and 5	`4.5.()`
A list containing 3, 4, and 5	`3.4.5.()`
A list containing 2, 3, 4, and 5	`2.3.4.5.()`
A list containing 1, 2, 3, 4, and 5	`1.2.3.4.5.()`
A list containing 0, 1, 2, 3, 4, and 5	`0.1.2.3.4.5.()`

Figure 2.5
Examples of the inductive set `list of natural numbers`, defined using two rules

Each example in the figure is built using the previous example, a strategy that we will use frequently when working with inductive sets.

Similar to the definition of the inductive set `natural`, whose inductive rules provide a check whether a particular element is a member of that set. For instance, to check whether 2 is a member of the set `natural`, we can argue that 0 is a member of `natural`, and so the successor of 0 that is 1 is a member of `natural`, and the successor of 1 that is 2 is also a member of `natural`.

2.2.3 Binary Trees

As another example, consider the set of `binary tree of natural numbers`. Similar to lists, we cannot write all elements of this set, but we can define it as an inductive set with just two rules, as discussed next.

```
tree  ::=                                  Tree of Natural Numbers
        leaf natural                              Leaf
        | root natural tree tree                  Tree
```

Figure 2.6
The inductive set `tree of natural numbers`, defined using two rules

The first rule says that a tree can be just a natural number, often referred to as the *leaf node* of a tree. The second rule says that a more complex tree can be formed by combining three elements: a natural number (the *root node*) and two trees. Due to their positions, the first tree is often referred to as the *left subtree* and the second tree is referred to as the *right subtree*. In other words, a leaf node is a tree, and a combination of a root node, left subtree, and right subtree is a tree.

Some example trees are presented here:

- A tree with just leaf node 6   leaf 6
- A tree with just leaf node 5   leaf 5
- A tree containing 4 at the root node   root 4 leaf 5 leaf 6
- A tree with just leaf node 2   leaf 2
- A tree with just leaf node 3   leaf 3
- A tree containing 1 at the root node   root 1 leaf 2 leaf 3
- A tree containing 0 at the root node   root 0 root 1 leaf 2 leaf 3 root 4 leaf 5 leaf 6

The first two trees are just leaf nodes containing the natural numbers 6 and 5, respectively. The third tree is formed by combining the first two trees with the natural number 4 at the root of the tree. The fourth and the fifth trees are also just leaf nodes containing the natural numbers 2 and 3, respectively. The first tree, like the third tree, is formed by combining the fourth and the fifth tree with the natural number 1 at the root of the tree. The seventh tree has the sixth tree as its left subtree, the third tree as its right subtree, and 0 at the root of the tree.

2.3 Functions over Inductive Sets

We will now study some mathematical functions over inductive sets. Recall from chapter 1 the notation for writing the signature of a function:

$$f : D \rightarrow R$$

Here, f is the name of the function, D is the *domain* of the function (the set of input), and R is the *range* of the function (the set of output).

Let us define some functions over the inductive type `boolean`, starting with negation. The signature of this function is as follows:

$$neg \ : \ bool \ -> \ bool$$

The definition of negation is as expected. This function should produce `false` if the input is `true` and produce `true` if the input is `false`:

$$neg(b) = \begin{cases} false & \text{if } b = true \\ true & \text{if } b = false \end{cases}$$

To review the function notation, `false` is the output of the function and if $b = true$ is the condition under which that output is produced. Similarly, `true` is the output of the function and if $b = false$ is the condition under which that output is produced. If the conditions on the right do not completely cover all cases of the input, then a default output of the function ought to be specified. Here, the input b can be either `true` or `false`. Therefore, it is not necessary to specify the default output.

We can similarly write functions over the inductive set `digit`. Let us begin with a simple function, `nextdigit`, from the set `digit`. The signature of this function would be the following:

$$nextdigit \ : \ digit \ -> \ digit$$

We would like this function to behave like a wheel in a tally counter like the one shown in figure 2.7. A single wheel in the tally counter rotates from 0 to 9 and then back to 0.

The *piecewise function*, shown in figure 2.8 defines `nextdigit` by defining the output of the function for each rule in the definition of the inductive set `digit` in figure 2.1. The cases for 0–8 say that the output of the function is the next digit 1–9, respectively.

Figure 2.7
A simple mechanical tally counter
Image courtesy of Wikimedia Commons

$$nextdigit(d) = \begin{cases} 1 & \text{if } d = 0 \\ 2 & \text{if } d = 1 \\ 3 & \text{if } d = 2 \\ 4 & \text{if } d = 3 \\ 5 & \text{if } d = 4 \\ 6 & \text{if } d = 5 \\ 7 & \text{if } d = 6 \\ 8 & \text{if } d = 7 \\ 9 & \text{if } d = 8 \\ 0 & \text{if } n = 9 \end{cases}$$

Figure 2.8
An inductive function `nextdigit` modeling one number wheel of the tally counter

The case for 9 is interesting, and it says that the output of the function is the digit 0. This models the behavior of the number wheel that rotates back to 0 after 9.

$$evendigit(d) = \begin{cases} true & \text{if } d = 0 \\ false & \text{if } d = 1 \\ true & \text{if } d = 2 \\ false & \text{if } d = 3 \\ true & \text{if } d = 4 \\ false & \text{if } d = 5 \\ true & \text{if } d = 6 \\ false & \text{if } d = 7 \\ true & \text{if } d = 8 \\ false & \text{if } n = 9 \end{cases}$$

Figure 2.9
An inductive function `evendigit`

How do we check if we have defined `nextdigit` properly (i.e., correctly for each possible digit)? All we have to do is to check each inductive rule for `digit`. The function definition must handle each rule properly. Checking off each rule in the definition of the input (here, `digit`) and defining the function's output constitute a great way to ensure that the function defines output for each possibility of input. In fact, we will see a recipe for writing inductive functions in more detail in the next section, which builds on this intuition.

Let us define another function, `evendigit`, from one inductive set to another. This function is meant to produce `true` if the input is an even digit, and `false` otherwise. The signature of this function would be the following:

```
evendigit : digit -> bool
```

The definition of this function presented in figure 2.9 is as expected. The function produces the Boolean value *true* if the input digit is even (0, 2, 4, 6, 8) and false otherwise. Once again, we can check to see if evendigit is so defined by checking to see if it is so defined for each case of the inductive input type digit.

How should we define functions over inputs that are defined by one or more base elements and one or more inductive rules? Quite similarly. The function definition would define how to handle each kind of input. To illustrate this point, consider a function that, given a natural number, produces the previous natural number. The signature of this function would be as follows, and its definition is shown in figure 2.10:

```
predecessor : natural -> natural
```

$$predecessor(n) = \begin{cases} 0 & \text{if } n = 0 \\ n' & \text{if } n = succ\ n' \end{cases}$$

Figure 2.10
An inductive function predecessor that produces the previous natural number

The function states that if the input natural number n is 0, then the predecessor is 0. Otherwise, if the input natural number n is of the shape succ n', then the predecessor is n'. The statement if $n = succ\ n'$ can also be read as: Let n' be some natural number, such that n is the successor of that natural number. Clearly, since n is the successor of n', it must be formed using the second rule in figure 2.3.

Consider another function that, given a natural number, tells us whether it is an even natural number. The signature of this function would be the following:

```
even : natural -> bool
```

The definition of this function is shown in figure 2.11:

$$even(n) = \begin{cases} true & \text{if } n = 0 \\ b & \text{if } n = succ\ n',\ b' = even(n'),\ and\ b = neg(b') \end{cases}$$

Figure 2.11
An inductive function even that tests whether a natural number is even.

Like the predecessor function, the even function is defined for both inductive rules of natural numbers. The first case is immediate because 0 is an even number. The second case is when the natural number is nonzero (i.e., $n = succ\ n'$ for some n'). The definition says that if n' is even, then n is not even and if n' is not even, then n is even.

2.4   Functions over Inductively Specified Lists

Let us study some functions over lists that are written similarly. For instance, let us write a function to test whether a list is empty. The signature of this function is as follows, and its definition is given in figure 2.12:

$$\texttt{null : list-of-naturals -> bool}$$

$$null(l) = \begin{cases} true & \text{if } l = () \\ false & \text{if } l = n \textbf{ . } l' \end{cases}$$

Figure 2.12
An inductive function `null` that tests whether a list is empty.

Like previous inductive functions, this function is defined for both inductive rules for the list. The definition for the first case is immediate; if the list is an empty list, then the function returns true. The definition for the second case is also intuitive; if the list is any natural number followed concatenated with another list (the second inductive rule), then regardless of what the second list is, it follows that the list l is not empty.

A function that removes the first element of a list is only slightly more complicated:

$$\texttt{cdr : list-of-naturals -> list-of-naturals}$$

The function `cdr` shown in figure 2.13 defines removing the first element from an empty list to produce another empty list. The second case states that if the input list is formed by concatenating n with another list l', then removing the first element produces the list l'.

$$cdr(l) = \begin{cases} () & \text{if } l = () \\ l' & \text{if } l = n \textbf{ . } l' \end{cases}$$

Figure 2.13
An inductive function `cdr` that removes the first element from a list

2.5   Recipe for Recursion

So far, we have been writing simple functions over inductive sets. In more interesting functions, it is often useful to create *recursive function* definitions (i.e., using the function being defined within the definition of the same function). In general, **recursion** means defining a solution in terms of itself. It was developed by Giuseppe Peano in mathematics. Stephen Cole Kleene, Alonzo Church, Kurt Gödel, Alan Turing, and others introduced and further developed the concept in computer science. A recursive function is a very effective strategy for writing functions that operate over inductive sets. We saw an example of such a function, `even`, before. In this section, we will understand a systematic process of writing such recursive functions.

Writing recursive functions is often considered a hard conceptual task, but it doesn't need to be. The majority of the conceptual hurdle involves coming up with the output of the more complex cases from simpler cases. The intent of the recipe that we are about to learn is to alleviate this conceptual hurdle by decomposing it into smaller conceptual tasks. Experts in writing recursive functions apply this process implicitly in their heads. With some practice, the reader can expect to do the same, but for the purpose of this chapter, it would help to follow the process systematically to get some practice.

The recipe is shown in figure 2.14. It has four major steps: writing examples, specifying input and output inductive sets, developing an outline, and filling in the outline. Each major step builds on the result of the previous step. The purpose of writing examples is to provide us with an opportunity to understand the behavior of the function without concerning ourselves too much with how to define that behavior. The purpose of specifying the input and output inductive sets is to help us understand the structure of the function. The next step defines that outline, and the final step fills in empty places in that outline.

Recipe for Writing Recursive Functions

1. Write out examples

    i. Write out examples for the base case(s).
    ii. Write out a related, simpler example.

2. Specify the input and output inductive sets.
3. Use an outline for a function that matches the grammar for the input inductive set.
4. Fill in the outline by generalizing the examples.

    i. What's returned in the base case(s)?
    ii. How do we get the answer from

        (i) – recursive call's answer, and
        (ii) – other information?

Figure 2.14
A recipe for systematically writing recursive functions over inductive sets

To illustrate, let us define a function `length` over the inductive set list-of-naturals to find the length of the list. The first step in our recipe is to write examples. Specifically, we would like to write our examples of base cases and then write related simpler examples. Now, it is very tempting to start with a complex example that, when solved, gives us insight into the complete behavior of the function, but those examples do not provide insight into the construction of the recursive function. See the following successive set of examples:

Input	Output	Notes: Why was this example selected?
()	0	Base case
0 . ()	*succ* 0	Simple, builds immediately on the base example
0 . 0 . ()	*succ succ* 0	Builds immediately on the previous example
0 . 0 . 0 . ()	*succ succ succ* 0	Builds immediately on the previous example

Notice that in the example given here, we are only using lists containing zeros. This is because intuitively, the value of the elements contained in the list is unimportant for this function, which is just concerned about counting the number of such elements. So, we could have used an example with other natural numbers, but the additional complexity would not have played a constructive role. One of the most important guidelines for selecting examples is to ensure that each example builds on the previous one. Doing so allows us to visualize how the output of the function for a larger example would be formed using the output of the function for smaller examples. Selecting unrelated examples doesn't provide us the same benefits. In the examples in this chapter, we have intentionally formatted the input and output so it is easy to see the new part of the input and the new part of the output compared to the previous example.

The next step is to specify the input and output inductive sets of the function. We can do so by writing the signature of the function. The process of specifying the input and output inductive sets clearly references the inductive rules that we will use in the next step when creating an outline for the function:

```
length : list-of-naturals -> natural
```

The next step is to create an outline of the function. The outline of a function that takes one argument of an inductive type can be created by writing out a case for each inductive rule in the definition of the inductive type. Here, the function `length` accepts a single argument of type `list-of-naturals`. Therefore, we can write two cases for each inductive rule in the definition of the type `list-of-naturals` as shown in figure 2.15.

$$length(l) = \begin{cases} \underline{\hspace{3cm}} & \text{if } l = () \\ \underline{\hspace{3cm}} & \text{if } l = n \ . \ l' \end{cases}$$

Figure 2.15
The outline of an inductive function length that computes the length of a list. The outline is derived from the inductive rules in the definition of the set list-of-naturals.

The next step is to fill in the outline by generalizing the examples. What is returned in the base case? From the first example, we have that the length of () is 0. We can immediately fill in the blank for the base case, creating a refined outline:

$$length(l) = \begin{cases} \underline{\hspace{1.5cm} 0 \hspace{1.5cm}} & \text{if } l = () \\ \underline{\hspace{3cm}} & \text{if } l = n \ . \ l' \end{cases}$$

How do we get the answer from the recursive call answer and other information? From the second, third, and fourth examples, we have that the answer of the larger case is built by finding the successor of the answer for the previous case. To find the answer for the previous case, we can use the recursive call *length(l')*, where *l'* was the tail of the list. The successor of a natural number *n* is *succ n*. By combining these two pieces of information, we can obtain the answer for the inductive case and fill in the remaining blank:

$$length(l) = \begin{cases} \underline{\hspace{1.5cm} 0 \hspace{1.5cm}} & \text{if } l = () \\ \underline{succ \ length(n')} & \text{if } l = n \ . \ l' \end{cases}$$

This completes the outline of `length`, giving us its complete definition. At each step, we successively refined the outline produced by the previous step, leading to the full solution.

2.5.1 Multiple Inputs and Recipe for Recursion

For the next example, let us define a function, `listequal`, to compare two lists to find out if they have equal length. Since this problem is similar to another function, `equal`, to compare two natural numbers to find out if they are equal, let us tackle both together. The first step, according to our recipe, is to write examples. Specifically, we would like to write our examples of base cases and then write related simpler examples. Again, it is very tempting to start with a complex example that, when solved, gives us insight into the complete behavior of the function, but note that those examples do not provide insight into the construction of the recursive function.

Here are some examples of the `listequal` function:

Input 1	Input 2	Output	Notes
()	()	true	Base
()	0 . ()	false	Base case of the inputs
0 . ()	()	false	Base case of the inputs
0 . ()	0 . ()	true	Builds directly on the previous example
0 . 0 . ()	0 . ()	true	Builds directly on the previous example

The next step is to specify the input and output inductive sets of the function. We can do so by writing the signature of the function. The process of specifying the input and output inductive sets clearly references the inductive rules that we will use in the next step, when creating an outline for the function:

```
listequal : list-of-naturals -> list-of-naturals -> bool
```

The next step is to create an outline of the function. The outline of a function that takes two arguments, each of which is inductively defined, can be created by writing a case for each combination of inductive rules in the definition of the inductive types. Here, the function `listequal` accepts two arguments of type `list-of-naturals`. Therefore, we can write four cases for each combination of inductive rules in the definition of the type `list-of-naturals` as shown in figure 2.16.

$$listequal(l1, l2) = \begin{cases} \underline{\hspace{3cm}} & \text{if } l1 = (), \ l2 = () \\ \underline{\hspace{3cm}} & \text{if } l1 = (), \ l2' = n \ . \ l2' \\ \underline{\hspace{3cm}} & \text{if } l1 = n \ . \ l1', \ l2 = () \\ \underline{\hspace{3cm}} & \text{if } l1 = n \ . \ l1', \ l2' = n \ . \ l2' \end{cases}$$

Figure 2.16
The outline of an inductive function `listequal`, which compares two lists to determine if their lists are equal. The outline is derived from the inductive rules in the definition of the set list-of-naturals.

The next step is to fill in the outline by generalizing the examples. What is returned in the base case? From the first example, we have that two empty lists are equal. We can immediately fill in the blank for the base cases, creating a refined outline. From the first example, we get the definition for the first case:

$$
listequal(l1, l2) = \begin{cases} \underline{\quad\quad true \quad\quad} & \text{if } l1=(),\ l2=() \\ \underline{\quad\quad\quad\quad\quad\quad} & \text{if } l1=(),\ l2'=n\ .\ l2' \\ \underline{\quad\quad\quad\quad\quad\quad} & \text{if } l1=n\ .\ l1',\ l2=() \\ \underline{\quad\quad\quad\quad\quad\quad} & \text{if } l1=n\ .\ l1',\ l2'=n\ .\ l2' \end{cases}
$$

From the second example, we get the definition for the second case:

$$
listequal(l1, l2) = \begin{cases} \underline{\quad\quad true \quad\quad} & \text{if } l1=(),\ l2=() \\ \underline{\quad\quad false \quad\quad} & \text{if } l1=(),\ l2'=n\ .\ l2' \\ \underline{\quad\quad\quad\quad\quad\quad} & \text{if } l1=n\ .\ l1',\ l2=() \\ \underline{\quad\quad\quad\quad\quad\quad} & \text{if } l1=n\ .\ l1',\ l2'=n\ .\ l2' \end{cases}
$$

From the third example, we get the definition for the third case:

$$
listequal(l1, l2) = \begin{cases} \underline{\quad\quad true \quad\quad} & \text{if } l1=(),\ l2=() \\ \underline{\quad\quad false \quad\quad} & \text{if } l1=(),\ l2'=n\ .\ l2' \\ \underline{\quad\quad false \quad\quad} & \text{if } l1=n\ .\ l1',\ l2=() \\ \underline{\quad\quad\quad\quad\quad\quad} & \text{if } l1=n\ .\ l1',\ l2'=n\ .\ l2' \end{cases}
$$

How do we get the answer from the recursive call answer and other information? From the third and fourth examples, we have that the answer for the larger case is built by finding the tails for both $l1$ and $l2$, and then finding if their lengths are equal. If the lengths of the tail lists are equal, then the lengths of $l1$ and $l2$ are equal. Consider our fourth example; the tails of two lists are empty lists. Since the function `listequal` returns `true` for empty lists (by our first example), the function `listequal` would return `true` for two lists, $0\ .\ ()$ and $0\ .\ ()$. Next, consider our fifth example; the tails of two lists are $0\ .\ ()$ and $()$. The `listequal` function returns `false` for these two lists (by the third example). So, the `listequal` function would also return `false` for these two lists, $0\ .\ 0\ .\ ()$ and $0\ .\ ()$. By combining these two pieces of information, we can obtain the answer for the inductive case and fill in the remaining blank in the outline of the definition of the function `listequal`:

$$
listequal(l1, l2) = \begin{cases} \underline{\quad\quad true \quad\quad} & \text{if } l1=(),\ l2=() \\ \underline{\quad\quad false \quad\quad} & \text{if } l1=(),\ l2'=n\ .\ l2' \\ \underline{\quad\quad false \quad\quad} & \text{if } l1=n\ .\ l1',\ l2=() \\ \underline{listequal(l1', l2')} & \text{if } l1=n\ .\ l1',\ l2'=n\ .\ l2' \end{cases}
$$

2.5.2   Recursive Comparison Functions over Natural Numbers

Let us similarly define a function that compares two naturals to find out if the two natural numbers are equal. Here are some examples of the `equal` function:

Input 1	Input 2	Output	Notes
0	0	`true`	Base case for inputs
0	*succ* 0	`false`	Base case for inputs
succ 0	0	`false`	Base case for inputs
succ 0	*succ* 0	`true`	Builds on the first example for base
succ succ 0	*succ* 0	`false`	Builds on the third example for base
succ 0	*succ succ* 0	`false`	Builds on the second example for base

Next, we have the outline of the function as shown in figure 2.17.

$$
equal(n1, n2) = \begin{cases}
\underline{\hspace{4cm}} & \text{if } n1 = 0,\ n2 = 0 \\
\underline{\hspace{4cm}} & \text{if } n1 = 0,\ n2 = succ\ n2' \\
\underline{\hspace{4cm}} & \text{if } n1 = succ\ n1',\ n2 = 0 \\
\underline{\hspace{4cm}} & \text{if } n1 = succ\ n1',\ n2' = succ\ n2'
\end{cases}
$$

Figure 2.17
The outline of an inductive function `equal`, which compares two natural numbers to determine if they are equal. The outline is derived from the inductive rules in the definition of the set `natural`.

From the first example, we get the definition for the first case:

$$
equal(n1, n2) = \begin{cases}
\underline{\quad true \quad} & \text{if } n1 = 0,\ n2 = 0 \\
\underline{\hspace{4cm}} & \text{if } n1 = 0,\ n2 = succ\ n2' \\
\underline{\hspace{4cm}} & \text{if } n1 = succ\ n1',\ n2 = 0 \\
\underline{\hspace{4cm}} & \text{if } n1 = succ\ n1',\ n2' = succ\ n2'
\end{cases}
$$

From the second example, we get the definition for the second case:

$$
equal(n1, n2) = \begin{cases}
\underline{\quad true \quad} & \text{if } n1 = 0,\ n2 = 0 \\
\underline{\quad false \quad} & \text{if } n1 = 0,\ n2 = succ\ n2' \\
\underline{\hspace{4cm}} & \text{if } n1 = succ\ n1',\ n2 = 0 \\
\underline{\hspace{4cm}} & \text{if } n1 = succ\ n1',\ n2' = succ\ n2'
\end{cases}
$$

From the third example, we get the definition for the third case:

$$
equal(n1, n2) = \begin{cases}
\underline{\quad true \quad} & \text{if } n1 = 0,\ n2 = 0 \\
\underline{\quad false \quad} & \text{if } n1 = 0,\ n2 = succ\ n2' \\
\underline{\quad false \quad} & \text{if } n1 = succ\ n1',\ n2 = 0 \\
\underline{\hspace{4cm}} & \text{if } n1 = succ\ n1',\ n2' = succ\ n2'
\end{cases}
$$

And, from the last two examples, we get the definition for the last case:

$$equal(n1, n2) = \begin{cases} \underline{\qquad true \qquad} & \text{if } n1 = 0, \ n2 = 0 \\ \underline{\qquad false \qquad} & \text{if } n1 = 0, \ n2 = succ\ n2' \\ \underline{\qquad false \qquad} & \text{if } n1 = succ\ n1', \ n2 = 0 \\ \underline{equal(n1', n2')} & \text{if } n1 = succ\ n1', \ n2' = succ\ n2' \end{cases}$$

As another example, let us define a function, `plus`, that adds two naturals to produce another natural number that is the sum of the two. Here are some examples of the `plus` function:

Input 1	Input 2	Output	Notes
0	0	0	Base
0	*succ* 0	*succ* 0	Base
succ 0	0	*succ* 0	Base
succ 0	*succ* 0	*succ succ* 0	Builds on the previous example
succ succ 0	*succ* 0	*succ succ succ* 0	Builds on the previous example

Next, we have the outline of the function:

$$plus(n1, n2) = \begin{cases} \underline{\qquad\qquad} & \text{if } n1 = 0, \ n2 = 0 \\ \underline{\qquad\qquad} & \text{if } n1 = 0, \ n2 = succ\ n2' \\ \underline{\qquad\qquad} & \text{if } n1 = succ\ n1', \ n2 = 0 \\ \underline{\qquad\qquad} & \text{if } n1 = succ\ n1', \ n2' = succ\ n2' \end{cases}$$

From the first example, we get the definition for the first case:

$$plus(n1, n2) = \begin{cases} \underline{\qquad 0 \qquad} & \text{if } n1 = 0, \ n2 = 0 \\ \underline{\qquad\qquad} & \text{if } n1 = 0, \ n2 = succ\ n2' \\ \underline{\qquad\qquad} & \text{if } n1 = succ\ n1', \ n2 = 0 \\ \underline{\qquad\qquad} & \text{if } n1 = succ\ n1', \ n2' = succ\ n2' \end{cases}$$

From the second example, we get the definition for the second case:

$$plus(n1, n2) = \begin{cases} \underline{\qquad 0 \qquad} & \text{if } n1 = 0, \ n2 = 0 \\ \underline{\qquad n2 \qquad} & \text{if } n1 = 0, \ n2 = succ\ n2' \\ \underline{\qquad\qquad} & \text{if } n1 = succ\ n1', \ n2 = 0 \\ \underline{\qquad\qquad} & \text{if } n1 = succ\ n1', \ n2' = succ\ n2' \end{cases}$$

From the third example, we get the definition for the third case:

$$plus(n1,n2) = \begin{cases} \underline{\hspace{4em}0\hspace{4em}} & \text{if } n1=0,\ n2=0 \\ \underline{\hspace{4em}n2\hspace{4em}} & \text{if } n1=0,\ n2=succ\ n2' \\ \underline{\hspace{4em}n1\hspace{4em}} & \text{if } n1=succ\ n1',\ n2=0 \\ \underline{\hspace{7em}} & \text{if } n1=succ\ n1',\ n2'=succ\ n2' \end{cases}$$

And, from the last two examples, we get the definition for the last case:

$$plus(n1,n2) = \begin{cases} \underline{\hspace{4em}0\hspace{4em}} & \text{if } n1=0,\ n2=0 \\ \underline{\hspace{4em}n2\hspace{4em}} & \text{if } n1=0,\ n2=succ\ n2' \\ \underline{\hspace{4em}n1\hspace{4em}} & \text{if } n1=succ\ n1',\ n2=0 \\ succ\ succ\ plus(n1',n2') & \text{if } n1=succ\ n1',\ n2'=succ\ n2' \end{cases}$$

The advantages of following the recipe for writing recursive functions are manyfold:

- It provides a systematic approach for defining recursive functions over inductive sets that can help avoid mistakes in their definition.
- By following the recipe, you can be sure that all the cases of the input have been considered because we create an outline based on the inductive rules in the definition of the input.
- The examples created are small, and the examples are systematically designed that help see the solution to the problem in terms of the smaller steps.
- Finally, since this recipe provides an almost mechanical approach for filling in the outline based on examples, the majority of the efforts can be spent focusing on the interesting cases of the recursive function.

As with any recipe, it is helpful to practice it explicitly at first, until one is sufficiently adept. At that point, the majority of the steps can be carried out implicitly. The examples are still useful because they can become useful test cases in case the recursive function is to be implemented as part of a computer program.

Summary

To summarize, in this chapter, we introduced inductive sets that are very important for describing multiple aspects of programming languages since they allow us to describe the membership of a set by giving a finite number of rules for describing its members. An inductive set is defined by specifying the base and inductive cases as well as a closure rule. We saw several examples of these inductive sets, such as natural numbers, lists, and trees. We reviewed writing functions over these inductive sets. Specifically, we noted that a recursive formulation is often more natural when writing functions over these inductive sets. We also reviewed a recipe for writing recursive functions that relies on a systematic method for identifying small examples that start from the base case and successively build upon the previous example.

Exercises

2.5.1. Write down the signature and the definition of a function called `odddigit`. There are two ways of writing it. First is by using the definition of `evendigit` and the second is by doing it directly. Practice both styles of writing that definition.

2.5.2. Write down the signature and the definition of a function called `carry`, which produces `true` if incrementing the digit will produce a carry and false otherwise.

2.5.3. A hexadecimal number notation represents the numbers 0–15. The traditional digits 0–9 are represented using standard digits. The numbers 10, 11, 12, 13, 14, and 15 are represented as using the characters $a, b, c, d, e,$ and f, respectively. Using the notations discussed in this chapter, define a new inductive set, `hexdigits`, which models hexadecimal digits. Define a variant of the functions `nextdigits` and `evendigit` for this inductive set.

2.5.4. Write the signature and the definition of a function called `greater`, which accepts two natural numbers as arguments using the recipe discussed in this chapter. For this problem and for this entire chapter, we would suggest being explicit about how you are following the recipe for writing recursive functions in your solution.

2.5.5. Write the signature and the definition of a function called `listgreater`, which accepts two list-of-naturals and produces `true` if the first list has more element compared to the second, and false otherwise. For this problem and for this entire chapter, we would suggest being explicit about how you are following the recipe for writing recursive functions in your solution.

2.5.6. Write the signature and the definition of a function called `sum-of-tree`, which accepts a tree of natural numbers as the argument and produces the sum of all the numbers in that tree. For this problem and for this entire chapter, we would suggest being explicit about how you are following the recipe for writing recursive functions in your solution.

II BUILDING A PROGRAMMING LANGUAGE

3 Getting Started

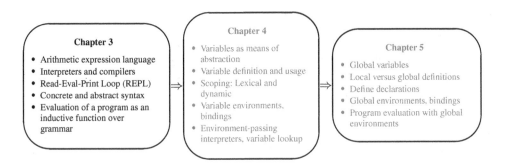

The secret of getting ahead is getting started. —*Mark Twain*

Now that we have covered the preliminaries, let us design and implement our first programming language together. In the process of designing and implementing our very own programming language, we will become familiar with some basic ideas behind the design and realization of any programming language (e.g., grammar, lexical analysis, parsing, and abstract syntax tree, etc.). We will also review some design ideas, including data abstraction, design for change, and the visitor design pattern that permeate throughout the programming language implementations discussed in this book.

3.1 Arithlang: An Arithmetic Language

We will get started by designing and implementing a simple programming language called *Arithlang*. You can think of this language as supporting all calculations that you could possibly do using a simple calculator like the one shown in figure 3.1.

The complete implementation of Arithlang is available with the book code, hosted at https://github.com/hridesh/arithlang. The reader is encouraged to download, set up, the implementation, and follow along with the descriptions and steps given in this chapter.

The primary goal of Arithlang is to write programs that can perform arithmetic. For example, a user of this programming language might write programs like the ones shown in figure 3.2.

These users can then expect such programs to produce the values 1, 2, 3, 4, and 5, respectively. Notice that the programs in Arithlang are written in a *prefix* notation instead of the *infix* notation that languages like Java use. In a prefix notation, operators such as +, −, *, and / appear before their operands. In the expression (+ 1 2), + is the operator and

Figure 3.1
A simple calculator
Image courtesy of Wikimedia Commons

An Arithlang program	Results
1	1
(+ 1 1)	2
(− (+ 2 2) 1)	3
(* (+ 1 1) (− 3 1))	4
(/ (* (− 6 1) 2) (+ 1 1))	5

Figure 3.2
Some Arithlang programs and their results

Table 3.1   Some Arithlang programs and their infix forms

An Arithlang Program	Equivalent Infix Form
1	1
(+ 1 1)	1 + 1
(− (+ 2 2) 1)	2 + 2 − 1
(* (+ 1 1) (− 3 1))	(1 + 1) * (3 − 1)
(/ (* (− 6 1) 2) (+ 1 1))	((6 − 1) * 2) / (1 + 1)

1 and 2 are operands. To be unambiguous, we delineate the start and end of an arithmetic expression with '(' and ')'. In Arithlang, the symbols +, −, *, and / represent addition, subtraction, multiplication, and division, respectively.

There are some distinct advantages to writing in a prefix notation (e.g., one can easily express operations that apply over multiple operands). For example, the arithmetic expression 2 + 4 + 6 + 5 can be written as (+ 2 4 6 5), which uses only one operator. Similarly, we can write 10 * 2 * 7 * 3 as (* 10 2 7 3), 5 − 4 − 1 as (− 5 4 1), and 6 / 3 / 2 as (/ 6 3 2). The prefix notation also helps eliminate the difficulties with operator precedence (as in infix notation). For example, in the third expression in table 3.1, we have to explicitly add parentheses to the infix form to state that (1 + 1) and (3 − 1) ought to be done prior to multiplying their results together.

In writing Arithlang programs, and for the remainder of the programming languages discussed in this book, it might be helpful to use indentation to match the open parenthesis with the closing parenthesis. An indented form of examples in table 3.1 is shown here:

Example 1

```
(+
    1
    1
)
```

Example 2

```
(-
    (+
        2
        2
    )
    1
)
```

Example 3

```
(*
    (+
        1
        1
    )
    (-
        3
        1
    )
)
```

Example 4

```
(/
    (*
        (-
            6
            1
        )
        2
    )
    (+
        1
        1
    )
)
```

The indentation is just for clarity; it has no impact on the semantics of Arithlang programs (unlike Python, where indentation begins a lexical scope). We will write the operator symbol on the same line as the open parenthesis to help clearly show the beginning and end of each operator. The operands of the same operator are indented by a tab (or four spaces). All operands of the same operator are aligned at the same indentation level.

Exercises

3.1.1. Convert the following arithmetic expressions written in infix notation to the prefix notation of Arithlang.

1. $2 + 3$
2. $2 + 3 * 4$
3. $5 * (6 + 4)$
4. $(5 - 1) / (2 * 2)$
5. $(2 + 3) * (6 - 1) / (7 - 2)$

3.1.2. Convert the following arithmetic expressions written in prefix notation to infix notation and count the increase in the number of operators.

1. $(+ 5 1 5)$
2. $(* (+ 4 3) (+ 4 0))$
3. $(/ (+ 4 3 4 9) (+ 5 1 5) 9)$

3.1.3. Write five different arithmetic expressions using the prefix notation of Arithlang, such that each expression produces the value 42. Each expression must use all four arithmetic operators: $+, -, *,$ and $/$.

3.2 Legal Programs

The objective of a valid implementation of the Arithlang programming language is to compute the value of the arithmetic expression represented by that program. Your simple calculator, if it supports prefix notation, is a valid implementation of such a programming language.

Not every text can be considered a valid program in this language. We need laws to distinguish valid programs from invalid ones. Moreover, these laws can also serve as guidance for creating new programs in this programming language. Such laws are encoded as the grammar of a programming language. We saw several grammars of inductive sets in chapter 2.

There are several possible notations for describing grammars depending on the tools used in constructing the implementation of the programming language. This book follows the Extended Backus-Naur Form (EBNF) notation. The grammar in the implementation of Arithlang follows the format used by ANTLR (www.antlr.org/), a tool for constructing language implementations. The appendix chapter reviews ANTLR syntax and usage. Going forward, we will present our grammar rules independent of the concrete ANTLR syntax. The ANTLR equivalent of the grammar in figure 3.3 is presented in figure A.1.

The simplest kind of arithmetic expression is a number. We can allow numbers to be valid programs in our programming language by defining our grammar as follows. The table header (in bold) is usually not included in a grammar description, but it is added here for clarification:

Nonterminal		Rule Body	Name of the Rule
Program	::=	Number	*Program*
Number	::=	Digit	*Number*
	|	DigitNotZero Digit$^+$	
Digit	::=	[0-9]	*Digits*
DigitNotZero	::=	[1-9]	*Nonzero Digits*

The first rule of this grammar says that a program (Program) can be a number (Number). From here on in this book, we will read x ::= y in grammars as "x can be y" or sometimes "x can be expanded to y." This is an example rule in this grammar. A rule contains two kinds of symbols: those that can be expanded (*nonterminals*), and those that can't be expanded further (*terminals*). The symbols Program and Number are nonterminals in this grammar of Arithlang.

The next rule defines legal numbers. It says that a number can be a digit (Digit) or (\|) and a nonzero digit (DigitNotZero), followed by one or more digits (represented as Digit+). Recall from chapter 2 that this is an example of specifying alternatives in grammar rules. The grammar also defines digit to be either the character '0' or '1' or '2' or '3' or '4' or '5' or '6' or '7' or '8' or '9'. The notation [0–9] means any character between '0' and '9'. Finally, this grammar defines DigitNotZero to be either the character '1' or '2' or '3' or '4' or '5' or '6' or '7' or '8' or '9'. In EBNF, a shorthand for writing all the characters from '1' to '9' is [1–9]. Here, '0' or '1' or '2' or '3' or '4' or '5' or '6' or '7' or '8' or '9' is a terminal.

According to this grammar, "0" is a valid program, and so is "1," and so on until "9." This is because '0' to '9' are valid digits, and since a number can be a digit, '0' to '9' are valid numbers; and since a program can be a number and the programs "0" to "9" does not contain any other characters besides '0' to '9', respectively, "0" to "9" are valid programs.

According to this grammar, "10" is a valid program. This is because '1' is a non zero digit, and since a number can be a non zero digit followed by one or more digits (according to the rule on the third line), and since '0' is another digit, '1' followed by '0' is a valid number. Since a program can be a number, '1' followed by '0' is a valid number, and "10" does not contain any characters other than '1' and '0', then "10" is a valid program.

> ## Terminals and Nonterminals
>
> In grammars, those symbols that can be expanded are called *nonterminals*, whereas those that are leaf nodes and cannot be expanded are called *terminals*. In our grammar for `Arithlang`, `program`, `exp`, `numexp`, `addexp`, `subexp`, `multexp`, and `divexp` are nonterminals. Special characters like '(', ')', as well as digits, are terminals.

Unlike previous valid programs, "01" is not a valid program. This is because there is no such rule in this grammar where '0' can be followed by any other digit. Similarly, "001" is also not a valid program, which we can determine by following the same reasoning process.

Numbers are nice programs, but to fulfill the objective of Arithlang implementation, the grammar must be able to support more complex programs. We can extend the grammar as shown in figure 3.3 in order to allow such programs.

Nonterminal		Rule Body	Name of the Rule
Program	::=	Exp	*Program*
Exp	::=		*Expressions*
		Number	*NumExp*
	|	(+ Exp Exp$^+$)	*AddExp*
	|	(− Exp Exp$^+$)	*SubExp*
	|	(∗ Exp Exp$^+$)	*MultExp*
	|	(/ Exp Exp$^+$)	*DivExp*
Number	::=	Digit	*Number*
	|	DigitNotZero Digit$^+$	
Digit	::=	[0-9]	*Digits*
DigitNotZero	::=	[1-9]	*Nonzero Digits*

Figure 3.3
Grammar for the Arithlang language. See figure A.1 in appendix chapter for the ANTLR form of the same grammar.

We have already seen the rules for `Number`, `Digit`, and `DigitNotZero`. The rule for `program` is now extended to allow several kinds of arithmetic expressions. This rule says that a program can be an expression (abbreviated as `Exp`). An expression can be either a number expression (`Number` for short), an addition expression (noted as the `AddExp` rule), a subtraction expression (noted as the `SubExp` rule), a multiplication expression (noted as the `MultExp` rule), or a division expression (noted as the `DivExp` rule). These are several different kinds of expressions that are now allowed in the Arithlang language.

The rule for a number expression (`NumExp`) says that an expression can be a `number`. As a result of this rule, we can still give an argument about why "0" to "9" are valid programs, and "10" is a valid program, but "01" is not a valid program. The argument, however, gets a bit lengthy. To argue that "0" is a valid program, we will first observe that a program can be an expression (`Exp`), an expression can be a number (by the `NumExp` rule), and a number can be `digit`, and since "0" contains the digit '0', only we do not need to apply any other rule. Therefore, "0" is a valid program.

The remainder of the rules define what constitute legal addition, subtraction, multiplication, and division expressions.

Each of these rules has a similar structure, so let us focus on the rule for an addition expression (`AddExp`). This rule says that an addition expression starts with an open parenthesis character '(' followed by a '+' character, and it ends with a close parenthesis character ')'. The middle section of this rule is important for allowing an addition expression to be formed out of subexpressions. It says that an addition expression can contain an expression followed by *one or more* expressions. The notation (X)+ represents one or more of X. This definition allows us to write programs like (+ 0 0 0). Other rules for subtraction, multiplication, and division arithmetic expressions can be similarly understood.

Exercises

3.2.1. How many nonterminals and terminals are present in the grammar for the Arithlang language shown in figure 3.3? List them.

3.2.2. Extend the grammar of Arithlang to support a unary minus expression. Compare the production rule of the unary minus expression with the production rule for `SubExp`.

3.2.3. Rewrite the grammar of Arithlang to avoid having to duplicate the common form `ExpExp+`.

3.3 Syntax Derivation

The process of creating an argument (proof) in support of the assertion that "a string is a valid program in a particular programming language" is called a *derivation* of that string (or derivation for short). An example of derivation for an assertion that "0" is a valid program in Arithlang is given here:

Step	Sentential form at that step	Production rule from figure 3.3
1.	*Program* →	`Program ::= Exp`
2.	*Exp* →	`Exp ::= Number`
3.	*Number* →	`Number ::= Digit`
4.	*Digit* →	`Digit ::= '0'`
5.	'0'	

At each step, a nonterminal is replaced by one or more nonterminals or terminals by applying the production rules from the Arithlang grammar. The intermediate results (e.g., on steps 2–4), of a derivation are in *sentential form*; that is, they are not yet a sentence in the grammar. The derivation as an argument can be read backward or forward. For example, "0" is a legal program because '0' is a `Digit`, which is a `Number`, which is an `Exp`, which is a `Program`. We could also say that `Program` can be expanded to `Exp`, which can be expanded to a `Number`, which can be expanded to a `Digit`, which can be expanded to the character '0'. Since "0" has no other characters, "0" is a legal program. Both of these are equally reasonable ways to understand the notion of syntax derivation.

A syntax derivation stops either when the sentential form under consideration has no remaining nonterminals or there is not a grammar rule that can be applied to the remaining nonterminals in the sentential form. For example, the derivation presented here stopped at step 6 because no nonterminals are remaining at that step.

While it might be tempting to replace several nonterminals in a single step, for both theoretical and practical reasons it is preferred to replace one nonterminal at a time. This allows syntax derivations to be more predictably understood. Furthermore, backtracking can be harder if one replaces several nonterminals in a single step. Backtracking here can be understood as reversing the replacement done at a particular step of the derivation. Backtracking is necessary when it is found that a particular syntax derivation is unlikely to yield a valid proof that a string is a valid program. An example where such backtracking is necessary is given here:

Step	Sentential form at that step	Production rule from figure 3.3
1.	*Program* →	`Program ::= Exp`
3.	*Exp* →	`Exp ::= Number`
4.	*Number* →	`Number ::= DigitNotZero Digit+`
5.	backtrack to previous	
6.	*Number* →	`Number ::= Digit`
7.	*Digit* →	`Digit ::= '0'`
8.	'0'	

In step 4, instead of using the first alternative for `number`, this derivation uses the second alternative. Notice that this derivation cannot be used to prove that "0" is a valid program. Thus, using the second alternative for `number` was not a good idea, and backtracking is necessary to return to the previous state. From there, the derivation can proceed by selecting the first alternative in the same manner as before. When writing derivations by hand, it is customary to perform this forward thinking implicitly, and write only the steps that are the correct derivation for a string.

Step	Sentential form at that step

1. *Program* →
2. *Exp* →
3. '(' '+' *Exp* (Exp)+ ')' →
4. '(' '+' *Number* (Exp)+ ')' →
5. '(' '+' *Digit* (Exp)+ ')' →
6. '(' '+' '0' *(Exp)+* ')' →
7. '(' '+' '0' *Exp* (Exp)+ ')' →
8. '(' '+' '0' *Number* (Exp)+ ')' →
9. '(' '+' '0' *Digit* (Exp)+ ')' →
10. '(' '+' '0' '0' *(Exp)+* ')' →
11. '(' '+' '0' '0' *Exp* ')' →
12. '(' '+' '0' '0' *NumExp* ')' →
13. '(' '+' '0' '0' *Number* ')' →
14. '(' '+' '0' '0' *Digit* ')' →
15. '(' '+' '0' '0' '0' ')'

Figure 3.4
A leftmost syntax derivation of the program "(+ 0 0 0)"

To understand the notion of syntax derivation further, let us first construct an informal argument to show that "(+ 0 0 0)" is a valid Arithlang program according to the grammar defined in figure 3.3. From our previous discussion, we know that "0" is a valid expression as per the NumExp rule. Since a program can be an addition expression, and an addition expression can be '(' '+' Exp (Exp)+ ')', if we replace Exp with a valid expression, we will continue to get a program—that is, '(' '+' 0 (Exp)+ ')' continues to be a valid program. You can think of occurrences of Exp in the addition expression given here as a placeholder, which can be replaced by any other valid expression. Since (Exp)+ represents one or more instances of Exp, we can replace it by two valid expressions and still have a valid program—that is, '(' '+' 0 Exp Exp ')' continues to be a valid program. By following our previous argument, we can substitute two later expressions with "0" and continue to have a valid program '(' '+' '0' '0' '0' ')' in Arithlang. We can write this argument more systematically, as shown in figure 3.4. We leave it as an exercise to identify the production rules from figure 3.3 that are applied at each of these steps.

Previously, we have said that it is customary to expand only one nonterminal in a single step. Depending on which nonterminal is selected for replacement, a syntax derivation can be a leftmost derivation or a rightmost derivation.

In the derivation shown in figure 3.4, at each step, the emphasized nonterminal is replaced by its expansion. The terminal symbols are never expanded (e.g., '0' or '+'). Also notice that at each step, the leftmost symbol is expanded. This kind of derivation is known as a *leftmost derivation*.

Another example of leftmost derivation is given in figure 3.5.

A *rightmost derivation* is where the rightmost available nonterminal is expanded first. For example, the rightmost derivation for (+ 1 2) is shown in figure 3.6. Compare this derivation with the leftmost derivation presented in figure 3.5. Notice that in step 3, instead of the leftmost nonterminal Exp, the rightmost nonterminal (Exp) + is expanded.

Step	Sentential form at that step
1.	Program →
2.	Exp →
3.	'(' '+' *Exp* (Exp)+ ')' →
4.	'(' '+' *Number* (Exp)+ ')' →
5.	'(' '+' *Digit* (Exp)+ ')' →
6.	'(' '+' '1' (Exp)+ ')' →
7.	'(' '+' '1' *Exp* ')' →
8.	'(' '+' '1' *Number* ')' →
9.	'(' '+' '1' *Digit* ')' →
10.	'(' '+' '1' '2' ')'

Figure 3.5
A leftmost derivation of the program "(+ 1 2)"

Step	Sentential form at that step
1.	Program →
2.	Exp →
3.	'(' '+' Exp *(Exp)+* ')' →
4.	'(' '+' Exp *Exp* ')' →
5.	'(' '+' exp *numexp* ')' →
6.	'(' '+' Exp *Number* ')' →
7.	'(' '+' Exp *Digit* ')' →
8.	'(' '+' *Exp* '2' ')' →
9.	'(' '+' *Number* '2' ')' →
10.	'(' '+' *Digit* '2' ')' →
11.	'(' '+' '1' '2' ')'

Figure 3.6
A rightmost derivation of the program "(+ 1 2)"

For the kind of grammars that we are studying in this chapter, both leftmost and rightmost derivations are equivalent. The sentential forms in the derivations can be different. For example, the sentential forms in steps 5–14 in figure 3.5 and figure 3.6 are completely different, even though both of these derivations are deriving the same program.

The main differences between leftmost and rightmost derivations are apparent when parsing programs. A leftmost derivation can consume the terminals of the program as they are read from left to right. Compared to that, a rightmost derivation stores terminals until the end of the nonterminal is read and consumes the terminals right to left. Interested readers may also want to learn about the roles of leftmost derivation and rightmost derivation in constructing a top-down parser and a bottom-up parser, respectively.

Exercises

3.3.1. Write the leftmost derivations for the following programs in Arithlang.

1. 3
2. (+ 3 4)
3. (+ (+ 3 4) 2)
4. (+ (* 3 4) (– 2 0))
5. (/ 2 (– 4 3))

3.3.2. Write the rightmost derivations for the programs in the previous exercise.

3.3.3. Arithlang grammar supports positive integers. Extend this grammar to support negative integers.

3.3.4. Arithlang grammar supports positive integers. Extend this grammar to support double values.

3.4 Two Possibilities for Implementation

Now that we have a specification of legal programs in Arithlang, we can begin to create an implementation. The main objective of this implementation would be to take an Arithlang program and compute its value.

Grace Hopper and Compiler

Grace Hopper and her team were among the first to implement a compiler. This team is also credited with inventing the term compiler.
Source: Hopper, Grace Murray, "The Education of a Computer," Proceedings of the ACM National Meeting, Pittsburgh, PA, USA, 1952.

We can realize this implementation in one of two ways. Either we can build a *compiler* or an *interpreter*. The programming language used to implement the compiler or the interpreter is called the *defining language*. The programming language that is being implemented is called the *defined language*.

A compiler is a program that reads *source program*s in the defined language and translates them into another program in a different language, often called the *target language*, so that when the resulting program in the target language runs, it will perform the computation that the source program is intended for. For example, a compiler for the Java programming language is a program that reads the source program in Java and translates the program into another program in the Bytecode target language. When this Bytecode program is run, it will perform the computation that the Java program was intended for. The implementation of the Java programming language employs both compilers and interpreters. The front-end `javac` is a program that takes a program written in the source language (here, Java) and produces another program in the Bytecode language. This resulting program is stored in one or more `.class` files and can be run later to perform the computation that the source program was intended to do. The back-end `java` is a program that takes a program written in the Bytecode language and immediately performs the computation that the program is intended for. We will learn later that even that step is usually divided into two parts: a compiler and an interpreter; but for now, we will not worry about those details. Similarly, a compiler for the C# programming language is a program that reads a C# source and translates it into another program in the Common Intermediate Language (CIL). Some compilers also produce programs in a target language, which have to be compiled further. For example, there is a range of languages whose compilers translates code to another program in JavaScript, such as Dart, CoffeeScript, TypeScript, and so on.

On the other hand, an *interpreter* is a program that reads the instructions of the source program and immediately performs the computation that the instruction is intended for. An interpreter is a program that runs a loop that reads new programs from the user (Read), evaluates the value of those programs (Eval), and prints those values (Print). So the main component of an interpreter are also sometimes referred to as the Read-Eval-Print-Loop (REPL). LISP, Perl, PHP, Python, R, Smalltalk, and VBScript are some widely used programming languages whose canonical implementations are interpreters.

> LISP was the first interpreted language implemented in 1958.

A programming language whose canonical implementation technique has been a compiler is called a *compiled language*, whereas programming languages whose canonical implementations are interpreters are called *interpreted languages*.

There are pros and cons to both kinds of implementation techniques. For example, interpreter-based techniques tend to be simpler, so they are easier to implement. On the other hand, since they often repeat certain steps every time a program is run (e.g., reading a program and converting it into abstract syntax trees), they can be inefficient at times. Due to the tremendous amount of research and engineering efforts that has gone into the design and implementation of interpreters, many modern implementations of interpreted languages often have comparable performance to compiled languages.[1]

In this book, since our primary purpose is to focus on understanding and modeling programming language concepts, we will favor simplicity and realize our programming languages as interpreters.

3.5 Reading Programs

A program is provided to an interpreter as a string. The main objective of the read phase is to convert this string into a more structured form, known as the *abstract syntax tree* (AST), so that the later Eval phase can compute its value. This action usually consists of the following steps:

---

1. One common implementation technique used to speed up computation is *Just-In-Time* (JIT) compilation, which compiles portions of the program prior to running it. Then, instead of interpreting the program, this compiled version is run.

1. Dividing the program string into symbols, called *tokens*
2. Organizing the tokens according to the rules of the programming language grammar into a tree structure called the *parse tree*
3. Converting the parse tree to an AST by ignoring the tokens irrelevant for evaluating the program

The first step is called *lexical analysis*. Legal tokens in a program are prescribed by its grammar. For example, the grammar of Arithlang in figure 3.3 defines '0' through '9', '+', '−', '*', '/', '(', and ')' as legal tokens. Programs can have zero or more legal tokens. For example, the only legal token in the program "3" is the digit 3, whereas legal tokens in the program "(+ 3 4)" are '(', '+', the digit 3, and the digit 4, ')' in that order.

The second step is called *syntax analysis*, or more commonly *parsing*. Parsing is the process of automatically creating a syntax derivation. It organizes all the tokens in the program as a parse tree according to the rules of the grammar of the programming language. The output of the parsing step is a *parse tree*. Figure 3.7 shows an example of a parse tree that conforms to the grammar in figure 3.3. A block in this parse tree can be either a terminal or a nonterminal. For example, Program is a nonterminal and '+' is a terminal. A line between two blocks can be read as "expands-to" or "made-up-of" (from top to bottom). For instance, a Program expands to an Exp, which expands to the terminal '(', followed by terminal '+', followed by a nonterminal Number, followed by another nonterminal Number, followed by a terminal ')', according to the rule AddExp in figure 3.3.

In the third step, unnecessary concrete tokens are eliminated to create a more abstract representation of the program, called *abstract syntax tree* (AST). An AST is a compact internal representation of the program. The primary consumers of AST are interpreters,

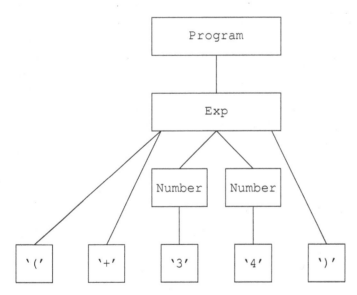

Figure 3.7
A parse tree for the Arithlang program "(+ 3 4)"

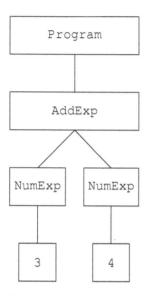

Figure 3.8
An abstract syntax tree for the Arithlang program "(+ 3 4)"

compilers, and other tools that operate over programs, such as for checking errors in programs. An AST for the example program is shown in figure 3.8. Notice that tokens that belong to the concrete syntax, such as '(', '+', ')', and whitespace, are not represented in this AST. To understand the intuition behind eliminating '(', '+', ')', consider the production rule for addexp in figure 3.3. Notice that the production rule itself provides the information that the parsed expression must have started with a '(', followed by '+', and ended with a ')'. Therefore, these tokens are redundant and can be reconstructed based on the knowledge of the AddExp production rule.

The determination that a token can be eliminated is dependent on the intended usage of the AST. For example, if an AST is to be used for code transformations that must preserve spacing, we would need to preserve white space, line breaks, and tabs.

It is also possible that the abstract syntax structure of a programming language implementation may differ substantially from its concrete grammar. In that case, conversion from parse tree to AST could be more involved. In Arithlang and the remaining languages discussed in this book, abstract syntax structure is very similar to the concrete grammar, modulo tokens such as '+', '−', '*', '/', '(', and ')', that do not exist in the abstract syntax.

Given the grammar of a programming language, it is possible to generate code for lexical analysis and parsing automatically. In fact, Arithlang's implementation uses ANTLR to generate a lexical analyzer and a parser. Using ANTLR for generating lexical analysers and parsers is reviewed in the appendix chapter, along with a direct translation of Arithlang grammar in figure A.1 to concrete ANTLR syntax.

Scope: The focus of this book is on understanding programming language designs and their semantics. Thus, we focus less on the implementation of lexical analysis and parsing components of an interpreter. Generating lexical analyzers and parsers is an interesting area of study, but it is typically covered in greater detail in courses and books focusing on theory of computation and compilers. Interested readers can learn more about construction of lexical analyzers and parsers using complementary resources.[2,3]

Exercises

3.5.1. Draw the parse tree of the following Arithlang programs.

1. (+ 5 1 5)
2. (* (+ 4 3) (+ 4 0))
3. (/ (+ 4 3 4 9) (+ 5 1 5) 9)

Next, draw ASTs for the same programs. Finally, report on the compression ratio achieved by the AST representation. The compression ratio is defined as (the number of nodes in the parse tree − the number of nodes in the AST) / the number of nodes in the parse tree.

3.5.2. In a previous exercise, you wrote five different programs using the prefix notation of Arithlang and all four arithmetic operators +, −, *, and /, such that each expression produces the value 42. Draw the parse tree and the AST for these programs.

3.6 Storing Programs

The output of the read phase of an interpreter is typically an AST.

In this section, we consider one possible AST representation for Arithlang. We derive this object-oriented representation from the grammar of Arithlang. In an abstract form (i.e., after ignoring concrete tokens like '(', '+', '−', '*', '/', ')', etc.), the grammar of Arithlang in figure 3.3 can be thought of as *entities*. Their relationships are shown in figure 3.9.

A program consists of an expression, represented as the relation "has" between the `Program` and `Exp` entity nodes. Expressions can be numeric expressions, addition, subtraction, multiplication, and division. This is represented as the relation "can be" between `Exp` and `NumExp`, `AddExp`, `SubExp`, `MultExp`, and `DivExp` entities. Furthermore, since each of the last four kinds of expressions (`AddExp`, `SubExp`, `MultExp`, and `DivExp`) can have one or more expressions as its subexpressions, we have a 1-to-many

---

2. For more information about grammar, parsing, syntax analysis, and other aspects of compiler construction, see Alfred V. Aho, Monica S. Lam, Ravi Sethi, and Jeffrey D. Ullman, *Compilers: Principles, Techniques, and Tools*, 2nd ed. (Addison Wesley, 2006).

3. For more information about the ANTLR syntax and semantics, see Terence Parr, *The Definitive ANTLR 4 Reference*, The Pragmatic Bookshelf, Release P2.0 (2015).

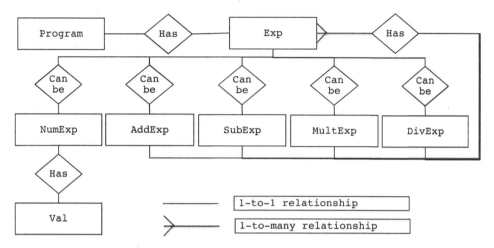

Figure 3.9
An entity relationship (ER) diagram for the Arithlang grammar in figure A.1

"has" relation between each kind of expression and `Exp`. The `NumExp` expression has a numeric value.

In the object-oriented representation, it would be convenient to deal with each entity uniformly (i.e., `Program`, `Exp`). So in that representation, shown in figure 3.10, we introduce a top-level class called `ASTNode`. The object-oriented representation uses a design notation known as a Unified Modeling Language (UML) diagram. In this notation, object-oriented classes are represented as three part boxes. The top part has the name of the object-oriented class. The middle part represents fields that are declared within that class. Finally, the bottom part represents methods that are declared within that class. An arrow with a triangular head from one class to another depicts an inheritance relationship. For instance, the arrow between `ASTNode` and `Program` in figure 3.10 says that `ASTNode` is the parent class for `Program`.

Both programs and expressions are AST nodes, so the classes `Program` and `Exp` are designed to be subclasses of the class `ASTNode`. This class provides only one abstract method, `accept`, for the Arithlang implementation. This method is part of the implementation of the visitor pattern that we will frequently use to examine ASTs. We will discuss this pattern in greater detail in section 3.7, later in this chapter. Concrete implementation of the classes `ASTNode`, `Program`, and `Exp` is shown in figure 3.11.

Since there are five kinds of expression in Arithlang as defined by its grammar, we can create a subclass of `Exp` for each kind so that the subclass can implement the behavior specific to that kind of expression. Each of these kinds needs to store information about subparts of that expression. For example, the `NumExp` expression in figure 3.11 ought to store the actual value of number for later use in program evaluation, printing, and other functions. Similarly, an addition expression "(+ 3 4 2)" would need to store subexpressions "3," "4," "2," and a multiplication expression "(* 3 (+ 4 2))" would need to store subexpressions "3" and "(+ 4 2)" for later use.

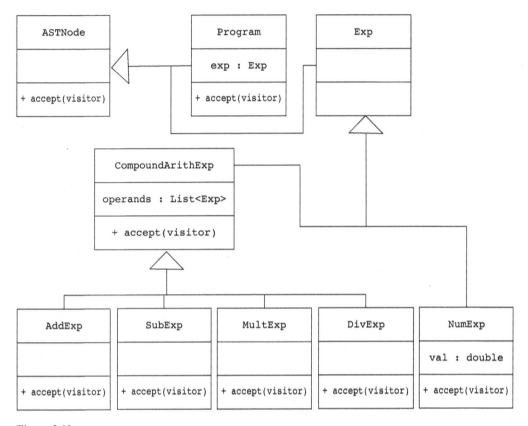

Figure 3.10
A UML diagram for the AST hierarchy designed to store Arithlang programs as defined by the grammar in figure A.1. The concrete Java code is shown in figures 3.11 and 3.12.

One straightforward design of these classes representing expression nodes in the AST would have the `AddExp` class maintain a list of argument expressions and operations to manipulate that list. However, notice from the grammar that `addexp`, `subexp`, `multexp`, and `divexp` all have a similar structure in terms of subexpressions. Each expression can have one or more subexpressions as operands. By realizing this commonality, we can improve our initial object-oriented design. We can allow code reuse if we can create a subclass of `Exp` that implements commonalities, and then create four subclasses that implement expression-specific variabilities. The object-oriented design shown in figure 3.10 utilizes this strategy. An implementation of this design strategy is shown in figure 3.12.

Implementation of the other expressions, `SubExp`, `DivExp`, and `MultExp`, are similar to `AddExp`.

In later chapters, we will not be showing the object-oriented design such as the one in figure 3.10, but leaving it as an exercise for the reader. The reader is also encouraged to consider the pro and cons of merging the functionality of `CompoundArithExp` with `Exp` in terms of code reuse and storage.

```
1    class ASTNode {
2      public abstract <T> T accept(Visitor<T> visitor);
3    }

5    class Program extends ASTNode {
6      Exp _e;
7      public Program(Exp e) { _e = e; }
8      public Exp e() { return _e; }

10     public <T> T accept(Visitor<T> visitor) {
11       return visitor . visit (this);
12     }
13   }

15   abstract class Exp extends ASTNode { }

17   class NumExp extends Exp {
18     double _val;
19     public NumExp(double v) { _val = v; }
20     public double v() { return _val; }

22     public <T> T accept(Visitor<T> visitor) {
23       return visitor . visit (this);
24     }
25   }
```

Figure 3.11
Concrete implementation of `ASTNode`, `Program`, `Exp`, and `NumExp` in Java

Exercises

3.6.1.   Draw an AST diagram for the expression (+ (− 6 3) (* 4 1) (/ (+ 7 2 1) 5)).
See figure 3.8 for an example. Make sure that you understand why certain nodes are
leaf nodes in this tree. What is the maximum depth of this AST? How many leaf
nodes are present in this AST? List them.

3.6.2.   Write an alternative implementation for the AST for Arithlang, one in which
`CompoundArithExp` stores a field of enum type `OperatorKind`, modeling the
concrete operator with four values, `Add`, `Sub`, `Mult`, and `Div`.

3.6.3.   Extend the implementation of the AST for Arithlang to include an AST node
for the negation expression "− Exp."

```
1    abstract class CompoundArithExp extends Exp {
2      List<Exp> _rep;
3      public CompoundArithExp(List<Exp> args) {
4        _rep = new ArrayList<Exp>();
5        _rep.addAll(args);
6      }
7      public List<Exp> all() {
8        return _rep;
9      }
10   }
11   class AddExp extends CompoundArithExp {
12     public AddExp(List<Exp> args) {
13       super(args);
14     }
15     public <T> T accept(Visitor<T> visitor) {
16       return visitor . visit (this);
17     }
18   }
```

Figure 3.12
Concrete implementation of `CompoundArithExp` and `AddExp`

3.7 Analyzing Programs

Recall from section 3.4 that an interpreter runs a three-step loop (REPL). The first step is to read (or consume) a program and produces an AST representing the program. In section 3.6, we learned about one possible realization of as AST. The next step is to evaluate (or consume) an AST and produces its value. This process is much like tree traversal, which you may have come across in courses on data structure, where the value of an expression depends on its subexpression. For example, the value of a multiplication expression "(* 3 (+ 4 2))" would depend on the value of the subexpressions "3" and "(+ 4 2)."

Program evaluation is not the only task that requires AST traversal. If you have ever used the code formatter of your integrated development environment (IDE), you have come across another consumer of AST that produces formatted strings.

There are two design strategies for realizing the functionalities that consume an AST, and require traversing it. In the first strategy, we can extend the implementation of each class representing AST nodes to implement the functionality. For example, classes corresponding to constant, addition, subtraction, multiplication, and division are all extended to implement code formatting, evaluation, and other actions. In the second strategy, we can extend the implementation of each class representing AST nodes to implement a generic traversal functionality. Concrete traversal strategies can extend the generic behavior.

In the first strategy, implementation of the evaluation behavior (evaluation concern) is spread across implementation of AST-related classes. Similarly, implementation of the formatting behavior (formatting concern) is spread across implementation of AST-related classes. In other words, evaluation and formatting concerns are scattered across such classes and could be considered to be tangled with each other. That makes it harder to modify them if needed. In the second strategy, this behavior is localized in one class, which makes it easier to maintain it.

3.7.1 Visitor Design Pattern

In this book, we will use the second strategy also known as the *visitor design pattern* in object-oriented program design.[4] We will illustrate this pattern by implementing a code formatter.

Recall from the AST representation discussed in section 3.6 that each concrete class implemented a method `accept`, which takes an object of type `Visitor` as a parameter and invokes the method `visit` on that object. We reproduce the relevant parts from figure 3.11 and figure 3.12 here for convenience. Notice that the code for AST representation does not contain any functionality for other parts of the interpreter, such as formatting, printing, and evaluating. Rather, it just provides a structure to facilitate the separation of concerns between the AST concern and the formatting or the evaluation concern.[5] This makes it possible to develop and maintain these concerns independently, as we will see shortly.

```
1   class ASTNode {
2     public abstract <T> T accept(Visitor<T> visitor);
3   }

5   class Program extends ASTNode {
6     ...
7     public <T> T accept(Visitor<T> visitor) {
8       return visitor . visit (this);
9     }
10  }

12  abstract class Exp extends ASTNode { }

14  class NumExp extends Exp {
15    ...
16    public <T> T accept(Visitor<T> visitor) {
17      return visitor . visit (this);
18    }
19  }
```

The definition of the type `Visitor` is given in figure 3.13. This interface provides the method `visit` for each concrete AST node. A functionality (e.g., formatting) that requires

---

4. For more information about the visitor and other object-oriented design patterns, see Erich Gamma, Richard Helm, Ralph Johnson, and John Vlissides, *Design Patterns: Elements of Reusable Object-Oriented Software* (Addison-Wesley Longman, 1995).

5. Separation of concerns, an idea first formally articulated by Edsger Dijkstra in his seminal paper "On the Role of Scientific Thought," *Selected Writings on Computing: A Personal Perspective* (Springer-Verlag, 1982, pp. 60–66), is a principle for separating a program into pieces so that the developer can understand these pieces for their own sake.

AST traversal is implemented in its own class that extends the `Visitor` interface. Thus, it has to provide an implementation for each `visit` method declared in the `Visitor` interface. An example appears in figure 3.14.

```
1   interface Visitor <T> {
2     T visit (NumExp e);
3     T visit (AddExp e);
4     T visit (MultExp e);
5     T visit (SubExp e);
6     T visit (DivExp e);
7     T visit (Program p);
8   }
```

Figure 3.13
The `Visitor` interface

```
1   class Formatter implements AST.Visitor<String> {
2     String  visit (Program p) {
3       return (String) p.e().accept(this);
4     }
5     String  visit (NumExp e) {
6       return "'' + e.v();
7     }
8     String  visit (AddExp e) {
9       String result = "(+ '';
10      for(AST.Exp exp : e.all())
11        result += (" '' + exp.accept(this));
12      return result + ") '';
13    }
14    ...
15  }
```

Figure 3.14
A code formatter: an example of `visitor`

The purpose of a code formatter is to print an AST. Since a code formatter is a concrete class and it implements the `Visitor` interface, it must provide an implementation for each method declared in that interface. The listing in figure 3.14 shows some of those methods, while others are elided because they are very similar to the `visit` method for `AddExp`.

The code formatter is an excellent example of how values for an AST node are built using values for its component AST nodes. Take the `visit` method, which takes a `Program` as a parameter, as an example. Since in Arithlang, a program consists of an expression, the formatted string of a program is the same as the formatted string of its expression. The formatted string for the expression (`p.e()`) is computed by invoking the `accept` method with the current `visitor` as the parameter. Take the `visit` method, which takes AddExp as a parameter, as another example. Since in Arithlang, an addition expression consists of one or more subexpressions, the formatted value of an addition expression is "(+," followed by the formatted value of each subexpression, followed by ")."

Note also that the Formatter class just represents the formatting concern. It doesn't include the implementation of the AST classes. Thus, separation of the formatting and the AST concern has been achieved by this design of the interpreter.

3.7.2 Control Flow of Visitor Pattern

The flow of a program using the visitor pattern can be a little difficult to understand at first due to extra indirections, but it helps to remember that (1) the logic for handling each kind of AST node is in the corresponding visit method, and (2) calling the accept method is a way to jump back to the suitable visit method in the current class.

To illustrate, let prog be an AST object of type Program corresponding to the program "3." We can manually construct this AST object as follows:

```
1    Exp exp = new NumExp(3);
2    Program prog = new Program(exp);
```

We can then try to find the formatted form of this program as follows:

```
3    Formatter f = new Formatter();
4    prog.accept(f);
```

As shown in figure 3.15, a call to the accept method causes the visit method (Program p) in class Formatter on line 2 in figure 3.14 to run, which is reproduced here:

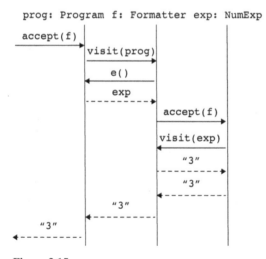

Figure 3.15
A sequence diagram showing the control flow of the prog.accept(f) call. The vertical lines represent objects that are specified on top of the line as obj:Class. The solid arrows represent method calls, and the dashed arrows represent returns from method calls. The value at the top of each arrow is the return value from the call.

```
// In Formatter class
public String  visit (Program p) {
  return (String)  p.e().accept(this);
}
```

This method calls the getter method e on the Program object to obtain the expression (in this case, exp). Then, it invokes accept as shown in the code here and in the sequence diagram shown in figure 3.15.

Recall that the accept methods are defined for each class representing an AST node. These methods accept a visitor object as a parameter, and their logic (mostly) is to call the visit method on the visitor object, passing the current object (a subtype of ASTNode as an actual parameter). In all concrete implementations of the Visitor interface, a method is defined for each kind of ASTNode. See figure 3.14 for an example of this. When the AST node object is passed, the object-oriented method call dispatch mechanism automatically picks the right method to execute, whose formal parameter matches the type of the actual parameter. In this case, the following method accept within the class NumExp is run with the object f of class Formatter as the argument:

```
// In NumExp class
public <T> T accept(Visitor<T> visitor) {
  return visitor . visit (this);
}
```

The accept method then invokes the visit method on the Formatter object f, passing it the current object this as an argument. This causes the corresponding visit method in the Formatter class to run reproduced here:

```
// In Formatter class
public String  visit (NumExp e) {
  return " '' + e.v();
}
```

This visit method for f returns the string format of the NumExp "3" that returns control to the accept method within the NumExp class. This method finishes returning "3" and the control to the visit (Program p) method within the Formatter class. Finally, the visit (Program p) method finishes returning "3."

The visitor pattern is said to use the "double-dispatch" pattern, in which the visitor calls the accept method on the object to be visited, which in turn invokes the visit method on the visitor, with itself as the actual argument. Using the current object as the actual argument uses the method dispatch based on the type of the actual argument to invoke the correct variation of the visitor method corresponding to the object.

A double dispatch is a programming language feature for routing a function call to an appropriate function based on two runtime arguments.[6] A single dispatch routes a function

---

6. SMALLTALK is the first language credited with supporting double dispatch, or rather its more general form, multiple dispatch.

call to an appropriate function based on just the receiver object, such as for a function call o.f(...), the selection of which f to run is based just on the runtime type of o. In contrast, in double dispatch for a function call o.f(o'), the selection of which f to run is based on the runtime type of o and o'.

The visitor pattern is a technique for simulating the double dispatch pattern in programming languages that do not support that mechanism. Here, the selection of which v.visit(T o) method to run depends on both the runtime type of the visitor object, v, and the runtime type of the object that is being visited, o. The call to accept selects based on the runtime type of the visitor object v, and the subsequent call to visit within the accept method selects an appropriate function based on the runtime type of the visited object o.

Building on our previous example, let prog be an AST object of type Program corresponding to the program "(+ 3 4 2)." We can manually construct this AST object as follows:

```
1    Exp exp3 = new NumExp(3);
2    Exp exp4 = new NumExp(4);
3    Exp exp2 = new NumExp(2);
4    List<Exp> expList = new ArrayList<Exp>();
5    expList.add(exp3);
6    expList.add(exp4);
7    expList.add(exp2);
8    AddExp addExp = new AddExp(expList);
9    Program prog = new Program(addExp);
```

We can then try to find the formatted form of this program as follows.

```
10    Formatter f = new Formatter();
11    prog.accept(f);
```

As shown in figure 3.16, as in the previous example, a call to the accept method causes the visit (Program p) method in the Formatter class on line 2 in figure 3.14 to run. When the AST node object is passed, the object-oriented method call dispatch mechanism automatically picks the right method to execute whose formal parameter matches the type of the actual parameter. For example, if the visit method is called with an actual parameter prog, since prog is of type Program, the visit (Program p) method is run.

This method then invokes the accept method on the object addExp, which in turn causes the visit (AddExp e) method in the Formatter class on line 8 to run. This method iterates over the component expressions exp3, exp4, and exp2 and invokes the accept method on each object. That in turn causes the visit (NumExp e) method in the Formatter class on line 5 to run three times, returning result strings "3," "4," and "2," respectively. Consequently, the return value of the visit (AddExp e) method is the string "(+ 3 4 2)." Therefore, the return value of the visit (Program p) method is also the string "(+ 3 4 2)," and as a result, the value of the expression prog.accept(f) is also the string "(+ 3 4 2)."

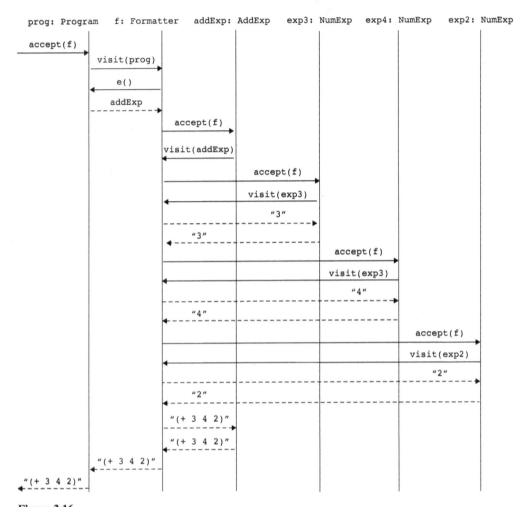

Figure 3.16
A sequence diagram showing the control flow of prog.accept(f) call. The vertical lines represent objects that are specified on top of the line as obj:Class. The solid arrows represent method calls, and the dashed arrows represent returns from method calls. The value at the top of each arrow is the return value from the call.

Exercises

3.7.1. *[AST node counter]* Use the visitor design pattern to create another example of a visitor class, say ASTCounter, which counts the number of AST nodes. The methods in ASTCounter should not use any global or static variables. The ASTCounter class should not have any fields.

3.7.2. *[Number collector]* Use the visitor design pattern to create another example visitor class, say NumberCollector, which collects all numbers that appear in the AST in a list. For example, three numbers, "3," "4," and "2," appear in the AST of the program "(+ 3 4 2)." The methods in `NumberCollector` also should not use any global or static variables. The `NumberCollector` class should not have any fields.

3.8   Legal Values

Output of a program in a programming language is defined and constrained by the legal values that it can produce. For Arithlang, only legal values are numerical values. This is because all expressions in Arithlang (as defined by its grammar in figure 3.3) can only produce numeric values.

```
Value    ::=                                                  Values
              NumVal                                     Numeric Values
NumVal   ::=   (NumVal n), where n ∈ the set of doubles      NumVal
```

Figure 3.17
The set of legal values for the Arithlang language

We can define this set of legal values as shown in figure 3.17, which says that only legal values are elements of `NumVal`. The `NumVal` is defined in terms of the double data type in the defining language. In other words, the definition of Arithlang is not independent of the defining language, but for the moment, we will tolerate this dependence in favor of simplicity.

3.8.1   Notations
From here on, we will use a prefix declarative form for writing values, as opposed to using their imperative form. So `v = (NumVal 342)` is the same as `NumVal v = new NumVal(342)`. When we use the name of an abstract class such as `Value`, we mean that all its subclasses can be used at that location. In other words, the relation is valid for all subclasses of that value. If some name from the left side of equality matches that on the right side of equality, they are the same object.

3.8.2   Implementation
We can create data structures to realize this definition as shown in figure 3.18. A note for readers not familiar with Java: in the programming language, it is possible to define *static* classes as part of an interface, as shown on line 3 in figure 3.18. These classes are referred to by appending their containing interface name in front of their name (e.g., `Value.NumVal`) to refer to the `NumVal` class in figure 3.18. This mechanism allows keeping related classes in a single compilation unit.

In the design of the value type hierarchy, we have created an interface called `Value` as a supertype of all kinds of values. This decision allows design for change. In particular, we would like to allow other kinds of program values in the future. So it made sense

```
1   public interface Value {
2     public String toString () ;
3     static class NumVal implements Value {
4       private double _val;
5         public NumVal(double v) { _val = v; }
6         public double v() { return _val; }
7         public String toString () { return " " + _val; }
8     }
9   }
```

Figure 3.18
Values in Arithlang

to create an interface so that we can protect clients of Value that do not need to refer to concrete kinds of values from the effect of adding new kinds of values. This concept, called *data abstraction*, plays a significant role in both the definition and implementation of programming languages.

3.9 Evaluating Programs to Values

To evaluate programs to values, we will follow a case-by-case recursive approach similar to formatter. We will realize this functionality as Evaluator, which is a kind of visitor, but first, let us learn about this evaluation procedure more abstractly.

A program in Arithlang consists of an expression. So what is the value of a program? It is the value of this expression.

3.9.1 Notations
Let Program be the set of all programs in Arithlang, Exp be the set of all expressions in Arithlang, and Value be the set of all values that can be produced by Arithlang programs. Also, let p be a program (i.e., it is in set Program), and e be an expression (i.e., it is in set Exp), such that e is the inner expression of p.

From here on, we will use a prefix declarative form for writing AST nodes, as opposed to using their imperative form. So p = (Program e) is the same as Program p = new Program(e). When we use the name of an abstract class such as Exp, we mean that all its subclasses can be used at that location. In other words, the relation is valid for all subclasses of that AST node. If some name from the left side of equality matches that on the right side of equality, they are the same object.

3.9.1.1 Value relation We will write the statement "value of a program" more precisely as the following mathematical relation:

$$\text{value : Program -> Value}$$

Here, think of value as a mathematical function that takes the program AST node as an argument, such as p.

We will write the statement "value of an expression" more precisely as the following mathematical relation:

```
value : Exp -> Value
```

3.9.1.2 Logical rules In describing the intended semantics of programming languages, we will often need to make statements like "B is true when A is true." We will state this relation as follows:

RELATION BIFA

$$\frac{A}{B}$$

Similarly, the relation "C is true when both A and B are true" is stated as follows:

RELATION CIFAANDB

$$\frac{A \quad B}{C}$$

We take the conjunction of the conditions above the line.

A relation "A is unconditionally true" is stated as follows:

RELATION AUNCONDITIONALLY

$$A$$

3.9.2 Value of a Program

With these two relations in place, we can write the statement "value of a program p is the value of its inner expression e" more precisely as the following mathematical relation:

VALUE OF PROGRAM

$$\frac{\texttt{value e = v}}{\texttt{value p = v}}$$

You should read the relation here as follows: *the result of applying the function* `value` *on a program* p *with inner expression* e *is* v *if the result of applying the function* `value` *on the expression* e *is* v.

The implementation of `Evaluator` mimics this mathematical relation:

```
class Evaluator implements Visitor<Value> {
  Value valueOf(Program p) {
    // Value of a program is the value of the expression
    return (Value) p.accept(this);
  }
  ...
}
```

Clients of `Evaluator` will call the `valueOf` method to find values of the argument program p.

This method uses the visitor functionality to find the value of the program. Recall from before that the `accept` call will eventually transfer control to the case `Program` of the visitor:

```
Value visit (Program p) {
  return (Value) p.e().accept(this);
}
```

This case says that the value of the program is the value of the expression that forms the program. This `accept` call will eventually run a case for the expression depending on the type of the result `p.e()`. We will now examine each of these possibilities.

3.9.3   Value of a Numeric Expression

First, the simplest case is when the result turns out to be a NumExp expression (literal). A numeric expression is a leaf AST node in any Arithlang program, and it doesn't have any component subexpressions. The value of a numeric expression is an NumVal value:

> VALUE OF NUMEXP
> value (NumExp n) = (NumVal n)

Here, n is a double. As before, `value` is a mathematical relation from expression to values. The notation (NumExp n) is the same as `new NumExp(n)`, and `Number` stands for all legal numbers.

Here are some applications of the relation shown here:

> value (NumExp 3) = (NumVal 3)
> value (NumExp 4) = (NumVal 4)
> value (NumExp 2) = (NumVal 2)

The implementation of this case in `Evaluator` also models this relation:

```
Value visit (NumExp e) {
  return new NumVal(e.v());
}
```

In this case, we extract the numeric value from the expression and then create a numeric value from that result. This models the semantics that the value of a literal is its numeric value [e.g., value of 10 is (NumVal 10)].

3.9.4   Value of an Addition Expression

Computing the value of an addition expression is different from literals because addition is a compound expression, whereas a numeric expression is a leaf expression.

To compute the value of a compound expression, we must first compute the values of its component subexpressions. Recall that an addition expression can have two or more subexpressions, such as (+ 300 40 2). The following mathematical relation specifies the value of an addition expression:

> VALUE OF ADDEXP
> $$\frac{\text{value } e_i = (\text{NumVal } n_i), \text{for } i = 0...k \qquad n_0 + ... + n_k = n}{\text{value (AddExp } e_0 ... e_k) = (\text{NumVal } n)}$$

Here, $e_0 ... e_n$ are expressions (i.e., they are in set Exp). All notations have the same meaning as before. Recall that the condition below the line holds if all conditions above the line hold. You should read this relation as: *If each of the component subexpressions* e_i *evaluates to a numeric value* (NumVal n_i) *and the sum of the numbers* n_0 *to* n_k *is* n, *then the value of the addition expression with* e_0 *to* e_k *as subexpressions is* n.

Here is an application of the previous relation:

```
value (AddExp (NumExp 4) (NumExp 2)) =

     value (NumExp 4) + value (NumExp 2)
```

Here is another application that recursively uses the same relation:

```
value (AddExp (NumExp 3) (AddExp (NumExp 4) (NumExp 2))) =

   value (NumExp 3) + value (AddExp (NumExp 4)(NumExp 2))
```

The implementation of this case in `Evaluator` also models this relation:

```
Value  visit (AddExp e) {
  List<Exp> operands = e.all();
  double result = 0;
  for(Exp exp: operands) {
    NumVal interim = (NumVal) exp.accept(this);
    result += interim.v();
  }
  return new NumVal(result);
}
```

The implementation technique that we use here has semantic implications; that is, it can change the intended meaning of addition in our programming language. For example, if an addition expression has three component subexpressions, we can compute their value at random, from first to last (which if you recall is equivalent to left to right textual order) or from last to first (equivalent to right to left textual order). Here, in our programming language, we chose to evaluate subexpressions left to right and sum up their values in an intermediate variable, `result`. The final value stored in `result` is the value of this addition expression.

Exercises

3.9.1. *[Semantic Variations]* Examine the following different interpretations of the value of the addition expression. What effect could it have on the value of programs?

- An addition expression evaluates its subexpressions at random.
- An addition expression treats any nonintegral value (not a `NumVal`) obtained from evaluating any of its subexpressions as 0.

3.9.5 Value of a Subtraction Expression

The value relation for a subtraction expression is also formulated in a manner similar to that of addition expression:

VALUE OF SUBEXP

$$\frac{\texttt{value } e_i \texttt{ = (NumVal } n_i), \text{ for } i = 0...k \qquad n_0 - ... - n_k = n}{\texttt{value (SubExp } e_0 \texttt{ ... } e_k) \texttt{ = (NumVal n)}}$$

All notations have the same meaning as before. Here is an application of the previous relation:

```
value (SubExp (NumExp 4) (NumExp 2)) =
    value (NumExp 4) - value (NumExp 2)
```

Here is another application that recursively uses the same relation:

```
value (SubExp (NumExp 3) (SubExp (NumExp 4) (NumExp 2))) =

  value (NumExp 3) - value (SubExp (NumExp 4)(NumExp 2))
```

The implementation of this case in `Evaluator` also models this relation:

```
public Value visit (SubExp e) {
  List<Exp> operands = e.all();
  NumVal lVal = (NumVal) operands.get(0).accept(this);
  double result = lVal.v() ;
  for(int i=1; i < operands.size(); i++) {
    NumVal rVal = (NumVal) operands.get(i).accept(this);
    result = result - rVal.v() ;
  }
  return new NumVal(result);
}
```

This implementation is only slightly different from the case for addition, in that we first compute the value of the first operand and then iteratively subtract other operands from this value.

3.9.6 Value of Multiplication and Division Expressions

The value relations for multiplication and division expressions are also formulated in a manner similar to that of addition expression, but for completeness we reproduce them here:

VALUE OF MULTEXP

$$\frac{\texttt{value } e_i \texttt{ = (NumVal } n_i), \text{ for } i = 0...k \qquad n_0 * ... * n_k = n}{\texttt{value (MultExp } e_0 \texttt{ ... } e_k) \texttt{ = (NumVal n)}}$$

VALUE OF DIVEXP

$$\frac{\texttt{value } e_i \texttt{ = (NumVal } n_i), \text{ for } i = 0...k \qquad n_0 / ... / n_k = n}{\texttt{value (DivExp } e_0 \texttt{ ... } e_k) \texttt{ = (NumVal n)}}$$

As an exercise, the reader can implement the cases for multiplication and division expressions in `Evaluator`.

3.10 Read-Eval-Print Loop

Now since we have all the components of the interpreter, we can put them together in a simple REPL and have the first working implementation of our Arithlang programming language:

```java
public class Interpreter {
  public static void main(String[] args) {
    Reader reader = new Reader();
    Evaluator eval = new Evaluator();
    Printer  printer = new Printer();
    try {
      while (true) { // Read-Eval-Print-Loop (also known as REPL)
        Program p = reader.read();
        Value val = eval.valueOf(p);
        printer . print (val);
      }
    } catch (IOException e) {
      System.out.println (" Error reading program.");
    }
  }
}
```

We can play with this interpreter to see how it works. In the *interaction log* below $ is the prompt of the interpreter, the text after $ is the program that the user writes, and the text on the next line is the value of this program:

```
$ 3
3
$ (* 3 100)
300
$ (- 279 277)
2
$ (/ 84 (- 279 277))
42
$ (+ (* 3 100) (/ 84 (- 279 277)))
342
```

Summary

In this chapter, we built our first complete (albeit tiny) programming language Arith-lang, which allowed us to compute over arithmetic expressions. In the process of building this language, we reviewed two possible implementations of a programming languages: interpreters and compilers. An interpreter is a program that converts a program in the defined language to a legal value in the defined language. A compiler is a program that converts a program in the defined language to another program in the target language. The program in the target language may be further processed by an interpreter or another compiler. For this chapter, we selected an interpreter as our language implementation.

We also learned about the grammar of a programming language, which consists of one or more rules to define legal program in that language. We reviewed nonterminals that are symbols that can be further expanded, and the grammar contains one or more rules for expanding nonterminals. We also reviewed terminals that are leaf nodes that can't be expanded. The grammar consists of one of more logical rules to expand nonterminals.

We reviewed data structures for storing programs so that they can processed further. The concrete syntax retains parts of the syntax that are apparent to the programmer, but it may not be relevant for the interpreter or the compiler. The abstract syntax ignores details in the concrete syntax that are there entirely for the benefit of the programmers. We created an object-oriented design and implementation for an object-oriented class hierarchy to store the AST of Arithlang programs. Given a grammar, tools such as ANTLR can generate code for parsing programs into the AST form.

We learned about the visitor pattern, an important object-oriented design pattern for implementing traversals over the AST. This pattern, by virtue of its indirection, allows the implementation of the functionality such as printing the AST, evaluating the AST, and so on, to be separated from the implementation of the AST classes.

Next, we reviewed the semantics of Arithlang and the process of evaluating expressions to values. All leaf expressions are directly evaluated to value, whereas composite expressions first evaluate component expressions to value and then combine the result of evaluating component expressions to compute the result of evaluating the composite expression. We learned about the order of evaluation for program expressions. We also reviewed expressing these rules for evaluating program expressions to values in the form of logical rules. Finally, we reviewed how the pieces of the interpreter are combined in a loop that reads programs, evaluate programs to values, and then prints those results.

Exercises

3.10.1. *[Least Common Multiple (LCM) Expression]* Extend the Arithlang programming language to support the least common multiple (LCM) expression, whose syntax should be (# list-of-operands). The LCM of integers is the smallest positive integer that is divisible by all integers. The following interaction log illustrates the intended semantics of this expression:

```
$ (# 2 0)
0
$ (# 2)
2
$ (# 2 4)
4
$ (# 2 4 9)
36
$ (# 2 4 9 12)
36
```

3.10.2. *[Value of Least Common Multiple (LCM) Expression]* Write the value relation for the LCM expression. Note that you would need to account for the case of 0.

3.10.3. *[Modulus Expression]* Extend the Arithlang programming language to support the modulus expression (% a b), also called a *remainder* sometimes. The following interaction log illustrates the intended semantics of this expression:

```
$ (% 8 3)
2
$ (% 8 3 2)
0
```

3.10.4. *[Value of Modulus Expression]* Write the value relation for the modulus expression.

3.10.5. *[Power Expression]* Extend the Arithlang programming language to support the exponential operation (** a b). The following interaction log illustrates the intended semantics of this expression:

```
$ (** 2 4)
16
$ (** 3 2 4)
6561
$(** 8 0)
1
```

3.10.6. *[Value of Power Expression]* Write the value relation for the power expression.

3.10.7. *[Greatest, Least Expressions]* Extend the Arithlang programming language to support two new expressions, *greatest-of* (>? a b) and *least-of* (<? a b). The following interaction log illustrates the intended semantics of this expression:

```
$(>? 3)
3
$(<? 3)
3
$ (>? 3 4 2)
4
$ (<? 3 4 2)
2
$ (>? 3 3)
3
$ (<? 3 3)
3
```

3.10.8. *[Value of Greatest, Least Expressions]* Write down the value relation for the greatest and least expressions.

3.10.9. *[Divide-by-Zero]* The current semantics of the Arithlang programming language does not account for divide-by-zero errors.

1. Write a program that uses all the arithmetic expressions defined in Arithlang and gives a divide-by-zero error.
2. Extend the Arithlang programming language so that the value of dividing any number by zero is a special kind of value of type `DynamicError`. This kind of value should give users some information about which expression caused the error. The following interaction log illustrates the intended semantics of this expression:

```
$ (/ 2 0)
Divide–by–zero error at:  (/ 2.0 0.0)
$ (– 279 (/ 2 0))
Divide–by–zero error at:  (/ 2.0 0.0)
$ (/ 84 (– 279 (/ 2 0)))
Divide–by–zero error at:  (/ 2.0 0.0)
$ (+ (* 3 100) (/ 84 (– 279 (/ 2 0))))
Divide–by–zero error at:  (/ 2.0 0.0)
```

3.10.10. *[Value with Divide-by-Zero]* Modify all the value relations for the Arithlang expressions to produce divide-by-zero errors, if necessary to support the semantics of that expression.

3.10.11. *[Memory Cell]* A typical calculator provides four operations to remember value: add to memory (M+), subtract from memory (M-), recall value stored in memory (MRec), and clear value stored in memory (Mclr). Extend the Arithlang programming language to support four expressions that model these operations.

1. Memory recall expression (`MrecExp`) with syntax (Mrec) should recall the current value stored in the interpreter's memory.
2. Memory clear expression (`MrecExp`) with syntax (Mclr) should clear the current value stored in the interpreter's memory.
3. Memory add expression (`MaddExp`) with syntax (M+ exp0 ... expn) should add the value of `exp0` to `expn` to the current value stored in the interpreter's memory.
4. Memory sub expression (`MsubExp`) with syntax (M- exp0 ... expn) should subtract the value of `exp0` to `expn` from the current value stored in the interpreter's memory.

3.10.12. *[Value of memory cell operations]* Write the value relation for the memory cell operations.

4   Varlang: A Language with Variables

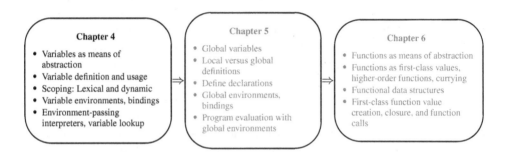

Chapter 4
- Variables as means of abstraction
- Variable definition and usage
- Scoping: Lexical and dynamic
- Variable environments, bindings
- Environment-passing interpreters, variable lookup

Chapter 5
- Global variables
- Local versus global definitions
- Define declarations
- Global environments, bindings
- Program evaluation with global environments

Chapter 6
- Functions as means of abstraction
- Functions as first-class values, higher-order functions, currying
- Functional data structures
- First-class function value creation, closure, and function calls

Our goal in this chapter is to learn about the following concepts:

- Variable definition and usage
- The notion of variable environment and variable binding
- Variable scope, entering and leaving scope
- Holes in variable scope
- Lexical and dynamic scoping
- Substitution-based programming language semantics

These concepts are often key elements of many programming language features such as functions, procedures, closures, classes, and modules.

The complete implementation of Varlang is available with the book code, hosted at https://github.com/hridesh/varlang.

4.1 Variables as Means of Abstraction

One of most important functionalities in computer programming languages is their *means of abstraction*; that is, the ability to create a proxy for certain program elements that hides certain concrete details while preserving those deemed important. The most elementary form of abstraction is variable definition, which is almost directly borrowed from the mathematical notion of variables. In a variable definition, the name of the variable is a proxy for the actual definition. When we define a variable, we abstract away from its concrete definition and give the clients of the variable the ability to refer to the (potentially complex) definition by referring to the name of the variable. For example, the variables x and y here stand for the definitions on the right:

$$x = \frac{-b \pm \sqrt{b^2 - 4ac}}{2a} \qquad y = \frac{-b' \pm \sqrt{b'^2 - 4a'c'}}{2a'}$$

which allows us to write $x * (y - x)$ instead of the following more complex form:

$$\frac{-b \pm \sqrt{b^2 - 4ac}}{2a} * (\frac{-b' \pm \sqrt{b'^2 - 4a'c'}}{2a'} - \frac{-b \pm \sqrt{b^2 - 4ac}}{2a})$$

Abstractions are important for scalability of programming as an intellectual activity, as well as for efficiency of programs. Both benefits can be seen in the previous example. Since we can understand the shorter form $x * (y - x)$ much easier than the more complex form, our ability to understand mathematical expressions is more effectively leveraged. Also, notice that in the shorter form, the quadratic root x is computed only once and used twice, whereas in the longer form, it is computed twice. That can be more efficient in some languages. It is for these reasons that variable definitions and usage are important components of most computer programming languages.

There are two kinds of variable definitions that are commonly included in programming language designs. These differ in terms of *scope* (i.e., the extent during which the variable definition is valid). In this chapter, we study the former kind, in which once defined, a variable definition has a limited scope. Then, in chapter 5, we will look at a different kind of variable definition that, once defined, is perpetually valid until it is redefined.

4.2 Variable Definition and Usage

We will get started by designing and implementing a simple programming language called *Varlang*. Varlang is an extension of Arithlang, the language developed in the previous chapter. When we say that a language extends another one, we will mean that the former has all the features of the latter and more. So, Varlang has all the features of Arithlang and more.

The primary goal of Varlang, and its advantage over Arithlang, is that it allows its programmer to write programs that can perform arithmetic using both numbers and defined variables. For example, a user of this programming language might write some of the programs shown in table 4.1. The table shows programs on the left and their results on the right.

The users of Varlang can then expect such programs to produce the values 1, 2, 3, 4, and 5, respectively. Notice that, like Arithlang, the programs in Varlang are also written in the prefix notation, as opposed to the infix notation that languages like Java use. To recall, in

Table 4.1 Some Varlang programs and their results

Varlang Program	Result of Program
(let ((x 1)) x)	1
(let ((x 1) (y 1)) (+ x y))	2
(let ((x 1) (y 1)) (let ((z 1)) (+ x y z)))	3
(let ((x 1)) (let ((x 4)) x))	4
(let ((x 5)) (let ((y x)) y))	5

a prefix notation, operators such as +, −, *, /, %, and `let` appear before their operands. To be unambiguous, we delineate the start and end of a Varlang expression with '(' and ')'.

These programs show two main features: variable definition and variable usage. Variable definition is done using the *let expression*, which is similar to variable definitions in mathematics, where we often write statements like

```
Let x be 1, and y be 1. Then, the result is x + y.
```

In the syntax of Varlang, the `let` expression starts with an open parenthesis '(' and the keyword '`let`' and ends with a close parenthesis ')'. The rest of the `let` expression has the following two parts:

- Open parenthesis '(', followed by one or more variables that are defined, followed by close parenthesis ')'
- The expression for which the definition would be effective, referred to as the scope of the variable definition

Each variable definition has the following form: an open parenthesis '(', followed by the name given to the variable, followed by the expression whose value will be given to the variable, followed by a close parenthesis ')'. So in Varlang, the informal statement given here will be written as the following expression:

```
(let
  ( (x 1) (y 1) ) // List of two definitions .
  (+ x y)   // Body of the let expression
)
```

Let expressions can be nested inside each other. For example, we can also define two variables x and y as follows:

```
(let
  ( (x 1) )
  (let
    ( (y 1) )
    (+ x y)
  )
)
```

In this example, the first `let` expression declares the variable x, and the second `let` expression declares the variable y. Let us look at another example:

```
(let
  ((x
   (let
     ((x 41))
     (+ x 1))
   )
  )
  x
)
```

In this example, the first `let` expression is assigning the value of the entire second `let` expression to `x`. The value of the entire `let` expression is the value of `(+ x 1)` in that context, which is `42`. Therefore, the value of this program is `42`.

Exercises

4.2.1. Convert the following arithmetic expressions, written in an informal notation, to the notation of Varlang. Also, check and write the value of each expression.

```
1. Let x be 1. Then, the result is x.
2. Let x be 4 and y be 2. Then, the result is x - y.
3. Let x be 1. Let y be 2. Then, the result is x + y.
4. Let x be 7, y be 1, and z be 2. Then, the result is
   x - y - z.
5. Let x be 10, y be 2. Then, the result is x / y.
```

4.2.2. Write five different arithmetic expressions using the syntax of Varlang, such that each expression produces the value 342. Each expression must use all four arithmetic operators +, –, *, and / and the new `let` expression.

4.2.3. Building on the last problem, write five different arithmetic expressions using the syntax of Varlang such that each expression produces the value 342. Each expression must use all four arithmetic operators +, –, *, and / and the new `let` expression. The first expression should use one `let` expression, the second expression should use two nested `let` expressions, the third expression should use three nested `let` expressions, and so on.

4.2.4. Using the `let` expression, write a Varlang program that declares a variable `pi` with value `3.1415` and then uses that variable in the body of the `let` expression to compute the area of a circle of radius 2.

4.2.5. Using the `let` expression, write a Varlang program that declares a variable `g`, the gravitational acceleration constant, with value `9.80655`, another variable `m`, for the mass of an object, with value `50`, and uses these two declarations to compute the value of gravitational force acting on that object.

4.2.6. Given two variables, `m` that stands for the mass of a *rigid* object and `v` that stands for the velocity of that object, write a Varlang program that computes the kinetic energy of that object. You may want to test it using several declared values of `m` and `v`.

4.3 Variable Scoping

When thinking about variable definitions, their validity span is an important concern. It is important to understand the extent to which the same variable definition would be in effect, and whether later variable definitions can supersede prior definitions. For example, consider the statement: "Let x be 1. Then, the result is x + 1." Here, we can see that the meaning of x in the second sentence is the same as that in the first sentence. In a different statement, "Let x be 1. Let x be 42. Then, the result is x + 1," the meaning of x in the third sentence is not the same as that given by the first sentence. In general, in writing, variable definitions supersede previous definitions and remain effective until the next variable definition with the same name or the end of discussion, whichever comes earlier. The previous sentence is an example of the *scoping rule*.

The *scope* of a variable refers to those locations in the program where the variable definition is visible and has an effect. A variable is accessible at program locations that are within scope.

4.3.1 Lexical or Static Scoping

A popular scoping rule is called *lexical* or *static scoping*. As the name implies, if a programming language implements static scoping, then the scope of variables in that language is determined by syntax. For example, consider a sequence of statements in a member of the ALGOL family of languages like C, C++, or Java: `int x = 1; { int x = 42; res = x + 1; }`. For these languages, the beginning of the scope of a variable definition is usually marked with an open brace '{', and the end of the scope is marked with a close brace '}'. So one can say that the definition of x that assigns 42 will be effective for the statement `res = x + 1;`. This allows programmers to look at the code and determine whether a variable definition would have an effect without running the program.

In Varlang, we adopt lexical scoping rules. The name defined in a `let` expression would be effective only within the body of the `let` expression, which can be found by examining the `let` expression. In other words, by observing the static code of a Varlang program, it will be possible to determine the extent of each variable definition. In the Varlang example here, the scope is marked by the syntax of the `let` expression. Comments are added for clarity:

```
(let
  ((x 3) (y 4) (z 2) )
  // Scope begin.
  (+ x y z)
  // End scope.
)
```

Lexical scopes can be nested. The example shown here has three nested scopes:

```
(let
  ((x 3))
  // Scope of x begin.
  (let
```

```
((y 4))
// Scope of y begin.
(let
  ((z 2))
  // Scope of z begin.
  (+ x y z)
  // End scope of z.
)
// End scope of y.
)
// End scope of x.
)
```

The syntax of Varlang doesn't allow scopes to partially overlap. In other words, a scope is either entirely contained within another scope or entirely outside another scope.

4.3.2 Dynamic Scoping

An alternative scoping rule is called *dynamic scoping*. It is available in some languages, such as Perl and Logo. In dynamic scoping, a variable's value is defined by the current scope at runtime, not by the lexical scope where the variable was declared. The notion of dynamic scoping will become clearer in the context of functions, which we will study in chapter 6. For the moment, it suffices to say that if a function has no definitions for certain variables, the values for those variables are taken from the surrounding scope in the case of lexical scoping, and from the runtime scope in the case of dynamic scoping. Dynamic scope allows a piece of code to be parameterized by more than the formal parameters of the function. On the other hand, this scoping rule can complicate program understanding, as variables can be accidentally take values from unintended variable definitions.

4.3.3 Hole in the Scope

A redefinition of a variable creates a hole in the scope of the original definition. For example, consider the following program in Varlang, which has two `let` expressions:

```
(let
  ( (x 1) )
  (let
    ( (x (+ x 2)) )
    (+ x 1)
  )
)
```

In this program, the second `let` expression redefines x. This redefinition has an effect within the body of the second `let` expression. This is referred to as "creating a hole in the scope" of the first `let` expression where the first definition of x is not effective.

As another example, consider the following program in Varlang, which has two `let` expressions:

```
(let
  ( (x 1) (y 1) )
  (let
    ( (x (+ x 2)) )
    (+ x y)
  )
)
```

The scope of *y*'s definition in this program is the entire body of the first `let` expression, whereas the scope of the first *x*'s definition is only the expression `(+ x 2)`. After evaluating this expression, the value of *x* is overridden with a new definition. The scope of this new definition is the expression `(+ x y)`. Redefining a name creates a hole in the scope of the original scope. So the expression `(+ x y)` is a hole in the scope of the first definition of *x*.

Holes in the scope can be nested as shown in the example here:

```
(let
  ((x 3))
  // Scope of x begin.
  (let
    ((x 4))
    // Scope of x, hole in the scope of outer x begin.
    (let
      ((x 2))
      // Scope of x, hole in the scope of middle x begin.
      (+ 300 x)
      // End hole in the scope of middle x.
    )
    // End hole in the scope of outer x.
  )
  // End scope of x.
)
```

Here, successive definitions of *x* create a hole in the scope of the outer definitions.

4.3.4 Free and Bound Variables

Related to variable definition and scoping is the concepts of a *free variable* and a *bound variable*. A variable occurs free in an expression if it is not defined by an enclosing `let` expression. For example, in program "x," the variable *x* occurs free. In the Varlang program "`(let ((x 1)) x)`," the variable x is bound because it is defined by an enclosing `let` expression. So *x* is not a free variable in this program. Normally, programs with free variables will produce undefined variable errors unless they are defined as global variables, as we will see in chapter 5.

In the program shown here, x is a free variable and y is a bound variable. This is because y is bound by the variable definition in the enclosing `let` expression, whereas x is not defined by that expression:

```
( let
  ((y 42))
  (+ x y)
)
```

Now consider a variation of this example. The next example has two definitions of x and y, both at line 2, two usages of x at lines 2 and 3, and one usage of y at line 3:

```
1 ( let
2    ((y ( let ((x 42)) x)))
3    (+ x y)
4 )
```

For this entire expression, x appears free because the usage of the variable at line 3 is not bound by an enclosing let expression. The usage of x at line 2 is not free because it is enclosed by a let expression that defines x; however, for the entire program at lines 1–4, the variable x appears free because it appears free at line 3.

Similarly, in the next example, x is free since the immediate let expression and the outer let expression do not have a binding for x:

```
( let
  ((y 300))
  ( let
      ((z 42))
      (+ x y z)
  )
)
```

In the example here, x is bound:

```
( let
  ((y 300))
  ( let
      ((z 40))
      ( let
        ((x 2))
        (+ x y z)
      )
    )
)
```

The variable x is bound in the previous example, or more precisely, it is bound at least once because there is a let expression in the example that defines x.

The free variables of a piece of code can be defined by variable definitions in the lexical context (in the case of a lexical scoping rule) or the dynamic context (in the case of a dynamic scoping rule). As we will see in chapter 6, the representation of a function as a value includes bound values for free variables in its body from the lexical scope.

Exercises

4.3.1. Write all the free and bound variables in each of the following Varlang programs. If a program has none of a particular kind, state None.

1. `(let ((x 1)) x)`
2. `(let ((x 1) (y 1)) (+ x y z))`
3. `(let ((c 3) (l p)) (let ((s 2)) (+ c l s)))`
4. `(let ((x 1)) (let ((x 4)) x))`
5. `(let ((q 5)) (let ((r q)) s))`

4.3.2. Are there holes in the scope of top-level variable definitions in each of the following Varlang programs? If a program has none, state None. Otherwise, write the portions of the program that represent the hole.

1. `(let ((x 1)) x)`
2. `(let ((x 1)) (let ((x 4)) x))`
3. `(let ((x 1) (y 1)) (+ x y z))`
4. `(let ((c 3) (l 4)) (let ((c 2)) (+ c l)))`
5. `(let ((q 5)) (let ((r q)) r))`

In the rest of this chapter, we will understand various aspects of the semantics of variable definitions and usage by building an implementation of Varlang. As with Arithlang, we will build an interpreter as opposed to a compiler. Fortunately, we have the Arithlang implementation to work with. So, the interpreter discussed in this chapter will build on that. To follow along, get the implementation of Varlang from https://github.com/hridesh /varlang and try some examples.

4.4 Reading Let and Var Expressions

Recall that an interpreter typically consists of three steps: read, eval, and print. The read step consists of reading a program in the programming language as a string, dividing the string into smaller, atomic pieces called *tokens*, organizing the tokens according to the grammar rules of the language into a parse tree, and finally converting the parse tree in to an abstract syntax tree (AST). We already looked at the grammar rule for the Arithlang programming language in the previous chapter. Since Varlang has a few more expressions, we will need to extend those rules. This extended grammar is given in figure 4.1.

The rule for programs is the same—a program can be an expression in Varlang. The rule for expression (`exp`) has two additional alternatives (highlighted in bold in the figure): `varexp` (short for "`var` expression") and `letexp` (short for "`let` expression"). The rule for `varexp` says that a variable name can be an `Identifier`. An `Identifier` can be a letter followed by zero or more letters or digits (e.g., `a1` is a valid identifier, but `1a` is not). As discussed earlier, the rule for `letexp` says that a `let` expression begins

```
Program        ::=  Exp                                    Program
Exp            ::=                                       Expressions
                    Number                                   NumExp
               |    (+ Exp Exp⁺)                             AddExp
               |    (- Exp Exp⁺)                             SubExp
               |    (* Exp Exp⁺)                            MultExp
               |    (/ Exp Exp⁺)                             DivExp
               |    Identifier                               VarExp
               |    (let ((Identifier Exp)⁺) Exp)            LetExp
Number         ::=  Digit                                    Number
               |    DigitNotZero Digit⁺
Digit          ::=  [0-9]                                     Digits
DigitNotZero   ::=  [1-9]                             Non-zero Digits
Identifier     ::=  Letter LetterOrDigit*                 Identifier
Letter         ::=  [a-zA-Z$_]                                Letter
LetterOrDigit  ::=  [a-zA-Z0-9$_]                     LetterOrDigit
```

Figure 4.1
Grammar for the Varlang language

with an open parenthesis and the 'let' keyword and ends with a close parenthesis, and
it contains one or more variable definitions '(' ('(' Identifier exp ')')+
')', followed by the body exp. In our grammars, when we say (x y)+, that means that a
sequence of *x* followed by *y* repeated one or more times, such as ('(' Identifier
exp ')')+.

Similar to Arithlang, we can write syntax derivations for example programs in Varlang.
One such derivation is shown in figure 4.2. In this derivation, new expressions are expanded
in step 3, which expands the let expression, and step 12, which expands the variable
expression into Identifier. Also, note the expansion of the + form on step 5, where it
is expanded to exactly one '(' Identifier exp ')' pair.

Exercises

4.4.1. Write the leftmost derivations for the following programs in Varlang.

1. (let ((c 3)) c)
2. (let ((c 3)(d 4)) d)
3. (let ((c 3)(d 4)) (+ c d))

4.4.2. Modify the grammar of the Varlang language so that the let expression can
declare exactly one variable. Is this design less expressive than the previous design,
where multiple variables could be declared? Why or why not?

4.4.3. Modify the grammar of the Varlang language so that the let expression has
a Haskell-like syntax. An example of such a let expression is let x = 3 in x.

1. *program* →
2. *exp* →
3. *letexp* →
4. '(' 'let' '(' ('(' *Identifier exp* ')')+ ')' exp ')' →
5. '(' 'let' '(' '(' *Identifier* exp ')' ')' exp ')' →
6. '(' 'let' '(' '(' *Letter* exp ')' ')' exp ')' →
7. '(' 'let' '(' '(' 'x' *exp* ')' ')' exp ')' →
8. '(' 'let' '(' '(' 'x' *numexp* ')' ')' exp ')' →
9. '(' 'let' '(' '(' 'x' *Number* ')' ')' exp ')' →
10. '(' 'let' '(' '(' 'x' *DIGIT* ')' ')' exp ')' →
11. '(' 'let' '(' '(' 'x' '1' ')' ')' *exp* ')' →
12. '(' 'let' '(' '(' 'x' '1' ')' ')' *varexp* ')' →
13. '(' 'let' '(' '(' 'x' '1' ')' ')' *Identifier* ')' →
14. '(' 'let' '(' '(' 'x' '1' ')' ')' *Letter* ')' →
15. '(' 'let' '(' '(' 'x' '1' ')' ')' 'x' ')'

Figure 4.2
A leftmost syntax derivation for the program (let ((x 1)) x)

4.5 AST Nodes for Let and Var

The read phase of the interpreter produces an AST representation of the program for other phases. In the AST representation of Arithlang, we didn't have suitable data structures for storing var and let expressions. So we extend the AST data structure to include two new kinds of AST nodes: VarExp, representing variables, and LetExp, representing let expressions. The modified Unified Modeling Language (UML) diagram for this AST node representation is shown in figure 4.3. The two new classes (on the bottom right) also inherit from the Exp class.

The source code for these new node kinds are shown in figure 4.4. Since both kinds of nodes are also expressions, their implementation extends the Exp class. Internally, VarExp stores the name of the variable, a string. The LetExp class stores the names of defined variables, their initial values, and the *let body*, an expression during which variable definitions will have an effect (the scope).

Since our overall interpreter framework uses the visitor design pattern, these new AST nodes also implement the delegating method accept. Recall that the role of the accept method is to invoke the method with the signature visit(LetExp e, Env env) declared in any subclass of the Visitor class.

Finally, the interface Visitor is extended to support these two new expressions (the new methods on lines 9–10 in figure 4.5). You will also notice that each existing method is extended to include an additional formal parameter of type Env, which stands for environment. We will discuss the notion of environment in section 4.7, later in this chapter. Since Formatter is a kind of visitor, this change requires updating it as well.

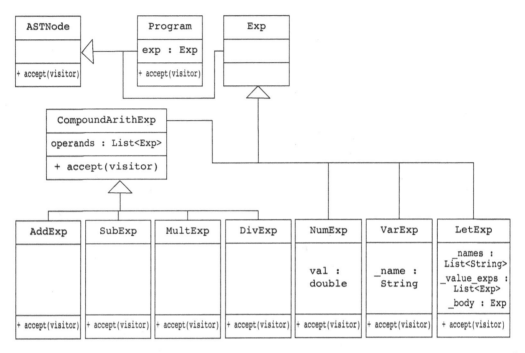

Figure 4.3
A UML diagram for the AST hierarchy designed to store Varlang programs as defined by the grammar in figure 4.1. The concrete Java code for two new AST nodes is shown in figure 4.4.

To summarize, to extend the front end of the Arithlang language to support new expressions for variable definition and usage we have taken the following steps:

1. Extended the language's grammar to support parsing new expressions
2. Extended the abstract syntax tree data structure to add new classes for each new kind of expression
3. Extended the visitor structure to support new kind of expressions
4. Updated existing visitors to support new kind of expressions

In the rest of this book, by saying "extending the front end," we will refer to these steps.

4.6 Lexically Scoped Variable Definitions

What is the value of (let ((x 1)) x)? For this simple expression, it is easy to guess that it may be 1. We can reason about the value of this expression as follows: "Let x be 1. Then, the result is x. Since x is 1, therefore the result is 1." So we might venture a guess and claim that the value of a let expression is the value of the let body. So the value of (let ((x 3)(y 4)) (+ x y)) is the value of (+ x y). We have realized the semantics of addition expression, so based on that, we can say that the value of the let expression is the value x added to the value of y, but how do we find the values of x and y?

```
1    class VarExp extends Exp {
2      String _name;
3      VarExp(String name) { _name = name; }
4      String name() { return _name; }
5      Object accept(Visitor  visitor , Env env) {
6        return visitor . visit (this, env);
7      }
8    }
9    class LetExp extends Exp {
10     List <String> _names;
11     List <Exp> _value_exps;
12     Exp _body;
13     LetExp(List<String> names, List<Exp> value_exps, Exp body) {
14       _names = names;
15       _value_exps = value_exps;
16       _body = body;
17     }
18     Object accept(Visitor  visitor , Env env) {
19       return visitor . visit (this, env);
20     }
21     List <String> names() { return _names; }
22     List <Exp> value_exps() { return _value_exps; }
23     Exp body() { return _body; }
24   }
```

Figure 4.4
New AST nodes for the Varlang language

```
1    public interface Visitor  <T> {
2      public T visit (AST.AddExp e, Env env);
3      public T visit (AST.NumExp e, Env env);
4      public T visit (AST.DivExp e, Env env);
5      public T visit (AST.ErrorExp e, Env env);
6      public T visit (AST.MultExp e, Env env);
7      public T visit (AST.Program p, Env env);
8      public T visit (AST.SubExp e, Env env);
9      public T visit (AST.VarExp e, Env env); // New for the Varlang
10     public T visit (AST.LetExp e, Env env); // New for the Varlang
11   }
```

Figure 4.5
The visitor interface for the Varlang language

There are two ways of thinking about this question. The first method, called *substitution-based semantics*, works as follows. The value of (let ((x 3)(y 4)) (+ x y)) is the value of a new expression created from the original let body (+ x y) by replacing x with 3 and y with 4. According to this approach, the value of the let expression is the value of (+ 3 4), which is 7. In this style, we do not need to define a meaning of "value of a variable" because we never need to find it. To further illustrate this, the value of (let ((x 3)) (let ((y 4)) (+ x y))) is the value of a new expression created from the original let body (let ((y 4)) (+ x y)) by replacing x with 3; that is, the value of (let ((y 4)) (+ 3 y)). The value of (let ((y 4)) (+ 3 y)) is the value of a new expression created from the let body (+ 3 y) by replacing y with 4.

Original program:	(let ((x 3)(y 4)) (+ x y))
Step 1 (replacing x by 3):	(let ((y 4)) (+ 3 y))
Step 2 (replacing y by 4):	(+ 3 4)
Step 3 (evaluate addition):	7

Figure 4.6
Illustrating substitution-based semantics of the let expression

Two examples are shown in figures 4.6 and 4.7, respectively.

The second method, called *environment-based semantics*, works as follows. The value of (let ((x 3)(y 4)) (+ x y)) is the value of the original let body (+ x y) in the presence of a dictionary, called the *environment*, which maps x to 3 and y to 4. The value of x is found by looking up x in that dictionary, and similarly, the value of y is found by looking up y in that dictionary.

Both strategies have some distinct advantages. In theoretical treatment of programming languages, the former approach is preferred. In this book, we will follow the environment-based style because it is closer to concrete implementations of programming languages.

In a nutshell, in environment-based semantics, all expressions have access to an environment, which is a dictionary that contains mapping from variable names to values. A let expression adds new mappings to the environment. These new mappings exist while running the let body. Afterward, these new mappings are discarded. We now illustrate this in figure 4.8 using an example.

Notice that new mappings from variables to values, such as x ↦ 1, are placed at the beginning of the environment. Also, observe from the evolution of the expression that the value of a variable is the first value on the left found in the environment. To implement this semantics, we will first build data structures for the environment.

Original program:	(let ((x 3)(y (let ((z 4)) z))) (+ x y))
Step 1 (replacing z by 4)	(let ((x 3)(y 4)) (+ x y))
Step 1 (replacing x by 3):	(let ((y 4)) (+ 3 y))
Step 2 (replacing y by 4):	(+ 3 4)
Step 3 (evaluate addition):	7

Figure 4.7
Illustrating substitution-based semantics of the let expression

Current Expression	Current Environment
`(let ((x 1)) (let ((y 2)) (let ((x 3)) x)))`	Empty
`(let ((y 2)) (let ((x 3)) x))`	$x \mapsto 1 :: \text{Empty}$
`(let ((x 3)) x)`	$y \mapsto 2 :: x \mapsto 1 :: \text{Empty}$
`x`	$x \mapsto 3 :: y \mapsto 2 :: x \mapsto 1 :: \text{Empty}$
`3`	$x \mapsto 3 :: y \mapsto 2 :: x \mapsto 1 :: \text{Empty}$
`(let ((x 3)) 3)`	$y \mapsto 2 :: x \mapsto 1 :: \text{Empty}$
`(let ((y 2)) 3)`	$x \mapsto 1 :: \text{Empty}$
`(let ((x 1)) 3)`	Empty
`3`	Empty

Figure 4.8
Illustrating environment for the Varlang language

4.7 Environment Abstraction

An environment is a data type that provides an operation to look up the value of a variable. The definition here models this intent, and the implementation in figure 4.9 realizes it:

```
get(env, var') = Error: No binding found,
        if env = (EmptyEnv)
get(env, var') = val, if var = var',
        env = (ExtendEnv var val env')
    otherwise get(env', var')
```

Here, `var, var'` ∈ `Identifier`, the set of identifier; `val` ∈ `Value`, the set of values in our Varlang language; and `env, env'` ∈ `Env`, the set of environments. As before, take the notation `(EmptyEnv)` to mean an environment constructed using a constructor of type `EmptyEnv`, and take `EmptyEnv` to mean all such elements (i.e., the entire set). Similarly, `(ExtendEnv var val env)` is an environment constructed using a constructor of type `ExtendEnv`, with `var, val, env` being values used to construct this environment.

This definition provides a single operation `get` to look up a variable from an environment, and says that looking up any variable in an empty environment leads to errors. Furthermore, it says that looking up a variable in an extended environment constructed using `var, val, env` is `val` if the variable being searched is the same as `var`, or else it is the same as the value obtained by looking up the variable in `env`.

An empty environment is the simplest kind of environment. It does not define any variables. The listing in figure 4.10 models this behavior.

```
1 public interface Env {
2    Value get (String search_var);
3 }
```

Figure 4.9
Environment data type for the Varlang language

```
1 class EmptyEnv implements Env {
2     Value get (String search_var) {
3         throw new LookupException("No binding found for: " + search_var);
4     }
5 }

7 class LookupException extends RuntimeException {
8     LookupException(String message){
9         super(message);
10    }
11 }
```

Figure 4.10
Empty environment for the Varlang language

```
1 class ExtendEnv implements Env {
2     private Env _saved_env;
3     private String _var;
4     private Value _val;
5     public ExtendEnv(Env saved_env, String var, Value val){
6         _saved_env = saved_env;
7         _var = var;
8         _val = val;
9     }
10    public Value get (String search_var) {
11        if (search_var.equals(_var))
12            return _val;
13        return _saved_env.get(search_var);
14    }
15 }
```

Figure 4.11
Extended environment for the Varlang language

Since this empty environment does not define any variables, for every variable lookup, it tells its client that the variable cannot be found by signaling an exception.

Another kind of environment is one that stores a mapping from a single variable to its value. This behavior is modeled by the environment class ExtendEnv, defined in figure 4.11. When a variable is looked up using the get operation in this kind of environment, it checks whether the variable being searched is the same as the variable stored. If so, it returns the stored value. Otherwise, it delegates.

The delegation behavior is interesting, in that it allows environments to be chained together in a singly linked list. The field _saved_env stores the next environment in the chain, and on line 13 in figure 4.11, we delegate to it.

Using these data types, we can create an environment that maps a variable a to value 3, b to value 4, and c to value 1 as follows:

```
Env env0 = new EmptyEnv();
Env env1 = new ExtendEnv(env0, "a", new NumVal(3));
Env env2 = new ExtendEnv(env1, "b", new NumVal(4));
Env env3 = new ExtendEnv(env2, "c", new NumVal(1));
```

Notice that since an empty environment marks the end of the list, each variable lookup that is not found in the environment will result in `LookupException`. We can also have two mappings for the same name in a chain of environments, such as in the environment `env4` given here, which has two mappings for the name "c":

```
Env env4 = new ExtendEnv(env3, "c", new NumVal(2));
env4.get("c");  // Result: new NumVal(2)
env4.get("b");  // Result: new NumVal(4)
env4.get("foo");  // Result: LookupException("No binding found for: foo")
```

We can look up some names in this created environment as shown previously. For each lookup, the reader is encouraged to trace through the listings for "extended environment" and "empty environment" to understand the exhibited behavior noted in the comments.

Exercises

4.7.1. *[ExtendEnvList]* Design and implement a new kind of environment, `ExtendEnvList`, that also implements the `Env` interface presented in this section. Unlike `ExtendEnv`, this kind of environment should allow storing multiple name-to-value mapping.

4.7.2. *[EmptyEnvNice]* Design and implement a new kind of empty environment, `EmptyEnvNice`, that also implements the `Env` interface presented in this section. Unlike `EmptyEnv`, which throws an exception when a name, say "x," is looked up, this kind of environment extends itself to add a mapping from "x" to the default value, "0." With this environment, could we distinguish between names that were given the default value "0" from undefined names?

4.8 Environment-Passing Interpreters

Now since we have a data type for representing environments, we can use it in our `evaluator`. Since environments can change when new variables are defined, and when the scope of variable definitions end, we need to pass around environments from parent expressions to subexpressions during expression evaluation. In this section, we enhance the interpreter of Varlang to include this functionality.

4.8.1   Value of a Program in an Environment

First things first: when a program starts running, what is the value of the environment?

Recall that a program consists of an expression, and previously we stated the semantics of a program as "the value of a program is the value of its component expression." Let `Program` be the set of all programs in Varlang, and `Exp` be the set of all expressions in Varlang. Also, let p be a program (i.e., it is in set `Program`) and e be an expression (i.e., it is in set `Exp`), such that e is the inner expression of p. On these assumptions, we can write the statement "value of a program is the value of its expression" more precisely as the following mathematical relation, where `Program` is the set of all programs, `Exp` is the set of all expressions, and `Value` is the set of all values:

VALUE OF PROGRAM
$$\frac{\texttt{value e = v}}{\texttt{value p = v}}$$

In the presence of environments, this changes slightly. We will state the semantics of a program in Varlang as "In an environment `env`, the value of a program is the value of its component expression in the same environment `env`." Here, env ∈ Env, the set of all environments:

VALUE OF PROGRAM
$$\frac{\texttt{value e env = v}}{\texttt{value p env = v}}$$

To illustrate this point, consider the program `(+ x y)`. Here, p is `(+ x y)` and e is an addition expression with two subexpressions, x and y. Now, imagine that this program is being run in an environment `env` that maps x to a value `300` and y to a value `42`. The semantics given here says that the value of p in `env` is going to be the same as that of e computed using the same `env`.

The case of program in the `Evaluator` (figure 4.12) implements this new meaning. Notice that the same environment `env` is passed forward to evaluate the component expression.

```
1 class Evaluator implements Visitor<Value> {
2   Value valueOf(Program p) {
3     Env env = new EmptyEnv();
4     return (Value) p.accept(this, env);
5   }
6   Value  visit (Program p, Env env) {
7     return (Value) p.e().accept(this, env);
8   }
9   ...
10 }
```

Figure 4.12
Evaluating a program to value in the Varlang language

Intuitively, when a program starts running, no variables have been defined yet. Therefore, we can start evaluating every program in an empty environment. This intended semantics is modeled on line 3 in figure 4.12 and defined as follows:

VALUE OF PROGRAM

$$\frac{\texttt{value e env = v, where env} \in \texttt{EmptyEnv}}{\texttt{value p = v}}$$

The reader is encouraged to think about environments that predefine certain constants for ease of programming. We will revisit this topic in chapter 5.

Recall from section 4.5 that to pass around environments, signatures of `accept` methods for each AST node were extended to take the environment as an extra parameter. Similarly, signatures of `visit` methods for the case of each AST node were extended to take the environment as an extra parameter.

4.8.2 Expressions That Do Not Directly Change Environment

Some expressions do not depend on the environment, such as `NumExp`:

VALUE OF NUMEXP

```
value (NumExp n) env = (NumVal n)
```

Some other expressions do not change the environment directly. They simply pass forward environments to their subexpressions. To illustrate this point, consider the case for addition expression:

VALUE OF ADDEXP

$$\frac{\texttt{value } e_i \texttt{ env = (NumVal } n_i), \text{ for i} = 0...k \qquad n_0 + ... + n_k = n}{\texttt{value (AddExp } e_0 \texttt{ ... } e_k) \texttt{ env = (NumVal n)}}$$

The addition expression neither defines new variable definitions nor removes any existing variable definitions. Therefore, an addition expression should have no *direct* effects on the environment. All its subexpressions are evaluated in the same environment.

To illustrate this point, consider the addition expression `(+ x y)` with two subexpressions `x` and `y`. Now, imagine that this expression is being evaluated in an environment `env` that maps `x` to a value `300` and `y` to a value `42`. The semantics given previously says that the environment in which we will compute the value of `x` and of `y` should be the same as the environment of the parent expression `(+ x y)`:

```
Value visit (AddExp e, Env env) {
  List<Exp> operands = e.all();
  double result = 0;
  for(Exp exp: operands) {
    NumVal intermediate = (NumVal) exp.accept(this, env);
    result += intermediate.v();
  }
  return new NumVal(result);
}
```

The semantics and implementation of subtraction, multiplication, and division expressions are similar to the addition expression. The reader is encouraged to review concrete implementation of these expressions in the companion code on the website before proceeding further.

Interesting cases that directly interact with the environment are `var` and `let` expressions.

4.9   Value of a Var Expression

The meaning of a `var` expression in a given environment is dependent on the environment in which we are evaluating that expression. For example, the value of a `var` expression x in an environment that maps name x to value 342 would be the numeric value 342. On the other hand, in an environment that maps name x to value 441, the value of the same `var` expression x would be the numeric value 441.

The value relation here models this semantics:

> VALUE OF VARExp
> ```
> value (VarExp var) env = get(env, var)
> ```

It says that the value of a `var` expression is the value obtained by looking up that variable name in the current environment.

The case for a `var` expression in the evaluator implementation also realizes this semantics as shown here:

```
public Value visit (VarExp e, Env env) {
  return env.get(e.name());
}
```

4.10   Value of a Let Expression

A `let` expression is the only expression in Varlang that changes the environment by adding new names to it. First, consider a `let` expression that can only define a single name-to-value mapping. The meaning of this expression can be given as

VALUE OF LETExp

$$\frac{\text{value exp env} = v' \qquad \text{env}' = (\text{ExtendEnv var } v' \text{ env}) \qquad \text{value exp}' \text{ env}' = v}{\text{value (LetExp var exp exp}') \text{ env} = v}$$

First and foremost, this definition says that the value of a `let` expression is the value of its body `exp'`, obtained in a newly constructed environment `env'`. This new environment isn't just any environment. It is obtained by extended the original environment of the `let` expression `exp` with new bindings (variable name-to-value mapping). In particular, we are mapping the name `var` to the value of `exp` that we previously computed.

Notice that besides variable definition, a `let` expression is also serving to combine two expressions, `exp` and `exp'`, into a larger expression. Therefore, it serves both as a *means of combination* and *abstraction* in this Varlang programming language.

We can now extend this definition to support the full `let` expression that allows defining several variables:

VALUE OF LETExp

$$\frac{\text{value exp}_i \text{ env}_0 = v_i, \text{for i} = 0...k \qquad \text{env}_{i+1} = (\text{ExtendEnv var}_i \; v_i \; \text{env}_i), \text{for i} = 0...k \qquad \text{value exp}_b \text{ env}_{k+1} = v}{\text{value (LetExp (var}_i \; \text{exp}_i), \text{for i} = 0...k \; \text{exp}_b) \text{ env}_0 = v}$$

Similar to the case of a single definition, the value of a let expression is the value of its body expression exp_b in a new environment env_{k+1}, which is created by extending the original environment env with bindings from variables var_i to their value v_i, obtained by evaluating them.

We already considered several examples of let expressions in previous sections. For the purpose of the discussion in this section, consider the let expression (let ((a 3) (b 4) (c 2)) (+ a b c)). For this expression, names that are being defined are "a," "b," and "c," and they are being defined to have the values of the expressions "3," "4," and "2," which are all constant expressions. In other words, names "a," "b," and "c" are defined to have the values new NumVal(3), new NumVal(4), and new NumVal(2), respectively. The body of the let expression is (+ a b c).

Against this background, consider the implementation of the LetExp case, which models the semantics of the let expression:

```
1   public Value  visit (LetExp e, Env env) {
2       List<String> names = e.names();
3       List<Exp> value_exps = e.value_exps();
4       List<Value> values = new ArrayList<Value>(value_exps.size());

6       for(Exp exp : value_exps)
7           values.add((Value)exp.accept(this, env));

9       Env new_env = env;
10      for (int i = 0; i < names.size(); i++)
11          new_env = new ExtendEnv(new_env, names.get(i), values.get(i));

13      return (Value) e.body().accept(this, new_env);
14  }
```

First, each expression on the right side is evaluated to its body on line 7. Then, the environment passed to this function is extended to include a mapping from the variable names to the corresponding values of the right-side expressions on lines 9–11. The body expression is evaluated using this new extended environment on line 13. Finally, notice that since the original environment passed to this function is not modified, these new bindings are no longer in the current environment after the evaluation of the let body is complete.

We can play with this interpreter to see how these features work. In the *interaction log* shown here, $ is the prompt of the interpreter, the text after $ is the program that the user writes, and the text on the next line is the value of this program.

```
$ (let ((a 3)) a)
3
$ (let ((a 3) (b 4)) a)
3
$ (let ((a 3) (b 4) (c 2)) (+ a b c))
9
$ (let ((a 3)) (let ((a 4)) (let ((a 2)) a)))
2
```

Summary

To summarize, in this chapter, we learned about a number of concepts related to variables: variable definition and usage, the notion of variable environment and variable binding, variable scope, entering and leaving scope, holes in variable scope, lexical and dynamic scoping, and substitution-based programming language semantics. We find these concepts in almost all programming language in existence today, although their concrete semantics may vary from Varlang's semantics.

To support variable definition and usage, we included a new abstraction environment, added support for var and let expressions in the read phase, supported new AST nodes to store var and let expressions, changed the evaluator to pass around environments from parent expressions to subexpressions, and added new cases for variable and let expressions in the evaluator. Those are the only components of the interpreter that need to be modified to provide support for the Varlang programming language.

Exercises

4.10.1. *[Initial Environment]* Extend the Varlang programming language such that all programs start running in a nonempty environment that predefines Roman numerals for 1–10 to their numeric values. The following interaction log illustrates the intended semantics of this change:

```
$ i
1
$ v
5
$ x
10
```

4.10.2. *[Expressive Environment]* Extend the environment interface and data types to define the following additional functionalities:

1. A predicate method isEmpty that returns true when the environment is empty and false otherwise
2. A predicate method hasBinding that accepts a variable name and returns true when the environment has binding for that name and false otherwise

4.10.3. *[isFree]* A variable occurs free in an expression if it is not bound by an enclosing let expression. Implement this predicate as an isFree method for each AST node, such that given a variable name of type String, the method returns true if that name occurs free in that AST node, and false otherwise.

4.10.4. *[Substitution-Based Let Expression]* Extend the Varlang programming language from the previous question to implement a *substitution-based variation* of the `let` expression (say a `lets` expression). Recall that a substitution-based semantics works as follows. The value of `(lets ((x 3)(y 4)) (+ x y))` is the value of a new expression created from the original `let` body `(+ x y)` by replacing x with 3 and y with 4. According to the substitution-based semantics, the value of the `let` expression is the value of `(+ 3 4)`, which is 7.

- The grammar of this new language feature should be exactly the same as the grammar of the `let` expression in the Varlang language, except for the keyword **lets**.
- Implement substitution as a `subst` method for each AST node such that given a list of variable names and a list of values, the `subst` method returns a copy of current AST node with each free variable name substituted for a corresponding value.

4.10.5. *[Unique Let Expression]* Notice from the semantics and from the implementation of the `let` expression that Varlang doesn't place any restriction on defining the same variable two or more times in the same `let` expression. In fact, a variable can be defined any number of times, and only the rightmost definition would have an effect in the body of the `let` expression. So the program `(let ((a 3) (a 4) (a 2) (a 342)) a)` would give the answer 342. Modify the semantics of the Varlang programming language so that all variable names defined in a `let` expression must be unique.

4.10.6. *[Disallow Hole in Scope]* The current semantics of the `let` expression in the Varlang language allows variable definitions to create a hole in the scope of the outer definition. Modify the semantics of the Varlang programming language so that redefinition of variables is prohibited and results in a dynamic error.

4.10.7. *[Encrypted Environment]* In some operating systems, when programs deallocate memory pages, those memory pages can be allocated to other programs without any changes. In such cases, other malicious programs can read the value stored in memory pages, which can cause information leakage. To avoid such an information leak due to environment storage, we can augment the Varlang language with a `lete` (encoded `let`) expression that encodes the value before storing in environment, and `dec` expression that decodes it prior to using it. Extend the Varlang programming language to support these two expressions. Implement an encrypted `let` (`lete` for `let` encrypted), which is similar to `let` but takes an additional parameter key, and a `dec` expression that is similar to `VarExp`. All values are stored by encrypting them with a key, and are read by decrypting them with a key.

```
> (lete 42 ((x 1)) x)
43
```

```
> (lete  42 ((x 1))  (dec 42 x))
1


> (lete  10 ((y 12)) y)
22


> (lete   10 ((y 12))  (dec 10 y))
12
```

4.10.8. *[Cascading Definitions]* The current semantics of the `let` expression allows Varlang programmers to define multiple variables (say, $var0, \dots, varN$) and give them the values of the expressions $exp0, \dots, expN$. These definitions have an effect within the body of the `let` expression, but not within $exp1, \dots,$ $expN$. Change the semantics of Varlang to implement cascading definitions in which $var0$ is defined within $exp1, \dots, expN$ and the body of the `let` expression, $var1$ is defined within $exp2, \dots, expN$ and the body of the `let` expression, and so on.

Here are some examples (without cascading definitions):

```
$ (let  ((x 1)(y x))  y)
 No binding found for name: x
$ (let  ((c1 641)(c2 c1)(c3 c2))  c3)
 No binding found for name: c1
```

Here are examples (with cascading definitions):

```
$ (let  ((x 1)(y x))  y)
 1
$ (let  ((c1 641)(c2 c1)(c3 c2))  c3)
 641
```

5 Definelang: A Language with Global Variables

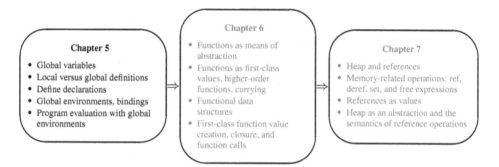

Our goal in this chapter is to learn about global definitions and usage and to contrast them with locally scoped definitions discussed in chapter 4. Early computer programming languages relied entirely on global variables.[1] Global variables are useful when several parts of a computer program need to all have access to shared information.

5.1 Local versus Global Definitions

So far in this discussion, each variable that we have defined in a `let` expression has had a local lexical scope. So in the `let` expression `(let ((a 3) (b 4) (c 2)) (+ a b c))`, variables a, b, and c are defined only during the evaluation of `(+ a b c)`, not outside it. Sometimes it is useful to define a variable and have it available for the entire duration of our interaction with the interpreter. For example, we can define the Roman numerals using such a feature:

$ (**define** i 1)

We will call this feature a *define declaration*. A define declaration has three parts: the `define` keyword, the name that is being defined (here, `i`), and the initial value given to the name (here, `1`). We can similarly define other Roman numerals:

$ (**define** ii 2)
$ (**define** iii 3)
$ (**define** iv 4)
$ (**define** v 5)

---

1. The Fortran programming language is credited with introducing the idea of scoped variables and lexically scoped variables. These variables in Fortran were scoped within subroutines.

We can then use these definitions in all our programs as shown here:

```
$ (+ (* iii iv v v) (* ii iv v) ii )
342
$ (− (* v v v v) (+ i ii iii iv) (* iii v v))
540
$ (+ (* v ii iv) i (* v v iv v))
541
$ (+ (+ v v v i) (* v v v v))
641
```

Note that this is different from extending the initial environment of programs in Varlang with predefined values. Those definitions would have effects on each run of the interpreter, whereas names defined by the `define` form during a particular run of the interpreter would not be automatically valid for the next run of the same interpreter.

Just like variables defined using the `let` expression, variables defined using define declarations can be redefined:

```
$ (define index 0)
$ index
0
$ (define index (+ index 1))
$ index
1
$ (define index (+ index 1))
$ index
2
```

This allows us to write programs that can communicate via global variables:

```
$ (define buffer 0)
$ (define buffer (+ buffer 2))  // Producer expression
$ buffer
2
$ (define buffer (− buffer 1))  // Consumer expression
$ buffer
1
```

The ability to communicate via a global variable can be both a blessing and a curse. On one hand, it allows flexibility in program design. Information that ought to be known globally can be communicated via global variables such as program configurations. On the other hand, programs that use global variables cannot be understood in terms of their inputs and outputs, which makes it difficult to understand them in general. Furthermore, a change in one part of the program may inadvertently affect other parts of the program via the global variables. Regardless of the challenges, global variables are an important tool for programmers. The remainder of this chapter discusses the syntax and semantics of an extension of Varlang that has global definitions.

```
Program         ::=   DefineDecl* Exp?                          Program
DefineDecl      ::=   (define Identifier Exp)                   Define
Exp             ::=                                             Expressions
                      Number                                    NumExp
                |     (+ Exp Exp⁺)                              AddExp
                |     (- Exp Exp⁺)                              SubExp
                |     (* Exp Exp⁺)                              MultExp
                |     (/ Exp Exp⁺)                              DivExp
                |     Identifier                                VarExp
                |     (let ((Identifier Exp)⁺) Exp)             LetExp
Number          ::=   Digit                                     Number
                |     DigitNotZero Digit⁺
Digit           ::=   [0-9]                                      Digits
DigitNotZero    ::=   [1-9]                                 Nonzero Digits
Identifier      ::=   Letter LetterOrDigit*                     Identifier
Letter          ::=   [a-zA-Z$_]                                   Letter
LetterOrDigit   ::=   [a-zA-Z0-9$_]                          LetterOrDigit
```

Figure 5.1
Grammar for the Definelang language

5.2 Define, Define

To support the define declaration, we extend the syntax of Varlang as shown in figure 5.1 to create a new language that is called *Definelang*.

There are two major changes in the grammar:

1. *Program syntax:* The syntax of the program changes in this language. A program in Definelang consists of zero or more definitions, represented as DefineDecl* followed by an optional expression, represented as Exp?. This allows several global variables to be defined in the same program. This syntax also allows a program to be just a collection of global variable definitions.

2. *Syntax of define declarations:* We have also added the syntax for define declarations. The syntax of DefineDecl takes an identifier (the name being defined) and an expression (the value of the name being defined). Note that we do not distinguish among the kinds of values, which (as we will see in chapter 6) allows us to also define functions as global variables.

Here are some additional examples:

```
$ (define R 8.3145) // The gas constant R
$ (define n 2) // 2 moles of gas
$ (define V 0.0224) // Volume of gas 0.0224 m^2
$ (define T 273) // Temperature of gas 273 K
$ (define P (/ (* n R T) V)) // Using Boyle's law to compute pressure
$ P     // What is the pressure?
202665.93750000003
```

Notice that the expression in a define declaration can use previously defined names, but it cannot utilize those that might appear later.

Each line in the previous example is a separate `Definelang` program according to the syntax in figure 5.1. Each of these programs defines a single variable, but it is possible to define multiple variables at once (e.g., both the Faraday and Rydberg constants):[2]

$ (**define** F 96454.56) (**define** R 10973731.6)

The Definelang language also permits the defining of one or more constants and then computing the value of an expression:

$ (**define** R 8.3145) (/ (* 2 R 273) 0.0224)
202665.93750000003

In this example, there is one define declaration, followed by an expression. The global variable declaration can be used within the expression.

As another example, the program here defines several variables and subsequently makes use of them. It is a variation of the example presented previously:

(**define** R 8.3145) // The gas constant R
(**define** n 2) // 2 moles of gas
(**define** V 0.0224) // Volume of gas 0.0224 m^2
(**define** T 273) // Temperature of gas 273 K
(/ (* n R T) V) // Using Boyle's law to compute pressure

Unlike the previous example, which presented six programs, the program given just here includes all the definitions and usage.

We will now explore the semantics and implementation of this new language feature, as well as changes in the semantics of programs to add define declarations.

5.2.1 Extending the AST, the Visitor, and the Formatter

Besides the grammar, we also need to extend the abstract syntax tree (AST) and the visitor infrastructure to accommodate these language changes. These changes include adding a new AST node called `DefineDecl`, modifying the AST node for `Program` to also store define declarations, modifying the visitor interface to support new AST node, and finally modifying the formatter to print the new AST node. The reader is encouraged to review these changes in the companion `code` on the website before proceeding further.

5.3 Semantics and Interpretation of Programs with Define Declarations

A correct Varlang program cannot have any free variables. On the other hand, a Definelang program can. For example, after starting the interpreter, if a Definelang programmer types the following program, the interpreter will evaluate the program to a dynamic error:

$ (/ (* 2 R 273) 0.0224)
No binding found for name: R

---

2. For the curious reader, the Faraday constant is the charge on a mole of electrons.

On the other hand, if the interaction of the programmer was like the following example, the same program would produce the anticipated value:

```
$ (define R 8.3145)
unit
$ (/ (* 2 R 273) 0.0224)
202665.93750000003
```

To understand the difference between these two behaviors, it would help to ask: when both of these programs start running, what was the value of the environment? In Varlang, when a program starts running, no variables have been defined yet. If you recall from the realization of Varlang, we started evaluating every program in an empty environment. The semantics of Definelang is slightly different—when an interpreter starts running, no variables have been defined yet; when a program starts running, all variables that have been declared since the interpreter started running are defined. To readers familiar with interpreters or similar systems, this distinction will not come as a surprise, but it is important to make a note of it as we develop the realization of Definelang.

Recall from previous chapters that in our interpreter, a single `Evaluator` object persists through the lifetime of the interpreter. In Definelang, we want definitions to be retained across runs, which can be achieved by making the initial environment an attribute of the `Evaluator` object. The following implementation changes model that:

```
1 class Evaluator implements Visitor<Value> {
2    Env initEnv = new EmptyEnv(); //New for definelang
```

What is the value of a program in Definelang? In Varlang, it was the value of the expression contained within the program in an empty environment. In Definelang, the value of the expression is computed in the context of the initial environment that retains the global variable definitions. This change is realized by altering the semantics of `valueOf` as shown here:

```
3    Value valueOf(Program p) {
4        return (Value) p.accept(this, initEnv);
5    }
```

If the program contains any global variables, they must be defined prior to evaluating the expression. At lines 9–10 in the following code, each define declaration is evaluated. Note that for evaluating these define declarations, the initial environment context is utilized instead of the empty environment. As we will see shortly, evaluation of the define declaration also extends the environment to add the new global variable definition. As a result, subsequent global variable definitions have access to all the definitions so far:

```
7    public Value visit (Program p, Env env) {
8        for(DefineDecl d: p.decls())
9            d.accept(this, initEnv);
10       return (Value) p.e().accept(this, initEnv);
11   }
12   ...
13 }
```

The implementation given here also imposes an order on the definition of variables going from the top to the bottom. This is the typical lexical order of variable definitions.

The set of legal values for Varlang was limited to `NumVal`; however, for Definelang, this set needs to be extended as shown in figure 5.2 to model the semantics that define declarations do not produce any values.

```
Value    ::=                                              Values
              NumVal                              Numeric Values
         |    UnitVal                                Unit Values
NumVal   ::=  (NumVal n), where n ∈ the set of doubles     NumVal
UnitVal  ::=  (UnitVal)                                    NumVal
```

Figure 5.2
The set of legal values for the Definelang language

The figure defines a new kind of value, `UnitVal`, for unit values. A `UnitVal` is like a `void` type in Java. It allows programming language definitions and implementations to uniformly treat programs and expressions as evaluating to a value, which could be a `UnitVal` when producing other kinds of value is not sensible.

The semantics of define declarations is very similar to that of `let` expressions, except that each definition changes the global `initEnv` to add a new binding from name to value:

```
1   public Value visit (DefineDecl d, Env env) {  // New for definelang.
2       String name = d.name();
3       Exp value_exp = d.value_exp();
4       Value value = (Value) value_exp.accept(this, env);
5       initEnv = new ExtendEnv(initEnv, name, value);
6       return new Value.UnitVal();
7   }
```

The implementation evaluates the value expression at line 4 and creates a new environment by extending the current value of `initEnv` at line 5. The value of a define declaration is a `UnitVal`. At line 4, the value expression is evaluated in the same environment as the define declaration.

Summary

To summarize, in this chapter, we considered a variation of variables: global variables that are effective throughout the program. These variables are useful for declaring constants and for passing information between unrelated portions of a program. At the same time, global variables can complicate program understanding as other parts of a program may change their values. We realized a language with global variables by extending Varlang. The extension required us to change the form of programs, add a global environment to keep track of global variables, and change the semantics of program evaluation. The value of a program is evaluated in an initial environment that stores bindings for global variables. The `define` declaration adds bindings to this initial environment. In the next chapter, we will learn about the usefulness of global variables to define standard utility functions.

Exercises

5.3.1. *[Volume of Sphere]* Define a constant `pi` with the usual value of `3.14159265359`. Define a constant `fourByThree`, with the value of `1.33333`. Using the definition of `pi` and `fourByThree`, compute the volume of a sphere with radius `1.42`. Recall that the volume of a sphere is `4/3 * pi * radius * radius * radius`.

5.3.2. *[Lazy Definitions]* Extend the Definelang programming language from this chapter such that it supports a variation of the define declaration, say `ldefine` declaration (short for "lazy define"). In a regular define declaration in an expression such as the following, first the value of the expression `(/ (* n R T) V)` is computed, and then the global environment is extended with a mapping from name `P` to this value:

```
$ (define P (/ (* n R T) V))
```

In a lazy define declaration, the value of the expression `(/ (* n R T) V)` will be computed when the name `P` is used. An example appears here:

```
$ (define P (/ (* n R T) V))
$ (define R 8.3145) // The gas constant R
$ (define n 2) // 2 moles of gas
$ (define V 0.0224) // Volume of gas 0.0224 m^2
$ (define T 273) // Temperature of gas 273 K
$ P       // What is the pressure?
202665.93750000003
```

Notice that the interaction given here would not have worked with the regular define declaration because the names n, R, T, and V would not be defined. In the lazy define declaration, since the value of the expression `(/ (* n R T) V)` is computed when P is looked up, the interaction works.

5.3.3. *[Macros]* Extend the Definelang programming language from this chapter such that it supports declaring macros and macro expansion.

A macro definition takes the following form:

```
$ (define (macro_name argument1, argument2, ...) expression )
```

Example:

```
$ (define (square x)  (* x x) )
$ (square 2) // This is expanded to (* 2 2)
4
```

```
$ (define (pressure n R T V)  (/  (* n R T) V))
$ (pressure 2 8.3145 273 0.0224 )
202665.93750000003
```

The macros described in the exercise were a simplified form of a more general idea known as *template metaprogramming*. Template metaprogramming, broadly, refers to a collection of techniques that consume user-facing syntax to generate more source code at compile time. Template metaprogramming is utilized by a number of programming languages (most notably C++), but also in Haskell and Curl.

5.3.4. *[Undefine]* Extend the Definelang programming language from this chapter such that it supports an undefine declaration. The goal of adding this new declaration is to clean up the global name space by removing those declarations that are no longer needed for the remainder of the program.

An undefine declaration has the following form:

```
$ (undefine Identifier  )
```

Some example usage of this declaration appears here:

```
$ (define R 8.3145)
unit
$ (/ (* 2 R 273) 0.0224)
202665.93750000003
$ (undefine R)
unit
$ (/  (* 2 R 273) 0.0224)
No binding found for name: R
```

A programmer can use define and undefine in the same program:

```
(define R 8.3145) // The gas constant R
(define n 2) // 2 moles of gas
(define V 0.0224) // Volume of gas 0.0224 m^2
(define T 273) // Temperature of gas 273 K
(define P (/  (* n R T) V)) // Using Boyle's law to compute pressure
(undefine R)
(undefine n)
(undefine V)
(undefine T)
(undefine T)
P
```

The result of this program should be 202665.93750000003.

5.3.5. *[cdefine]* Extend the Definelang programming language from this chapter such that it supports a `cdefine` declaration for a constant define declaration. The goal of adding this new declaration is to define a constant variable whose definition cannot be changed after it is defined.

A `cdefine` declaration has the following form:

$ (**cdefine** Identifier Exp)

Some example usage of this declaration appears here:

```
$ (cdefine R 8.3145)
unit
$ (/ (* 2 R 273) 0.0224)
202665.93750000003
```

In the example given here, `cdefine` declaration behaves exactly like a `define` declaration. Next, look at the example here:

```
$ (cdefine buffer 0)
$ (cdefine buffer (+ buffer 2)) // Producer expression
Cannot modify binding for name: buffer
$ buffer
0
$ (cdefine buffer (- buffer 1)) // Consumer expression
Cannot modify binding for name: buffer
$ buffer
0
```

A programmer can use `define` and `cdefine` in the same program. For example, the program here shows an attempt to change a constant defined by a `cdefine` using a `define` declaration, which also fails:

```
$ (cdefine buffer 0)
$ (define buffer (+ buffer 2)) // Producer expression
Cannot modify binding for name: buffer
$ buffer
0
$ (define buffer (- buffer 1)) // Consumer expression
Cannot modify binding for name: buffer
$ buffer
0
```

6 Funclang: A Language with Functions

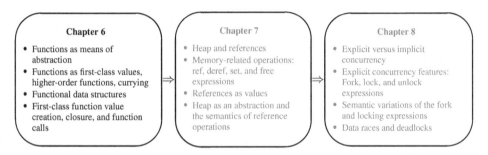

Chapter 6	Chapter 7	Chapter 8
• Functions as means of abstraction • Functions as first-class values, higher-order functions, currying • Functional data structures • First-class function value creation, closure, and function calls	• Heap and references • Memory-related operations: ref, deref, set, and free expressions • References as values • Heap as an abstraction and the semantics of reference operations	• Explicit versus implicit concurrency • Explicit concurrency features: Fork, lock, and unlock expressions • Semantic variations of the fork and locking expressions • Data races and deadlocks

Our goal in this chapter is to learn about functions in full detail. We will especially focus on first-class functions, lambda abstraction, closures, higher-order functions, currying, and on functional data structures. We will also learn about the essence of pairs and lists and techniques for flat recursion. The complete implementation of Funclang is available with the book code, hosted at https://github.com/hridesh/funclang.

6.1 Function as Abstraction

We have already discussed variables, the most elementary abstraction mechanism in computer programming languages, in previous chapters. A variable name is a proxy for a piece of computation. For example, the variables x and y here stand for the definitions on the right:

$$x = \frac{-b \pm \sqrt{b^2 - 4ac}}{2a} \quad y = \frac{-b' \pm \sqrt{b'^2 - 4a'c'}}{2a'}$$

which allows us to write $x * (y - x)$ instead of the following more complex form:

$$\frac{-b \pm \sqrt{b^2 - 4ac}}{2a} * \left(\frac{-b' \pm \sqrt{b'^2 - 4a'c'}}{2a'} - \frac{-b \pm \sqrt{b^2 - 4ac}}{2a} \right)$$

We can think of these variables as an opaque, fixed abstraction; once we define them, we cannot customize their functionalities. For some abstractions, it might be desirable to alter some portion of its functionality. For example, for the variable definitions x and y, it may be sensible to change the values of a, b, and c and get a different instantiation of the abstraction. Functions, procedures, and methods in computer programming languages provide such an abstraction. This ability to instantiate an abstraction by assigning concrete values in place of formal parameters is known as *parametrization*.

There are many variations of programming language features that can be used for the parametrization of a computation. Each such feature is a variation of two elementary concepts: the ability to define a procedure and the ability to call a procedure. In this chapter, we first focus on these concepts and then study some variations. We will gradually define a programming language with these features that called *Funclang*.

6.2   Function Definitions and Calls

We will start by studying two features: lambda abstraction and call. Think of a lambda abstraction as a tool for defining anonymous functions. Let us start with simple examples of such feature. For example, the listing here defines an anonymous function that takes a single parameter x and the value of the function is x. It may be useful for you to try these examples using the interpreter on the website for this chapter:

```
(
  lambda        // Lambda special function for defining functions
  (x)           // List of formal parameter names of the function
  x             // Body of the function
)
```

If you are familiar with the notion of procedure or methods in the ALGOL family of languages like C, C++, Java, and C#, you should notice three key differences in syntax and one key difference in semantics. The key differences in syntax are:

1. We are not specifying the name of the function.
2. The formal parameter name is neither preceded nor followed by the type of the formal parameter.
3. We don't have to write an explicit "return" statement to specify the value returned by the function. In the function definition given previously, the value of the formal parameter x is the return value of the function.

In the ALGOL family of languages as well as in lower-level languages like assembly language, procedures and methods are thought of as a subsection of the code section, procedure/method names are thought of as a proxy for the location of that subsection in the code section, and procedure/method call are thought of as a jump to that location after adjusting the environment. Unlike this mental model, it is perhaps best to think of a lambda abstraction as a generator of runtime values that represent functions. A lambda abstraction can be used to create many such function values, and each of these function values have a different identity. Each such function value can be used multiple times.

The following listing shows another anonymous function that takes a single parameter x and the value of the function is x + 1:

```
(
  lambda        // Lambda special form for defining functions
  (x)           // List of formal parameter names of the function
  (+ x 1)       // Body of the function
)
```

The listing here defines an anonymous function that takes two parameters x and y and the value of the function is x + y:

```
(lambda (x y) (+ x y))
```

We can call an anonymous function as well. Here, is an example of calling the identity function:

```
(                      // Begin function call syntax
  (lambda (x) x)       // Operator: Function being called
  1                    // Operands: List of actual parameters
)                      // End function call syntax
```

The value of this program is 1. Notice the prefix notation for function calls. The operator here is the function (lambda (x) x). Here is another example of calling the addition function:

```
(                      // Begin function call syntax
  (lambda (x) (+ x 1)) // Operator: Function being called
  1                    // Operands: List of actual parameters
)                      // End function call syntax
```

The value of this program is 2. The operator here is the function (lambda (x) (+ x 1)). Here is a third example of calling the function that adds two numbers. The value of this program is 2:

```
(
  (lambda (x y) (+ x y))
  1 1
)
```

If we desire, we can also give these lambda abstractions lexically scoped names using the let expression. For example, we can give the name identity to the lambda abstraction that we defined previously:

```
(let
  (( identity  (lambda (x) x)))     // Naming the function
  ( identity  1)                    // Function call
)
```

We can also give these functions globally scoped names using the define declaration:

```
$ (define identity  (lambda (x) x))
$ ( identity  1)
1
```

As usual, functions can be defined in terms of other helper functions:

```
$ (define square (lambda (x) (* x x)))
$ (square 1.2)
1.44
$ (define cube (lambda (x) (* (square x) x)))
$ (cube 1.2)
1.728
```

Exercises

6.2.1. *[Area]* Using the `define` declaration, define a constant `pi` with the standard value of `3.14159265359`. Use the definition of `pi` to define a function `area` of a circle that takes a radius and computes the area using the standard formula `pi * radius * radius`.

6.2.2. *[sumsquares]* Define a function called `sumsquares` that takes two integers as a parameter and computes the sum of square of numbers from the first number to the second number.

```
$ (sumsquares 0 0)
0
$ (sumsquares 1 2)
5
$ (sumsquares 3 5)
50
```

6.2.3. *[sumseries]* Define a function `sumseries` that takes a number n as argument and computes the series given here. Take the value of `(sumseries 0)` to be 0:

$$(1/2) - (1/4) + (1/8) - (1/16) + \ldots$$

```
$(sumseries 0)
0
$(sumseries 1)
0.5
$(sumseries 2)
0.25
$(sumseries 3)
0.375
```

6.3 Functions for Pairs and Lists

Most programming languages provide some built-in functions (i.e., functions that programmers do not have to define from scratch and can assume to be available). In Funclang, we have several such built-in functions, mostly related to list manipulation. Funclang programmers have access to the `list`, `car`, `cdr`, `cons`, and `null?` built-in functions. The functions `car`, `cdr`, `cons`, and `null?` operate on both pairs and lists in Funclang.

A pair in Funclang is a 2-tuple written as `(fst.snd)`. A list in Funclang is a pair where the second element is a list. There is a special list, *empty list*, which is not a pair. Not all pairs are lists, but each list except for the empty list is a pair.

The function `list` is a constructor for list, and it takes zero or more values as arguments and produces a list containing these values. The function `car` takes a single argument, a pair or a list, and produces the first element of that pair or list. The function `cdr` also takes a single argument, a pair or a list, and produces the second element of that pair or list. The function `cons` takes two values as arguments. If the second value is a list, it produces a new list with the first value appended to the front of the second value list. Otherwise, it produces a pair of two argument values. The function `null?` takes a single argument and evaluates to `#t` if that argument is an empty list. The exercises in this section will help you become more familiar with the semantics of these functions.

Using these basic functions, other functions over lists can also be defined. For example, the function `cadr` defined here returns the second element of the argument list:

```
(define cadr
  (lambda (lst)
    (car (cdr lst))
  )
)
```

Similarly, the function `caddr` defined here produces the third element of the argument list:

```
(define caddr
  (lambda (lst)
    (car (cdr (cdr lst)))
  )
)
```

The `length` function here computes the size of the list:

```
(define length
  (lambda (lst)
    (if (null? lst) 0
      (+ 1 (length (cdr lst)))
    )
  )
)
```

The `length` function is an excellent first example of a recursive function over a list. *A recursive function's definition should mirror the definition of the input data types.* For example, a list can be thought of as follows:

$$List := (list) \mid (cons \text{ val } List), \text{ where val} \in \texttt{Value}$$

The definition says that a list is either an empty list or a pair constructed by joining an element and another list. Notice that the function `length` is structured just like the definition of list into two cases. The first case handles empty lists. The second case handles nonempty lists.

The append function here combines two lists:

```
(define append
  (lambda (lst1 lst2)
    (if (null? lst1) lst2
      (if (null? lst2) lst1
        (cons (car lst1) (append (cdr lst1) lst2))
      )
    )
  )
)
```

Notice that for append, the definition of list suggests that the function's structure should have four cases:

- lst1 is empty, lst2 is empty.
- lst1 is empty, lst2 is not empty.
- lst1 is not empty, lst2 is empty.
- lst1 is not empty, lst2 is not empty.

On closer observation, we realize that the value of the function append in the first and second cases will be the same, so to optimize the function definition, we merge these two cases. Thus, we arrive at a suggested recursive function structure with three cases. In summary, when writing recursive functions that process data types such as lists, the structure of the data type provides useful hints for creating the structure of the function.

Exercises

6.3.1. Experiment with built-in functions for lists.

1. Use (list) to create an empty list,
2. Use (list 342) to create a list with a single element 342.
3. Use (car (list 342)) to get the first element of the previously defined list.
4. Use (cdr (list 342)) to get the rest of the elements of the previously defined list.
5. Use (null? (list)) to check if the list created in part 1 is an empty list.
6. Use (cons 541 (list 342)) to append an element at the beginning of the list created in part 2.
7. Use (cadr (list 541 342)) to get the second element of the list.
8. Use (caddr (list 641 541 342)) to get the third element of the list.
9. Use the function length to find the length of the list created by the expression (list).
10. Use the function append to concatenate a list with a single element 3 with another list with a single element 4.

6.3.2. *[Sum of Even Numbers]* Write a function, `sumeven`, that takes a list of numbers and returns the summation of the even numbers in this list. For example:

```
$ (sumeven (list 1 1 1 1 1)).
0
$ (sumeven (list 1 1 1 1 2))
2
```

6.3.3. *[Frequency]* Write a function, `frequency`, that takes a list, `lst`, and an element, `elem`, and returns the frequency of that element in that list. For example:

```
$ (frequency (list ) 5)
0
$ (frequency (list #t "hello") 5)
0
$(frequency (list #t 5 "hello") 5)
1
$(frequency (list #t 5 "hello" 5) 5)
2
```

6.3.4. *[Reverse]* Write a function, `reverse`, which takes a list, `lst`, and returns the reverse of that list. For example:

```
$(reverse ( list ))
()
$(reverse ( list 3))
(3)
$(reverse ( list 3 4))
(4 3)
$(reverse ( list 3 4 2))
(2 4 3)
```

6.3.5. *[Sum of 2^n]* Write a recursive function called `sumPower`, that takes a list of numbers, and computes the sum of 2 to the power of each element in the list.

The following interactions log illustrates the semantics of `sumPower`:

```
$ (sumPower (list))
0
$ (sumPower (list 0))
1
$ (sumPower (list 1))
2
```

```
$ (sumPower (list 3))
8
$ (sumPower (list 1 3))
10
```

6.3.6. *[Get books]* Write a function, `getbooks`, that takes in a list of lists with author/book string pairs and returns a single list of only the books. Assume that the author is the first element and the book is the second. For example:

```
$ (get–books (list ( list "C. S. Lewis" "The Last Battle")
                   ( list "Charles Dickens" "A Christmas Carol")
                   ( list "Arthur C. Clarke" "Rama")))
("The Last Battle" "A Christmas Carol" "Rama")
```

6.3.7. *[Triangle]* Write a function, `triangle`, which takes a number and produces a list, each element of which is a list of symbols.

When `triangle` is called with a nonnegative integer, n, it returns a list containing n number of lists. The first inner list has n elements, the second inner list has n–1 element, and so on until you reach the top with only one element list, which forms the shape of a triangle. Each of the inner lists contain only the numbers 0 and 1 and they alternate across lists. The result always has 0 as the first element of the first inner list, if any.

In the following examples, we have formatted the output to show the result more clearly, but your output will not look the same; it is sufficient to just get the outputs that are equal to those shown. Spaces in the lists are just for display purposes here; you are not required to print them:

```
$ ( triangle  0)
   ()

$ ( triangle  1)
   ((0) )

$ ( triangle  2)
   ((0  1)
    (1) )

$ ( triangle  3)
   ((0  1 0)
    (1  0)
    (0) )

$ ( triangle  4)
   ((0  1 0 1)
    (1  0 1)
    (0  1)
    (1) )
```

```
$ ( triangle  5)
   ((0  1 0 1 0)
     (1  0  1 0)
       (0  1 0)
         (1  0)
           (0))

$ ( triangle  6)
   ((0  1 0 1 0 1)
       (1 0 1 0 1)
         (0 1 0 1)
           (1  0 1)
             (0  1)
               (1))
```

6.3.8. *[Board]* Write a procedure, board, which takes a integer number as input and produces a list as an output, each element of which is a list of 0s and 1s.

When board is called with a nonnegative integer, n, it returns a list containing n lists, each of which has n elements. These lists form the shape of a square board. Each of the inner lists contain only numbers 0 and 1, and they alternate across lists. The result always has 0 as the first element of the first inner list, if any.

The following examples show a formatted output of the boards, but your output does not need look the same regarding spaces. For your output, it is sufficient to produce the list. Spaces in the lists are just for illustrative purposes here; you are not required to print them:

```
$ (board 0)
()

$ (board 1)
((0))

$ (board 2)
((0  1)
 (1  0))

$ (board 3)
((0  1 0)
 (1  0 1)
 (0  1 0))

$ (board 4)
((0  1 0 1)
 (1  0 1 0)
 (0  1 0 1)
 (1  0 1 0))
```

```
$ (board 5)
((0  1 0 1 0)
 (1 0 1 0 1)
 (0  1 0 1 0)
 (1 0 1 0 1)
 (0  1 0 1 0))

$ (board 6)
((0  1 0 1 0 1)
 (1 0 1 0 1 0)
 (0  1 0 1 0 1)
 (1 0 1 0 1 0)
 (0  1 0 1 0 1)
 (1 0 1 0 1 0))
```

6.3.9. *[Carpet]* Write a function `carpet` that takes one nonnegative natural number as the argument and produces a list as shown in the examples.

You may assume that the argument of `carpet` will always be a nonnegative natural number.

The following examples show a formatted output of the carpets, but your output does not need to look the same regarding spaces. For your output, it is sufficient to produce the list. Spaces in the lists are just for illustrative purposes here; you are not required to print them:

```
$ (carpet 0)
((0))

$ (carpet 1)
(( 1 1 1 )
 ( 1 % 1 )
 ( 1 1 1 ))

$ (carpet 2)
( ( 0 0 0 0 0 )
  ( 0 1 1 1 0 )
  ( 0 1 0 1 0 )
  ( 0 1 1 1 0 )
  ( 0 0 0 0 0 ))

$ (carpet 3)
( ( 1 1 1 1 1 1 1 )
  ( 1 0 0 0 0 0 1 )
  ( 1 0 1 1 1 0 1 )
  ( 1 0 1 0 1 0 1 )
  ( 1 0 1 1 1 0 1 )
  ( 1 0 0 0 0 0 1 )
  ( 1 1 1 1 1 1 1 ))
```

6.3.10. *Pascal's Triangle* The pattern you see here is called Pascal's Triangle:

```
   1
  1 1
 1 2 1
1 3 3 1
1 4 6 4 1
```

The numbers at the edge of the triangle are all 1, and each number inside the triangle is the sum of the two numbers above it.

Write a function `pascal` with the following output:

```
$ (pascal 1)
((1))

$ (pascal 2)
(  ( 1 )
   ( 1 1 )
)

$ (pascal 3)
(  ( 1 )
   ( 1 1 )
   ( 1 2 1 )
)

$ (pascal 4)
(  ( 1 )
   ( 1 1 )
   ( 1 2 1 )
   ( 1 3 3 1 )
)
```

You may assume that the argument will always be a natural number >= 1.

The examples given here show a formatted output of the Pascal triangles, but your output does not need to look the same. For your output, it is sufficient to produce the list. Spaces in the lists are just for illustrative purposes here; you are not required to print them.

6.4 Higher-Order Functions

A *higher-order function* is a function that accepts a function as the argument or returns a function as the value. In Funclang, we can define higher-order functions. For example, here is a function that returns (`lambda (x) c`), which is also a function:

```
(lambda (c)          // Lambda abstraction with a single argument
   (lambda (x) c)    // Result of running this lambda expression
)
```

If we call this function with argument 1 as follows:

```
(                                    // Function call
   (lambda (c)(lambda (x) c))        // Operator
   1                                 // Operand
)
```

the result would be (lambda (x) 1). If we call this function with argument 2 as follows:

```
(                                    // Function call
   (lambda (c) (lambda (x) c))       // Operator
   2                                 // Operand
)
```

the result would be (lambda (x) 2). So we can think of (lambda (c) (lambda (x) c)) as a constant function generator:

```
(define
   constgen
   (lambda (c) (lambda (x) c))
)
```

We can also define functions that take other functions as parameters. For example, the listing here defines a function that takes a function f and applies it to 1:

```
(define
   applytoone
   (lambda (f) (f 1))
)
```

To try this function, we can define another function:

```
(define add3
   (lambda (x) (+ x 3))
)
```

We can then use add3 as an argument to applytoone:

```
$ (applytoone add3)
4
```

We can also create a function on the fly and give it as an argument to applytoone:

```
$ (applytoone (lambda (x) x))
1
$ (applytoone (constgen 342))
342
```

The second call to function `applytoone` is especially noteworthy. It uses the previous higher-order function `constgen` to create a function that, when called, returns `342`, and calls `applytoone` with this function as the argument.

Higher-order functions can be particularly useful for defining reusable algorithmic structures. For example, the listing here shows a higher-order function that accepts an operation and a list and applies the operation to each element of the list:

```
(define map
  (lambda (op lst)
    (if (null? lst) (list)
      (cons (op (car lst)) (map op (cdr lst)))
    )
  )
)
```

Here are some examples of using this function:

```
$ (define num1to10 (list 1 2 3 4 5 6 7 8 9 10))
$ (define identity (lambda (x) x))
$ (map identity num1to10)
(1 2 3 4 5 6 7 8 9 10)
$ (define square (lambda (x) (* x x)))
$ (map square num1to10)
(1 4 9 16 25 36 49 64 81 100)
```

Exercises

6.4.1. Define a function `filter` with the following signature:

```
(define filter (lambda (test_op lst) ...) )
```

The function takes two inputs, an operator `test_op`, which should be a single argument function that returns a Boolean; and `lst`, which should be a list of elements. The function outputs a list containing all the elements of "`lst`" for which the `test_op` function returned #t:

```
$ (define gt5? (lambda (x) (if (> x 5) #t #f)))
$ ( filter gt5? (list ))
()
$ ( filter gt5? (list 1))
()
$ ( filter gt5? (list 1 6))
(6)
$ ( filter gt5? (list 1 6 2 7))
(6 7)
$ ( filter gt5? (list 1 6 2 7 5 9))
(6 7 9)
```

6.4.2. Define a function `foldl` (fold left) with three parameters, `op`, `zero_element`, and `lst`. The parameter `op` itself is a two-argument function, zero_element is the zero element of the operator function (e.g., 0 for plus function or 1 for the multiply function), and lst is a list of elements. (The `plus` function takes two parameters and adds them, and the multiply function takes two parameters and multiplies them.)

The function successively applies the `op` function to each element of the list and the result of the previous `op` function (where no such results exist, the zero element is used). The following interaction log illustrates the `foldl` function:

```
$ (define plus (lambda (x y) (+ x y)))
$ ( foldl plus 0 ( list ))
0
$ ( foldl plus 0 ( list 1))
1
$ ( foldl plus 0 ( list 1 2))
3
$ ( foldl plus 0 ( list 1 2 3))
6
$ ( foldl plus 0 ( list 1 2 3 4))
10
```

6.4.3. Define a function `foldr` (fold right) with three parameters, `op`, `zero_element`, and `lst`. The parameter `op` itself is a two-argument function, zero_element is the zero element of the operator function (e.g., 0 for '+' operator or 1 for the multiply operator), and lst is a list of elements. (The `plus` function takes two parameters and adds them, and the multiply function takes two parameters and multiplies them.)

The function successively applies the `op` function to each element of the list and the result of the previous `op` function (where no such results exist, the zero element is used). The following interaction log illustrates the `foldr` function:

```
$ (define minus (lambda (x y) (– x y)))
$ ( foldr minus 0 ( list ))
0
$ ( foldr minus 0 ( list 1))
1
$ ( foldr minus 0 ( list 1 2 3 4) )
$ –2
$ ( foldr minus 0 ( list 4 3 2 1) )
$ 2
```

6.4.4. *[Repeated]* If f is a numerical function and n is a positive integer, then we can form the `nth` repeated application of f, which is defined to be the function whose value at x is `f(f(...(f(x))...))`. For example, if `f` is the function `f(x) = x + 1`, then the `nth` repeated application of `f` is the function `f(x) = x + n`.

Define a function `repeated` that takes as input a procedure that computes `f` and a positive integer `n` and returns a function that computes the `nth` repeated application of `f`. Your function `repeated` should permit the following usage:

```
$ (define inc (lambda (x) (+ x 1)))
$ ((repeated inc 2) 3)
5
$ ((repeated inc 10) 3)
13
$ ((repeated inc 100) 3)
103
$ ((repeated inc 3) 0)
3
$ ((repeated inc 3) -1)
2
$ ((repeated inc 3) -23)
-20

$ (define quad (lambda (x) (+ (* 2 x) 1)))
$ ((repeated quad 2) 2)
11
```

In this example, `quad` is a function which, given a number x, returns `(+ (* 2 x) 1)`. `repeated` is a function that takes a function (`quad` in this case) and another number (2 in this case) and returns a function that applies the `quad` function twice on 2:

```
$ ((repeated quad 2) 3)
15
$ ((repeated quad 3) 2)
23
```

6.4.5. *[Smooth]* The idea of smoothing a function is an important concept in signal processing. If `f` is a function and `dx` is a small number, then the smoothed version of `f` is the function whose value at a point x is the average of `f(x - dx)`, `f(x)`, and `f(x + dx)`.

Write a function `smooth` that takes two inputs, a function that computes `f` and a smoothing parameter `dx`, and returns a function that computes the smoothed value of `f`. Your function `smooth` should permit the following usage:

```
$(define quad (lambda (x) (+ (* 2 x) 1)))
$ ((smooth quad 1) 10)
21
$ ((smooth quad 1) 1)
3
$ ((smooth quad 1) 0)
1
$ ((smooth quad 1) 30)
61
```

6.4.6. *[GCD]* The greatest common divisor (GCD) of two numbers a and b is defined as follows: If a > b, then (gcd a b) is gcd of a − b and b. Else, if a < b, then (gcd a b) is gcd of a and b − a. Otherwise, it is a.

1. Define a function gcd that computes the GCD according to the definition given here.

   The following interaction log illustrates the function:

   ```
   $ (gcd 4 2)
   2

   $ (gcd 12 15)
   3
   ```

2. Use the function gcd to define GCDs that takes two lists of numbers and produces a third list that contains the list of GCDs of corresponding elements from the first and the second list.

   The following interaction log illustrates the function:

   ```
   $(gcds (list) (list))

   ()

   $ (gcds (list 4) (list 2))
   (2)

   $ (gcds (list 4 12) (list 2 15))
   (2 3)
   ```

6.4.7. Define a higher-order function forloop that takes three arguments: an initial value (counter) representing the initial value of the loop counter, a function (condition) representing a test expression with a single argument, and a function (increment) representing the loop counter increment function with a single argument. It outputs another function that, when run with a function as argument (say, loopbody), runs loopbody starting with the initial value of the loop counter until the condition returns `false`, while incrementing the loop counter using the `increment` function.

The examples here assume the following function definitions:

```
(define inc (lambda (x) (+ x 1)))
(define inc2 (lambda (x) (+ x 2)))
(define test25 (lambda (x) (< x 25)))
(define test42 (lambda (x) (< x 42)))
(define body (lambda (x) (+ x 42)))
```

Some examples of using the `forloop` function are presented here:

```
$ ((forloop 0 test25 inc) body)
66
$ ((forloop 1 test25 inc) body)
66
$ ((forloop 0 test42 inc) body)
83
$ ((forloop 1 test42 inc) body)
83
$ ((forloop 43 test42 inc) body)
-1
$ ((forloop 43 test25 inc) body)
-1
```

6.5 Functional Data Structures

Our ability to define abstractions that represent a piece of computation is essential to creating meaningful software systems, but we also need to be able to represent data structures. Fortunately, first-class functions of Funclang can serve both purposes equally well.

To illustrate this point, imagine that we want to create a data type that holds a pair of values. In order to define the data type, from the perspective of the client of the data type, it would be sufficient to provide definitions for all operations that can be applied to that data type: a constructor for creating pairs, an observer for getting the first element of the pair, and another observer for getting the second element of the pair. We can define a constructor operation that can be used to create values of that data type as follows:

```
(define pair
  (lambda (fst snd)
    (lambda (op)
      (if  op fst snd)
    )
  )
)
```

We can then use this operator to create a new pair value:

```
$ (pair 3 4)
(lambda ( op ) ( if  op fst  snd))
```

Here, `pair` is a higher-order function. It returns a *function value* that takes a single parameter op and, based on the value of op, evaluates to `fst` or `snd`. We can also store this pair to use later:

```
$ (define apair (pair 3 4))
```

An important property to reemphasize here is that `apair` is a function value. This function can be called by providing a value for the parameter op, which will then run its body `(if op fst snd)`. The body of the function has two variables, `fst` and `snd`. So, in addition to the code, the function value `apair` also stores mappings from `fst` to 3 and `snd` to 4.

Now, we can define the observer operations `first` and `second`:

```
$ (define first  (lambda (p) (p #t)))
$ (define second (lambda (p) (p #f)))
$ ( first  apair)
3
$ (second apair)
4
```

The functions `first` and `second` assume that their argument p is a function. We can implement runtime checks, but for simplicity, let us disregard them at the moment. These functions then call p with the arguments `#t` and `#f`, respectively. Recall from the earlier discussion that when a function value created by the constructor `pair` is called with argument `#t` and `#f`, it returns the value of `fst` or `snd`, respectively.

Exercises

6.5.1. *[Procedural representation of records]* Define a function, `record`, which takes a list of strings, `fields`, and a list of values, `values`, and returns a procedural representation of record. Write a second procedure, `lookup`, which takes a procedural representation of record and a string and returns the *i*th element of the list `values` if *i* is the index of name in list `fields`. For example:

```
$ (define roman (record (list "i" "v" "x") ( list  1 5 10)))
$ (lookup roman "i")
1
$ (lookup roman "v")
5
$ (define empty (record ( list ) ( list )))
$ (lookup empty "a")
"error"
```

```
$ (define bad (record ( list ) ( list  1 2 3)))
$ (lookup bad "a")
"error"
$ (define bad2 (record ( list  a b c) ( list )))
$ (lookup bad2 "a")
"error"
```

6.5.2. *[Procedural representation of tree]* Define a procedural representation of a binary tree. A binary tree is either a terminal node that contains a value or a nonterminal node containing two children that are both binary trees. Define two constructors, leaf and interior, for creating terminal and nonterminal trees. Define an observer, traverse, that traverses the tree in a depth-first manner, applies op to each value stored in the tree, and applies combine to combine values from the root node, left subtree, and right subtree to produce a single value:

```
(define leaf (lambda (leafval) ... ))
(define interior (lambda (rootval lefttree  righttree ) ... ))
(define traverse (lambda (tree op combine) ... ))
```

6.6 Currying

All the functions that we have written so far are defined using lambda abstractions that could take zero or more arguments. The ability to take zero or more arguments isn't an essential property of a lambda abstraction. In fact, in a programming language with support for first-class functions, it is possible to model multiple argument lambda abstractions as a combination of single-argument lambda abstraction. Take the function plus, which we defined previously as follows:

```
(define plus
  (lambda (x y)
    (+ x y)
  )
)
```

We can easily redefine plus using single-argument lambda abstractions as follows:

```
(define plusCurry
  (lambda (x)
    (lambda (y)
      (+ x y)
    )
  )
)
```

This form in which a function is defined using only single-argument lambda abstractions is called its *curried form*. Since a curried form accepts only a single argument, calling it is slightly different. An example appears here:

```
$ ((plusCurry 3) 4)
7
```

Note that the expression (`plusCurry 3`) only partially evaluates the function. The value of this expression is a function, which when applied on 4 evaluates to the final value 7.

Exercises

6.6.1. *[volume]* Write a curried form of a function using a lambda abstraction that takes the length, width, and height of a cuboid and computes the volume of the cuboid by multiplying the length, width and height.

  Use that function to compute the volume of a cuboid with a length equal to 3, width equal to 4, and height equal to 2.

6.6.2. *[speed-mph]* Define a curried version of the following procedure, calling it `speed-mph`:

```
(define (speed kms kmToMile hours)
  (/ (* kms kmToMile) hours) )
```

  Test your code by executing the following:

```
$ // Speed of carA that traveled 150 km in 2 hours in mph
$ (speed 150 0.62 2)
46.5
$ // Speed of carB that traveled 250 miles in 3 hours in mph
$ (speed 250 0.62 3)
51.666666666666664
```

6.6.3. *[speed-miles-per-two-hours]* Using your solution from problem 6.6.2, define a procedure as follows:

```
speedMilesPerTwoHours
```

which takes a single number (kilometers) as an argument and computes the speed of a car in miles per 2 hours.

  Test your code by executing the following:

```
$ (speedMilesPerTwoHours 50)
$ (speedMilesPerTwoHours 120)
```

In the rest of this chapter, we will explore various aspects of the semantics of function definitions and calls by building an implementation of Funclang. As with Varlang, we will build an interpreter as opposed to a compiler. Fortunately, we have the Definelang implementation to work with. So the interpreter discussed in this chapter will build on that.

6.7 Syntax of Lambda and Call Expressions

We will first build support for lambda abstractions and calls, and discuss other features such as the list-related functions, if expression, and conditional expressions.

Program	::=	DefineDecl* Exp?	*Program*
DefineDecl	::=	(**define** Identifier Exp)	*Define*
Exp	::=		*Expressions*
		Number	*NumExp*
	|	(+ Exp Exp+)	*AddExp*
	|	(- Exp Exp+)	*SubExp*
	|	(* Exp Exp+)	*MultExp*
	|	(/ Exp Exp+)	*DivExp*
	|	Identifier	*VarExp*
	|	(**let** ((Identifier Exp)+) Exp)	*LetExp*
	|	(Exp Exp+)	***CallExp***
	|	(**lambda** (Identifier+) Exp)	***LambdaExp***
Number	::=	Digit	*Number*
	|	DigitNotZero Digit+	
Digit	::=	[0-9]	*Digits*
DigitNotZero	::=	[1-9]	*Non-zero Digits*
Identifier	::=	Letter LetterOrDigit*	*Identifier*
Letter	::=	[a-zA-Z$_]	*Letter*
LetterOrDigit	::=	[a-zA-Z0-9$_]	*LetterOrDigit*

Figure 6.1
Grammar for the Funclang language. Nonterminals that are not defined in this grammar are exactly the same as in Definelang.

Like the grammar for Definelang, in the grammar for Funclang shown in figure 6.1, a program consists of zero or more definitions (define declarations), followed by an optional expression (exp)?. We also have two new expressions, LambdaExp and CallExp. We have used the syntax of these expressions often in previous sections of this chapter. We also need to extend the abstract syntax tree (AST) representation to support these two new nodes, as shown in figure 6.2.

The AST node for a lambda expression has fields to store the formal parameter names and the body of the lambda expression, whereas the call expression has fields to store the operator expression and zero or more operand expressions.

We would also need to extend the visitor infrastructure to accommodate these language changes. That will include adding new methods to the Visitor interface for the

```
1    class LambdaExp extends Exp {
2      List<String> _formals;
3      Exp _body;
4      LambdaExp(List<String> formals, Exp body) {
5        _formals = formals;
6        _body = body;
7      }
8      List<String> formals() { return _formals; }
9      Exp body() { return _body; }
10     Object accept(Visitor  visitor , Env env) {
11       return visitor . visit (this, env);
12     }
13   }

15   class CallExp extends Exp {
16     Exp _operator;
17     List<Exp> _operands;
18     CallExp(Exp operator, List<Exp> operands) {
19       _operator = operator;
20       _operands = operands;
21     }
22     Exp operator() { return _operator; }
23     List<Exp> operands() { return _operands; }
24     Object accept(Visitor  visitor , Env env) {
25       return visitor . visit (this, env);
26     }
27   }
```

Figure 6.2
New AST nodes for the Funclang language

CallExp and LambdaExp types. The standard visitors, such as Formatter, would need to provide the functionality to handle AST nodes of these new types. The reader is encouraged to review these changes in the companion code on the website before proceeding further.

6.8   Value of a Lambda Expression

Functions are a *first-class feature* in Funclang since the values of type functions are treated just like numeric, string, Boolean, and list values. They can be passed as parameters, returned as values, and stored in environments.[1] This enables us to program higher-order functions, as well as procedural representation of data structure, as discussed in previous sections.

---

1. An expression (let ((identity (lambda (x) x))) ...) stores a 2-tuple: a name identity and a value of type FunVal in the environment.

Since the Funclang program and expressions can produce functions as values, it becomes essential to extend the set of legal values to include a new kind of value as follows: `FunVal`.

From our previous discussion about the lambda expression, recall that a lambda expression evaluates to a function value as follows:

VALUE OF LAMBDAEXP

$$\frac{(\texttt{FunVal var}_i, \texttt{for i = 0...k exp}_b \texttt{ env}) = v}{\texttt{value (LambdaExp var}_i, \texttt{for i = 0...k exp}_b) \texttt{ env} = v}$$

Value	::=		*Values*
		NumVal	*Numeric Values*
	|	FunVal	*Function Values*
NumVal	::=	(NumVal n)	*NumVal*
FunVal	::=	(**FunVal** var$_0$, .., var$_n$ e env)	*FunVal*
		where var$_0$, .., var$_n$ $\in$ Identifier,	
		e $\in$ Exp, env $\in$ Env	

Figure 6.3
The set of legal values for the Funclang language

Here, `FunVal` is a new kind of value for Funclang as shown in figure 6.3. It encapsulates the names of the formal parameter, the body of the lambda expression, and the current environment. A realization of `FunVal` is shown in figure 6.4.

```
1   class FunVal implements Value {
2       private Env _env;
3       private List<String> _formals;
4       private Exp _body;
5       public FunVal(Env env, List<String> formals, Exp body) {
6           _env = env;
7           _formals = formals;
8           _body = body;
9       }
10      public Env env() { return _env; }
11      public List<String> formals() { return _formals; }
12      public Exp body() { return _body; }
13  }
```

Figure 6.4
FunVal: A new kind of value for functions

The implementation of the lambda expression case in the interpreter is shown here:

```
Value visit (LambdaExp e, Env env) {
    return new Value.FunVal(env, e.formals(), e.body());
}
```

This implementation exactly models the semantics. It creates a function value that encapsulates the formal parameter names, function body, and current environment.

6.9   Value of a Call Expression

Evaluating a call expression includes three key steps:

1. *Evaluate the operator.* Evaluate the expression whose value will be the function value. For example, for the call expression (`identity i`), the value of the variable expression `identity` will be the function value.
2. *Evaluate the operands.* For each expression that is in place of a formal parameter, evaluate it to a value. For example, for the call expression (`identity i`), the value of the variable expression `i` will be the only operand value.
3. *Evaluate the function body.* This step has three parts:

   i. Find the expression that is the body of the function value.
   ii. Create a suitable environment for that body to evaluate.
   iii. Evaluate the body.

   For example, for the call expression (`identity i`), if the function value is (`lambda (x) x`), then the body of the function is `x`. A suitable environment for running the body of this function would have a binding from the formal parameter name `x` to the actual parameter value (`1` for our example call expression). Evaluating that body would result in the value `1`.

The value relation here models this intent:

VALUE OF CALLEXP

$$\frac{\begin{array}{c} \texttt{value exp}_b \texttt{ env}_{k+1} \texttt{ = v} \\ \texttt{value exp env = (FunVal var}_i\texttt{, for i = 0...k exp}_b \texttt{ env}_0\texttt{)} \\ \texttt{value exp}_i \texttt{ env = v}_i\texttt{, for i = 0...k} \\ \texttt{env}_{i+1} \texttt{ = (ExtendEnv var}_i \texttt{ v}_i \texttt{ env}_i\texttt{), for i = 0...k} \end{array}}{\texttt{value (CallExp exp exp}_i\texttt{, for i = 0...k) env = v}}$$

The first condition above the line says that the value of a call expression is the value of `body` in a new environment, env_{k+1}. The second condition says that evaluating `exp` results in a function value, and that function value has exp_b as the function body. We also get the names of the formal parameters var_i, for i = 0...k from the function value. The third condition says that evaluating each of the exp_0 to exp_k in the original environment results in the values v_0 to v_k, respectively. The fourth condition defines the extended environment env_{k+1}, which maps the formal parameter names to the corresponding actual parameter values.

The case for `CallExp` in the interpreter implements this semantics as discussed next. To improve user experience, it also implements some checks. For example, if the result of evaluating the operator is not a function value; for example, in expression (`1 2`), the result is a dynamic error. Similarly, if the number of formal parameters does not match the number of actual arguments, the call expression also results in a dynamic error.

6.9.1 Dynamic Errors

To support a dynamic error as a legal value, we redefine the set of legal values in Funclang as shown in figure 6.5. A dynamic error encapsulates a string s (e.g., for describing the cause of the error).

Value	::=		*Values*
		NumVal	*Numeric Values*
	|	FunVal	*Function Values*
	|	DynamicError	*Dynamic Error*
NumVal	::=	(NumVal n)	*NumVal*
FunVal	::=	(**FunVal** var_0, .., var_n e env)	*FunVal*
		where var_0, .., $var_n \in$ Identifier,	
		e $\in$ Exp, env $\in$ Env	
DynamicError	::=	(DynamicError s),	*DynamicError*
		where s $\in$ the set of Java strings	

Figure 6.5
The set of legal values for the Funclang language with new dynamic error values

There are no expressions that the programmer can use to produce dynamic errors directly with their own custom string. However, programmers can easily produce dynamic errors indirectly, such as by using a call expression incorrectly.

6.9.2 Implementation of a Call Expression

The implementation also mirrors the value relation and the informal semantics of call expressions:

```
Value  visit (CallExp e, Env env) {
  // Step 1: Evaluate operator
  Object result = e.operator().accept(this, env);
  if (!( result instanceof Value.FunVal))
    return new Value.DynamicError("Operator not a function");
  Value.FunVal operator = (Value.FunVal) result;
  List<Exp> operands = e.operands();

  // Step 2: Evaluate operands
  List<Value> actuals = new ArrayList<Value>(operands.size());
  for(Exp exp : operands)
    actuals.add((Value)exp.accept(this, env));

  // Step 3: Evaluate function body
  List<String> formals = operator.formals();
  if (formals.size()!=actuals.size())
    return new Value.DynamicError("Argument mismatch in call ");
  Env fenv = appendEnv(operator.env(), initEnv);
  for (int i = 0; i < formals.size(); i++)
    fenv = new ExtendEnv(fenv, formals.get(i), actuals.get(i));
  return (Value) operator.body().accept(this, fenv);
}
```

In the third step, evaluating in the function body, an environment for running the function body `fenv` is created by first appending the bindings from function value and the initial environment, and then successively adding mapping from the formal parameters to the actual parameters. The first step uses a recursively defined helper function `appendEnv` as follows:

```
Env appendEnv(Env fst, Env snd){
  if ( fst .isEmpty())
    return snd;
  ExtendEnv f = (ExtendEnv) fst;
  return new ExtendEnv(appendEnv(f.saved_env(),snd), f.var(),f.val());
}
```

In summary, to support function definitions and calls, we included a new kind of value, `FunVal`, for encapsulating aspects of a function definition, added support for `lambda` and call expressions in the read phase, supported new AST nodes to store lambda and call expressions, and changed the evaluator to add the semantics for lambda and call expressions. We also added a new kind of value, `DynamicError`, for representing error conditions in the evaluation of function calls.

Exercises

6.9.1. *[Environment optimization]* Optimize the function call semantics by reducing the size of the environment saved in `FunVal` so that it contains only mappings from free variables in the function body to their bindings in the current environment.

6.9.2. *[Substitution-Based Call Expression]* Extend the Funclang programming language from problem 6.9.1 to implement a *substitution-based variation* of the call expression (say [ ] expression). Recall that a substitution-based semantics works as follows. The value of [(lambda (x y) (+ x y)) 3 4] is the value of a new expression created from the original function body (+ x y) by replacing x with 3 and y with 4. According to substitution-based semantics, the value of the call expression is the value of (+ 3 4), which is 7.

The grammar of this new language feature should be exactly the same as the grammar of the `call` expression in the Funclang language, except for the syntax [ ].

Implement substitution as a `subst` method for each AST node, such that given a list of variable names and a list of values, the `subst` method returns a copy of the current AST node with each free variable name substituted for the corresponding value.

6.9.3. *[Tracing Lambda Abstractions]* Extend the Funclang programming language to implement a tracing lambda expression `tlambda`, which prints "Entering `a function"` before starting to run the function body, and `"Exiting a function"` after returning.

6.9.4. *[Dynamic Binding]* An alternative to static binding is *dynamic binding*, in which the function body is evaluated in an environment obtained by extending the environment at the function call point (instead of the environment at the function declaration point that is used for static binding).

Extend FungLang with a dynamic call expression that has the syntax `'('` `'dynamic'` `expr expr*` `')'`. A dynamic call expression is evaluated using dynamic binding.

The following examples illustrate the difference between dynamic and static bindings during function calls. Consider the program here:

```
(let
  ((a 3))
  (let
    ((p  (lambda (x) (– x a))))
    (let
      ((a  5))
      (– (p 11) (p 11))
    )
  )
)
```

The value of this program is 0. In the expression given here, variable *a* is bound to 3.

Now consider another version of the program that uses dynamic call expression:

```
(let
  ((a 3))
  (let
    ((p  (lambda (x) (– x a))))
    (let
      ((a  5))
      (– (p 11)  (dynamic p 11))
    )
  )
)
```

The value of this program is 2. Here, variable *a* is bound to 5.
Consider another program that uses static binding only:

```
(let
  ((a 3))
  (let
    ((p  (lambda (x) (– x a))))
```

```
  (let
    ((a  5))
    (− a (p 2))
  )
 )
)
```

The value of this program is 6. Here, variable *a* is bound to 3.

```
(let
  ((a 3))
  (let
    ((p  (lambda (x) (− x a))))
    (let
      ((a  5))
      (− a (dynamic p 2))
    )
  )
)
```

If the program used dynamic binding, since the variable *a* will be bound to 5, the value of this program will be 8.

6.9.5. *[Default parameters]* In this question, you will explore a semantic variation of function call and return.

A function definition can provide default values for the function's parameters. Extend the Funclang interpreter to support functions with the default value for their last parameters (not all parameters).

The following interaction log illustrates the syntax and semantics for our desired extension:

```
$ (define func (lambda ((v = 342))  v)  )
$ (func)
342

$ (func 541)
541

$ (define add (lambda (a (b = 5)) (+ a b))  )
$ (add 8)
13

$ (add 8 4)
12
```

6.9.6. *[Implicit parameters]* In this question, you will explore a semantic variation of function call and return.

A function can take an implicit parameter. Extend the Funclang language to support function calls that can optionally provide an implicit parameter, 'this.'

The following interaction log illustrates the syntax and semantics of our desired extension:

```
$ (define f (lambda () this))
```

Here, the function f is using the implicit parameter 'this' in its body:

```
$ (define obj ( list  3 4 2))
$ (obj.f)
(3 4 2)
```

In the function call, obj is being provided as the value of the implicit parameter 'this' to be used in the function body f.

Here are some more examples of defining and using such functions:

```
$ (define first  (lambda () (car this)))
$ (obj. first )
3
$ (define second (lambda () (car (cdr this))))
$ (obj.second)
4
```

6.9.7. *[Variable argument functions]* In this question, you will explore a semantic variation of function call and return.

A function can take a variable number of parameters. Such functions are known as *varargs* or *variadic functions*. Extend the Funclang language to support variable argument functions with the following syntax:

```
'(' lambda '(Identifier  ... ')'  exp ')'
```

This syntax (especially . . . three dots) allows a lambda expression with a variable number of parameters. Parameters of variadic functions are treated as a list in the body of the function. For example, `(lambda (x ...) (car x))` defines an anonymous function with variable parameters x, where the body of the function returns the first parameter of the function.

A variable number of arguments could be passed when calling a variadic function. For example, in the program `((lambda (x ...) (car x)) 8 2 3)`, the three parameters 8, 2, and 3 are passed to the function. The program returns the first argument in the list of arguments (i.e., it returns 8):

```
$ ( (lambda (x ...)  (car x)) 8 2 3)
8
$ ( (lambda (x ...)  (cdr x))  8 2 3)
```

```
(2 3)
$ ( define variadicFunc (lambda (y ...)  (car y)))
$ (variadicFunc 2)
2
$ (variadicFunc 2 3 4)
2
$ (variadicFunc 2 3 4 5)
2
```

6.10   Call-by-Name Evaluation

What is the value of the program shown here?

```
(define f
  (lambda (x)
    (f x)
  )
)

(define g
  (lambda (fx y)
    y
  )
)

(g (f 42) 42)
```

The function f is a recursive function that invokes itself unconditionally. Therefore, it creates an infinite loop. The function g takes two parameters and uses only the second parameter y. The function call (g (f 42) 42) invokes g with two parameters: the result of invoking f with 42 as the parameter, and 42. According to the call-by-value evaluation that we have studied in this section so far, the actual argument expressions (f 42) and 42 are evaluated to values, and then the function will be invoked. Since the evaluation of (f 42) causes the infinite loop to occur, the function g is never invoked. Depending on the size of the Java stack, this program will lead to errors after a number of recursive invocations of the function f. It really is a pity that the program stops trying to compute the value of fx, which is not even used by the function g.

Some programming languages use an evaluation strategy in which the actual argument is not evaluated prior to calling the function. This strategy is called *call-by-name evaluation*. When used in the context of parameter passing strategy, it is also called *call-by-name parameter passing*.

We can change the semantics of Funclang to realize the call-by-name strategy. The two rules that need changing are the function call rule that needs to wrap the expressions that are used in place of parameters instead of evaluating them directly, and the variable lookup rule. This special kind of value, which is an assurance to provide the parameter value later, is known as a *promise*.

The modified semantics of `CallExp` is shown here:

```
Value  visit (CallExp e, Env env) {
  Object result = e.operator().accept(this, env);
  if (!( result instanceof Value.FunVal))
    return new DynamicError("Operator not a function in call " + ts. visit (e,
        env));
  Value.FunVal operator = (Value.FunVal) result;
  List<Exp> operands = e.operands();

  // Call-by-name semantics
  List<Value> promises = new ArrayList<Value>(operands.size());
  for(Exp exp : operands)
    promises.add(new Value.Promise(env, exp));

  List<String> formals = operator.formals();
    if (formals.size() != promises.size())
    return new DynamicError("Argument mismatch in call " + ts.visit(e, env));

  Env fun_env = operator.env();
  for (int index = 0; index < formals.size(); index++)
    fun_env = new ExtendEnv(fun_env, formals.get(index), promises.get(index));

  return (Value) operator.body().accept(this, fun_env);
}
```

Instead of evaluating each expression to a value as before, in this call-by-name semantics, each argument expression is converted to a promise. Then, each promise is passed as a value to the function. A promise value is very similar to a `FunVal`, as shown here:

```
class Promise implements Value { //New for call-by-name
  private Env _env;
  private Exp _body;
  public Promise(Env env, Exp body) {
    _env = env;
    _body = body;
  }
  public Env env() { return _env; }
  public Exp body() { return _body; }
  public String tostring () {
    String result = "(promise ()";
    result += _body.accept(new Printer.Formatter(), _env);
    return result + ")";
  }
}
```

The main difference is that `Promise` doesn't require any parameters to evaluate, but like `FunVal`, it also stores both the expression and the environment that contains bindings for free variables in that expression.

Another change that is needed concerns the semantics of `VarExp`. The evaluation of this expression needs to distinguish between variable values that are promises and those that are not:

```
Value  visit (VarExp e, Env env) {
  Value v = env.get(e.name());
  if (v instanceof Value.Promise) {
    Promise promise = (Promise) v;
    v = promise.body().accept(this, promise.env());
  }
  return v;
}
```

When a variable value is looked up from the environment and it is a promise, that promise is evaluated to retrieve the actual value. In other words, function evaluation is done lazily and parameter evaluation is deferred until it is actually needed. It is for these reasons that the call-by-name evaluation strategy is also referred to as *lazy evaluation*.

In a version of Funclang that implements call-by-name, what would be the value of the program discussed at the beginning of this section? As was the case with call-by-value, the function name g would be looked up. Next, unlike call-by-value, where we would attempt to evaluate (f 42) and 42, a promise of both these values would be created. These promises would be passed as actual arguments to g. So the body of g will be evaluated in an environment that binds fx to a promise to evaluate (f 42), and y to a promise to evaluate 42. In the body of g, only y is used. Therefore, only the promise to evaluate 42 would be evaluated to the value 42. The promise to evaluate (f 42) will never be used. So the program will never invoke f, and instead of going into an infinite loop, it will terminate with the value 42.

Call-by-name evaluation as demonstrated here is particularly useful for saving unnecessary computations. One of the downsides of call-by-name, however, is that it can interact in an unintuitive way when expressions can modify memory locations, as we will see in later chapters. If an argument expression modifies a memory location, and an other expression relies on that modification, the modification might not even happen or it may happen in an unexpected order. This property may make it challenging to understand programs in languages that support both call-by-name and references.

Next, look at another property of call-by-name that often requires improvement. To illustrate it, consider the program here. How many times does this program invokes the function `factorial`?

```
(define factorial
  (lambda (n)
    ( if (= n 0) 1
      (* n ( factorial (- n 1)))
    )
  )
)
```

```
(define cube
  (lambda (x)
    (* x x x)
  )
)
```

```
(cube ( factorial  42))
```

Calling the function `cube` passes the value of (`factorial  42`) as the actual argument. In call-by-name, instead of computing the value of (`factorial  42`) and passing the value as in call-by-value, a promise to evaluate the expression (`factorial  42`) is created. This promise is passed to the function `cube`, where it is bound to the formal parameter name `x`. The body of the function `cube` looks up the value of the formal parameter name three times. Each such lookup leads to an evaluation of the expression (`factorial  42`). Thus, the function `factorial` is invoked three times. This might not be desirable for functions that are expensive to compute.

To address this problem, some programming languages provide a variation of call-by-name evaluation known as *call-by-need* evaluation. In this parameter passing variation, each promise is evaluated the first time it is used. Then, the value of the promise is cached. This is also referred to as *memoization*, where repeated computation of the promise that could be expensive is optimized. If the promise is used more than once, as is the case for the function `cube` discussed previously, the memoized value of the promise is used instead of evaluating the promise again. With call-by-need, the factorial function will be evaluated only once and its result used for the next two times that `x` is looked up in the function `cube`.

The call-by-need parameter passing strategy offers the advantages of both worlds. It delays the computation, as in call-by-name. It also evaluates the argument expression exactly once, as in call-by-value. In languages that support references, such as those that we discuss later in this book, call-by-need removes some of the limitations of call-by-name. If the argument expression has side effects such as writing to memory, those side effects will not be repeatedly produced. However, like call-by-name, the order in which expressions will be evaluated in call-by-need can still be unintuitive. Thus, understanding programs in languages that support both references and call-by-need can still be challenging.

Exercises

6.10.1. *[Optimized promises]* In the realization of call-by-name discussed so far, a promise is created for each argument expression. That might seem like overkill. For instance, we don't need promises for numeric values like 42 or Boolean values. Modify the semantics of the call-by-name Funclang interpreter to implement an optimized call-by-name that doesn't create promises for basic values like numeric values, Boolean values, string values, and unit values.

6.10.2. *[Call-by-need]* Modify the call-by-name Funclang interpreter to implement the call-by-need parameter passing strategy discussed previously.

6.11   Semantics of Conditional Expressions

We have also added a conditional expression, if, and three comparison expressions, <, =, and > to the Funclang language to improve expressiveness of the language. The syntax for these extensions is given in figure 6.6.

An if expression is different from the if statement in ALGOL-like languages. In Java, for example, an if statement can have a condition, a then block of statements, and optionally an else block of statements. An if expression in a function consists of three expressions: the condition expression, the then expression, and the else expression. All parts are mandatory, and all three of them are expressions.

The comparison expressions are standard, except that like other expressions in Funclang, they are written using the prefix form.

```
Exp   ::=                                          Expressions
        Number                                        NumExp
    |   (+ Exp Exp⁺)                                  AddExp
    |   (- Exp Exp⁺)                                  SubExp
    |   (* Exp Exp⁺)                                  MultExp
    |   (/ Exp Exp⁺)                                  DivExp
    |   Identifier                                    VarExp
    |   (let ((Identifier Exp)⁺) Exp)                 LetExp
    |   ( Exp Exp⁺)                                   CallExp
    |   (lambda (Identifier⁺) Exp)                    LambdaExp
    |   (if Exp Exp Exp)                              IfExp
    |   (< Exp Exp)                                   LessExp
    |   (= Exp Exp)                                   EqualExp
    |   (> Exp Exp)                                   GreaterExp
    |   #t | #f                                       BoolExp
```

Figure 6.6
Extended grammar for the Funclang language. Nonterminals that are not defined in this grammar are the same as those in figure 6.1.

To add these new expressions to the language, we should first decide about the legal values produced by these expressions. Here, we have two options:

1. Encode using NumVal: We could choose to use the domain of NumVal as legal values produced by the comparison expressions and those consumed by the if expressions. For example, a greater expression (> a b) could produce 0 as a value when a is not greater than b; otherwise, it can produce a nonzero value. Similarly, an if expression (if (> a b) ..) could assume that any value of its condition expression (> a b) greater than zero would be taken as true, and false otherwise.

2. Introduce new kind of values: We could also choose to introduce a new kind of value to model boolean conditions. A disadvantage of this option is that the language definition and implementation must support an additional feature. A distinct advantage is that the results of a boolean comparison may not be confused with the results of

Value	::=		*Values*
		NumVal	*Numeric Values*
	|	BoolVal	*Boolean Values*
	|	FunVal	*Function Values*
	|	DynamicError	*Dynamic Error*
NumVal	::=	(NumVal n)	*NumVal*
BoolVal	::=	(BoolVal true)	***BoolVal***
	|	(BoolVal false)	
FunVal	::=	(**FunVal** $var_0, ..., var_n$ e env)	*FunVal*
		where $var_0, ..., var_n \in$ Identifier,	
		$e \in$ Exp, env $\in$ Env	
DynamicError	::=	(DynamicError s),	*DynamicError*
		where s $\in$ the set of Java strings	

Figure 6.7
The set of legal values for the Funclang language with a new **Boolean value**

arithmetic operations since they would be values of a different kind. This has the potential to reduce errors, and so most modern languages introduce boolean as a new kind of value.

In Funclang, following recent trends, we will also extend the set of legal values produced by Funclang programs to include Boolean values. This extended set of values is shown in figure 6.7. A true literal is represented as #t and a false literal as #f, as shown in figure 6.6. A BoolVal can be either true or false.

With a new set of legal values and syntax, we can give the semantics of the three comparison expressions in Funclang as shown here:

VALUE OF GREATEREXP

$$\frac{\text{value } exp_0 \text{ env} = (\text{NumVal } n_0) \quad \text{value } exp_1 \text{ env} = (\text{NumVal } n_1) \quad n_0 > n_1 = b}{\text{value (GreaterExp exp0 } exp_1) \text{ env} = (\text{BoolVal } b)}$$

VALUE OF EQUALEXP

$$\frac{\text{value } exp_0 \text{ env} = (\text{NumVal } n_0) \quad \text{value } exp_1 \text{ env} = (\text{NumVal } n_1) \quad n_0 == n_1 = b}{\text{value (EqualExp exp0 } exp_1) \text{ env} = (\text{BoolVal } b)}$$

VALUE OF LESSEXP

$$\frac{\text{value } exp_0 \text{ env} = (\text{NumVal } n_0) \quad \text{value } exp_1 \text{ env} = (\text{NumVal } n_1) \quad n_0 < n_1 = b}{\text{value (LessExp exp0 } exp_1) \text{ env} = (\text{BoolVal } b)}$$

The semantics of the if expression is a bit more involved, and it is given by the two rules that follow. The first rule handles the case when the Boolean condition exp_{cond} evaluates to true, and the second rule handles the false case:

VALUE OF IFEXP - TRUE

$$\frac{\text{value } exp_{cond} \text{ env} = (\text{BoolVal true}) \quad \text{value } exp_{then} \text{ env} = v}{\text{value } (\text{IfExp } exp_{cond} \text{ } exp_{then} \text{ } exp_{else}) \text{ env} = v}$$

VALUE OF IFEXP - FALSE

$$\frac{\text{value } exp_{cond} \text{ env} = (\text{BoolVal false}) \quad \text{value } exp_{else} \text{ env} = v}{\text{value } (\text{IfExp } exp_{cond} \text{ } exp_{then} \text{ } exp_{else}) \text{ env} = v}$$

The reader is encouraged to review the implementation of these expressions in the companion code before proceeding further.

Exercises

6.11.1. *[Logical conjunction and disjunction expressions]* Extend the syntax and semantics of the Funclang language to add support for the logical conjunction (and) and logical disjunction (or) expressions.
   Examples:

```
$  (&& (< 3 4) (> 4 2))
#t
$  (|| (> 3 4) (> 4 2))
#t
```

6.11.2. *[Switch expression]* Extend the syntax and semantics of the Funclang language to add support for a switch expression.
   Examples:

```
$ (define x 0)
$ (switch (x) (case 0 3) (case 1 4) (case 2 2))
3
$ (define x 1)
$ (switch (x) (case 0 3) (case 1 4) (case 2 2))
4
$ (switch ((+ x 1)) (case 0 3) (case 1 4) (case 2 2))
2
$ (switch (x) (case 0 3) (case 1 4) (case 2 (+ 1 1)))
2
```

6.12   Semantics of Pairs and Lists

A Funclang programmer also has access to pair values, list values, and related expressions. Recall that a pair in Funclang is a 2-tuple. A list is either an empty list or a pair, where the second element is a list.

As shown in figure 6.8, Funclang supports several built-in expressions, such as `list` for creating a new list, `car` for getting the first element of a pair, `cdr` for getting the second element of a pair, `cons` for constructing a pair, and `null?` for checking for an empty list. Support for these expressions is orthogonal to function-related features (as discussed in section 6.5), but Funclang includes this support to make it easier to write interesting programs.

Exp ::=		*Expressions*
	`Number`	*NumExp*
|	`(+ Exp Exp`⁺`)`	*AddExp*
|	`(- Exp Exp`⁺`)`	*SubExp*
|	`(* Exp Exp`⁺`)`	*MultExp*
|	`(/ Exp Exp`⁺`)`	*DivExp*
|	`Identifier`	*VarExp*
|	`(let ((Identifier Exp)`⁺`) Exp)`	*LetExp*
|	`( Exp Exp`⁺`)`	*CallExp*
|	`(lambda (Identifier`⁺`) Exp)`	*LambdaExp*
|	`(if Exp Exp Exp)`	*IfExp*
|	`(< Exp Exp)`	*LessExp*
|	`(= Exp Exp)`	*EqualExp*
|	`(> Exp Exp)`	*GreaterExp*
|	`#t | #f`	*BoolExp*
|	`(car Exp)`	***CarExp***
|	`(cdr Exp)`	***CdrExp***
|	`(null? Exp)`	***NullExp***
|	`(cons Exp Exp)`	***ConsExp***
|	`(list Exp`[*]`)`	***ListExp***

Figure 6.8
Extended grammar for the Funclang language. Nonterminals that are not defined in this grammar are the same as those in figure 6.1.

To support these expressions, we include two additional kinds of value, `PairVal` and `Null`, as shown in figure 6.9. This is an inductively-defined value. A `ListVal` is either an empty list, represented as the type `EmptyList`, or a pair that consists of a value as the first element and a `ListVal` as a second element, represented as the type `ExtendList`. The new AST nodes `ListExp`, `CarExp`, `CdrExp`, `ConsExp`, and `NullExp` are also added to store these expressions.

The semantics of list-related expressions is given in terms of the list values. The value of a `ListExp` is given by the following relation:

value (ListExp exp_0 ... exp_n) env = (ListVal val_0 $lval_1$)

where exp_0 ... $exp_n \in$ Exp   env $\in$ Env
value exp_0 env = val_0, ..., value exp_n env = val_n
$lval_1$ = (ListVal val_1 $lval_2$), ...,
$lval_n$ = (ListVal val_n (EmptyList))

```
Value            ::=                                          Values
                     NumVal                          Numeric Values
                 |   BoolVal                          Boolean Values
                 |   FunVal                          Function Values
                 |   PairVal                              Pair Values
                 |   NullVal                               Null Value
                 |   DynamicError                       Dynamic Error
NumVal           ::=  (NumVal n)                            NumVal
BoolVal          ::=  (BoolVal true)                        BoolVal
                 |    (BoolVal false)
FunVal           ::=  (FunVal var₀,.., varₙ e env)           FunVal
```

FunVal   ::= (**FunVal** $var_0, .., var_n$ e env) *FunVal*
                     where $var_0, .., var_n \in$ Identifier,
                     $e \in$ Exp, env $\in$ Env

PairVal   ::= (PairVal v_0 v_1)   ***PairVal***
                     where $v_0, v_1 \in$ Value

NullVal   ::= (NullVal)   ***NullVal***

DynamicError   ::= (DynamicError s),   *DynamicError*
                     where $s \in$ the set of Java strings

Figure 6.9
The set of legal values for the Funclang language with new **pair and null values**

A corollary of the relation is

$$\text{value (ListExp) env = (EmptyList)}$$

The value of CarExp is given by

$$\text{value (CarExp exp) env = val}$$
$$\text{where exp} \in \text{Exp   env} \in \text{Env}$$
$$\text{value exp env = (ListVal val lval) where lval} \in \text{ListVal}$$

The value of CdrExp is given by

$$\text{value (CdrExp exp) env = lval}$$
$$\text{where exp} \in \text{Exp   env} \in \text{Env}$$
$$\text{value exp env = (ListVal val lval) where lval} \in \text{ListVal}$$

The value of a ConsExp is given by:

$$\text{value (ConsExp exp exp') env = (ListVal val lval)}$$
$$\text{where exp, exp'} \in \text{Exp   env} \in \text{Env value exp env = val}$$
$$\text{value exp' env = lval}$$

The value of a NullExp is given by:

$$\text{value (NullExp exp) env = \#t if value exp env = (EmptyList)}$$
$$\text{value (NullExp exp) env = \#f}$$
$$\text{if value exp env = (ListVal val lval') where lval'} \in \text{ListVal}$$
$$\text{where exp} \in \text{Exp   env} \in \text{Env}$$

Summary

In this chapter, we learned about functions that are a fundamental mechanism for enabling polymorphic abstraction in programming languages. Unlike functions in Java, the function feature developed in this chapter was a *first-class* feature, in that function values could be passed as parameters, returned as values, and stored in data structures. The design of function-related feature is inspired from the lambda calculus and supported anonymous function declarations and function call. We also learned about functions over lists.

One of the most important concepts covered in this chapter was higher-order functions, which are functions that accept other functions as parameters and can return functions as values. We saw that when using higher-order functions, reusable algorithms could be expressed as functions. Furthermore, functions that produce other specialized functions could be developed as higher-order functions.

Using first-class functions as a mechanism, we were also able to define data structures such as pairs and lists. The core idea there was to utilize the binding of free variables to store variable values in the lexical scope of the function. First-class function values acted as the runtime representation of the data structure that retained data. The logic of the data structure could be written in the function body to extract these pieces of data.

Next, we discussed the semantics of lambda expressions and call expressions. In particular, the lambda expression evaluates to a function value that encloses the body of the function, the environment at the lexical scope that contains the value of the free variables in the body of the function, and the names of the formal parameters. Evaluating a call expression includes three key steps: evaluating the expression whose value will be the function value, evaluating the operands, and evaluating the function body in a new environment that extends the function's environment with bindings from formal parameters to actual arguments.

Exercises

6.12.1. *[Pairs and Lists]* In some programming languages such as Scheme, pairs are the basic values and lists are defined in terms of pairs. Define a pair as a 2-tuple and redefine the value relations for `list`, `car`, `cdr`, `cons`, and `null?` in terms of pair values.

6.12.2. *[equal? expression]* Extend the Funclang language to support a new expression `equal?`, which takes two subexpressions and returns `#t` if their values are equal and `#f` otherwise.

The following interaction log illustrates the semantics of `equal`:

```
$(equal? #t #t)
#t
$(equal? #t 1)
#f
$(equal? #t "Hello")
#f
$(equal? (list) (list))
#t
$(equal? (list) (list 1))
#f
$(equal? (list (list 1)) (list (list 0)))
#f
$(equal? (list (list 1)) (list (list 1)))
#t
$(equal? (+ 2 3) (+ 2 3))
#t
$(equal? (let ((x 2)) x) (let ((y 2)) y))
#t
$(equal? (let ((x 2)) y) (let ((y 2)) x))
funclang.Env$LookupException: No binding found for name: y
```

6.12.3. *[List comprehension]* Extend the Funclang programming language to support a new list comprehension expression. A list comprehension is a concise way of representing higher-order functions that operate over a list. It should have the following syntax:

comp–exp : '[' exp '|'   identifier '<–' exp ',' exp ']'

The following interaction log illustrates the list comprehension expression:

```
$ (define add2 (lambda (x) (+ x 2)))

$ (define list1 (list 3 4 2))

$ [ (add2 x) | x <– list1 , #t]
(5 6 4)

$ [ (add2 x) | x <– (list) , #t]
()

$ [ (add2 x) | x <– list1 , (> x 2)]
(5 6)
```

III   REFERENCES AND CONCURRENCY

7 Reflang: A Language with References

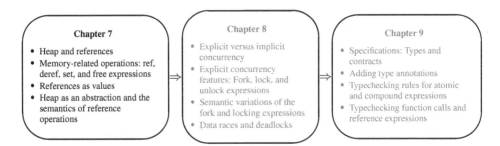

Most programming languages have features that can produce side effects (i.e., the programming language feature can change the state of the program besides its output). Some examples of side effects include:

- Reading or writing memory locations
- Printing on console
- Reading user input
- File read and file write
- Throwing exceptions
- Sending packets on network
- Acquiring mutual exclusion locks

Although understanding programs that use side effects is often more difficult compared to those that are functional,[1] side effects can be indispensable for certain use cases.

Although each kind of side effect mentioned here has some unique semantic properties, semantic issues and design trade-offs pertaining to reading or writing memory locations constitute a representative kind of effect.

7.1 Heap and References

To support reading or writing memory locations, programming languages typically include two new concepts in their definitions:

---

1. Pure functional programs can be understood in terms of their input and output. Given the same input, a functional program would produce the same output.

- *Heap:* An abstraction representing area in the memory reserved for dynamic memory allocation
- *References:* Locations in the heap

Since heap size is finite, programming languages adopt the following strategies to remove unused portions of memory so that new memory can be allocated:

- *Manual memory management:* In this model, the language provides a feature (e.g., free in C/C++) to deallocate memory, and the programmer is responsible for inserting memory deallocation at appropriate locations in their programs.
- *Automatic memory management:* In this model, the language does not provide explicit feature for deallocation. Rather, the language implementation is responsible for reclaiming unused memory. Languages like Java and C# adopt this model.

Programming languages also differ in how they support references:

- *Explicit references:* In some languages, references are program objects available to the programmer. Examples of such languages includes C and C++.
- *Implicit references:* In other languages, references are available only to the language implementation. Some actions of programs implicitly create references.

Languages also differ in what operations are supported on references:

- *Reference arithmetic:* In some languages, references are treated as positive integers and all arithmetic operations on references are available to the programmer. Examples of such languages includes C and C++.
- *Deref and assignment only:* In other languages, references can be used for only two operations: dereference, to get the value stored at that location in the heap; and assignment, to change the value stored at that location in the heap.

Last but not least, languages also differ in how individual memory locations in heap are treated:

- *Untyped heap:* The type of value stored at a memory location is not fixed; it can change during the program's execution.
- *Typed heap:* Each memory location has an associated type, and it can contain only values of that type. Therefore, the type of the value stored at a memory location doesn't change during the program's execution.

Exercises

7.1.1. *[Heap]* Design and implement Heap, a new abstraction representing area in the memory reserved for dynamic memory allocation. For testing, you can assume the capacity of the heap to be 8 KB.

- The heap abstraction internally maintains a contiguous space of memory and a *free list*, which is a collection of 2-tuple (location, size) representing available space. The collection of tuples representing available space starts with a single entry (0, size), where size is the capacity of the heap.

- The `heap` abstraction provides four operations: `alloc`, `get`, `set`, and `free`.
- The `alloc` operation takes a single parameter, the size of desired memory space, which is a numeric value in the language. It scans the free list and finds the first available space sufficient for allocation, returns that location, and adjusts the free list to reflect this memory allocation.

  If contiguous space is not available, the `alloc` operation throws an exception of type `InsufficientMemoryException`.
- The `get` operation takes a single parameter: location, which is a numeric value in the language, and returns the value stored at that location. If the location is in the free list, an exception of type `SegmentationFault` is raised. If the location is out of bounds of the heap, again an exception of type `SegmentationFault` is raised.
- The `set` operation takes two parameters: location, which is a numeric value in the language, and value, which is also a numeric value to be stored at that location. If the location is in the free list, an exception of type `SegmentationFault` is raised. If the location is out of bounds of the heap, again an exception of type `SegmentationFault` is raised. Otherwise, the heap is modified so that the value is stored at the location.
- The `free` operation takes two parameters, location and size, both of which are numeric values in the language. If the location is already in the free list, it does nothing. Otherwise, it puts the location in the free list.

7.1.2. *[Fragmented heap]* Create an example allocation and deallocation test case for heap, which allocates n chunks of memory of size s, where n is `size/s`. Here, size is the capacity of the heap. The test case then frees every alternate chunk of memory to effectively free approximately half the heap (i.e., zeroth chunk, second chunk, fourth chunk, and so on). Finally, the test case should try to allocate a chunk of memory with size 2 s.

7.1.3. *[Array allocation and access]* Extend the heap abstraction with three operations: `allocArray`, `getAt`, and `setAt`, which allows for treating a chunk of memory as a two-dimensional array. Given the row and column sizes, `allocArray` allocates a chunk of memory sufficient to hold the array. If contiguous space is not available, the `allocArray` operation throws an exception of type `InsufficientMemoryException`.

Given the location of the memory chunk, row number, column number, row size, and column size, the `getAt` operation returns the value stored at that location in the chunk. If the accessed element is outside the legal bounds of the array, the operation throws an exception of type `IndexOutOfBoundsException`.

Given the location of the memory chunk, row number, column number, row size, column size, and a new value, the `setAt` operation changes the stored value at that location in the chunk so it is the new value. If the accessed element is outside the legal bounds of the array, the operation throws an exception of type `IndexOutOfBoundsException`.

7.1.4. *[Untyped access]* Allocate a chunk of memory of size 16 cells containing the consecutive natural numbers 1–16 using the `alloc` and `set` operations provided by the heap abstraction. Then treat this chunk of memory as a 4 x 4 array and use the `setAt` operation to set diagonal elements of this array to the value 0.

7.1.5. *[Array Val and Operations]* Extend the Funclang language to add *array of numeric values* as a new kind of value to the programming language. This would require adding three new kinds of expressions, `arrayexp`, `indexexp`, and `assignexp`. You will also need to generalize the array allocation and access operations for heap from the previous question.

To create an array with three rows, one can use `arrayexp` as follows:

```
$ (array 3)
[ 0
  0
  0 ]
```

In the output, we have adjusted spacing for clarity, but you are simply required to produce output that is equal to these.

To create an array with three rows and four columns, one can use `arrayexp` as follows:

```
$ (array 3 4)
[[0 0 0 0]
 [0 0 0 0]
 [0 0 0 0]]
```

To create a three-dimensional array with three rows, four columns, and height two, one can use `arrayexp` as follows:

```
$ (array 3 4 2)
[[[0 0 0 0]
  [0 0 0 0]
  [0 0 0 0]]
 [[0 0 0 0]
  [0 0 0 0]
  [0 0 0 0]]]
```

To access the second element in an array with three rows, one can use `indexexp` as follows:

```
$ (index (array 3) 1)
0
```

> To access the element in the second row and the first column in an array with three
> rows and four columns, one can use `indexexp` as follows:
>
> ```
> $ (index (array 3 4) 1 0)
> 0
> ```
>
> To assign the second element in an array with three rows, one can use `assignexp`
> as follows:
>
> ```
> $ (assign (array 3) 1 342)
> [ 0
>   342
>   0 ]
> ```
>
> To assign the element in the second row and the first column in an array with three
> rows and four columns, one can use `indexexp` as follows:
>
> ```
> $ (assign (array 3 4) 1 0 342)
> [[0  0 0 0]
>  [342 0 0 0]
>  [0  0 0 0]]
> ```

7.2 Memory-Related Operations in Reflang

In the rest of this chapter, we will develop *Reflang*, a language with references. Reflang
contains expressions for allocating a memory location, dereferencing a location reference,
assigning a new value to an existing memory location, and freeing a previously allocated
memory location. For example, we can allocate a new piece of memory using the *reference
expression* as follows:

```
$ (ref 1)
loc:0
```

A reference expression is like the *malloc* statement in C, C++. It will result in a memory
cell being allocated at the next available memory location. That location will contain value
1. The value of the reference expression is the *location* at which memory was allocated
(here, `loc:0`).

The reference expression is also different from the *malloc* statement in C and C++.
Unlike *malloc*, which accepts the size of the memory that is to be allocated, the argument
of the reference expression is a value that is to be stored at the newly allocated location.
From this concrete value, both the type of the value and the size required to store it can be
derived.

In the Reflang language, we can explicitly free a previously allocated memory location
using the *free expression* as follows:

```
$ (free (ref 1))
```

A free expression is like its namesake in languages like C, C++. It results in a memory at the location that is the value of the expression to be deallocated (`ref 1`).

We can also dereference a previously allocated memory location using the dereference expression

```
$ (deref (ref 1))
1
$ (let ((loc (ref 1))) (deref loc))
1
```

Dereferencing a memory location is a way to find out what is stored at that location. So a dereference expression takes a single expression, one that evaluates to a memory location, and the value of the dereference expression is the value stored at the memory location.

We can also mutate the value stored at a memory location using the assignment expression

```
$ (let ((loc (ref 1))) (set! loc 2))
2
$ (let ((loc (ref 3))) (set! loc (deref loc)))
3
$
```

An assignment expression `set!` has two subexpressions, a left-hand-side (LHS) expression that evaluates to a memory location, and a right-hand-side (RHS) expression that evaluates to a value; and the value of RHS expressions is stored at the memory location that is the value of the LHS expression.

Reflang has an untyped heap (i.e., the type of the value stored a memory location in heap may change over time). We can mutate a memory location to store different kinds of values:

```
$ (let ((loc (ref 1))) (set! loc "2"))
2
$ (let ((loc (ref 3)) (loc2 (ref 4))) (set! loc loc2))
loc:1
$
```

In the two examples given here, initially at the location `loc`, a number is stored. In the first example, the assignment expressions stores a string "1" at that location. In the second example, the assignment expression stores a memory location `loc2` at that location.

7.3   Parsing Reference-Related Expressions

The main changes in the grammar for Reflang are bolded in figure 7.1. This grammar builds on the grammar for the Funclang language.

The notation . . . in figure 7.1 is a shorthand that means that the definition of `exp` includes all the alternatives defined for the Funclang language.

```
Program      ::=  DefineDecl* Exp?                Program
DefineDecl   ::=  (define Identifier Exp)            Define
Exp          ::=                                  Expressions
                  Number                            NumExp
             |    (+ Exp Exp⁺)                       AddExp
             |    (- Exp Exp⁺)                       SubExp
             |    (* Exp Exp⁺)                      MultExp
             |    (/ Exp Exp⁺)                       DivExp
             |    Identifier                         VarExp
             |    (let ((Identifier Exp)⁺) Exp)      LetExp
             |    ( Exp Exp⁺)                        CallExp
             |    (lambda (Identifier⁺) Exp)      LambdaExp
             |    (ref Exp)                          RefExp
             |    (deref Exp)                      DerefExp
             |    (set! Exp Exp)                  AssignExp
             |    (free Exp)                        FreeExp
```

Figure 7.1
Grammar for the Reflang language. Expressions in bold are new to the language. Nonterminals that are not defined in this grammar are exactly the same as those in Funclang.

New expressions also follow the prefix form that we have been using up to this point. To store these new expressions, we also need to introduce four new abstract syntax tree (AST) nodes: `RefExp`, `DerefExp`, `AssignExp`, and `FreeExp`. As usual, adding new AST nodes requires extensions to other parts of the interpreter that must process each kind of expression (e.g., the `Visitor` interface, expression formatter, and other elements).

7.4 RefVal: A New Kind of Value

For the Funclang language, the set of normal values is given by

```
Value : NumVal | BoolVal | StringVal | PairVal | FunVal
```

We also have unit and null values:

```
Value : ... | NullVal | UnitVal
```

Finally, we have a value that represents the abnormal state of programs:

```
Value : ... | DynamicError
```

To support memory-related operations, we add a new kind of value, `RefVal`, to the Reflang language:
```
Value : ... | RefVal
```

The choice to create a separate kind of value, as opposed to using `NumVal` to represent references, has several consequences:

- NumVal cannot be mistaken for references in Reflang programs, which prevents Reflang programs from accessing arbitrary locations in memory. On the other hand, standard locations (e.g., the memory address of memory-mapped devices) cannot be easily encoded.

- Operations on NumVal such as addition, subtraction, and multiplication cannot be applied to references, which also prevents Reflang programs from accessing arbitrary locations in memory. This facilitates understanding of Reflang programs. On the other hand, optimized (in terms of size) representation of certain data structures, such as messages sent on a network, cannot be easily created.

- Extra metadata about references may be encoded in the representation of RefVal. This has the advantage of encapsulating related information in a single abstraction. A separate table of metadata indexed by the reference's numeric value can also be created, but that will require additional maintenance.

7.5 Heap Abstraction

As discussed previously, Heap is an abstraction that represents dynamically allocated memory locations. In essence, a heap maps each reference value to another value as follows:

$$\text{Heap : RefVal -> Value}$$

It may be the case that the heap maps some reference values to the error value Dynamic-Error. The listing in figure 7.2 shows an implementation of the heap abstraction.

```
1 public interface Heap {
2    Value ref  (Value value) ;
3    Value deref  (RefVal loc) ;
4    Value setref  (RefVal loc, Value value) ;
5    Value free  (RefVal value) ;
6 }
```

Figure 7.2
The heap abstraction in the Reflang language

7.6 Semantics of Reflang Expressions

Now, since we have defined two essential concepts, heap and references, we can give semantics to Reflang programs.

Let Program be the set of all programs in Reflang, and Exp be the set of all expressions in Reflang. Also, let p be a program (i.e., it is in the set Program) and e be an expression (i.e., it is in the set Exp), such that e is the inner expression of p. With these assumptions, in the presence of environments, we stated the semantics of a program as, "In an environment env, the value of a program is the value of its component expression in the same environment env" as shown below

$$\text{value p env = value e env}$$

Here, e is an expression, and env is an environment. In the presence of declarations, we further extended this rule, but for simplicity, let us disregard declarations for the moment.

In the presence of heaps, the value relation is extended further:

$$\text{value p env h = value e env h}$$

We can state this relation as, "In an environment env and a heap h, the value of a program is the value of its component expression e in the same environment env and the same heap h."

7.6.1 Semantics of Expressions That Do Not Affect Heap

There are three kinds of expressions in Reflang—those that do not affect heap either directly or indirectly, those that only affect heap via their subexpressions, and those that directly affect heap.

A constant expression is an example of an expression in any Reflang program that does not affect heap directly, and since it doesn't have any component subexpressions, it cannot indirectly affect heap either. The value of a constant expression is a NumVal value. Let e be a constant expression that encapsules the numeric value n. Then,

$$\text{value e env h = (NumVal n) h}$$

where n is a Number, env is an environment, and h is a heap.

The meaning of a variable expression in a given environment and heap is simple. As in previous languages, it is the value obtained by looking up that variable name in the current environment. We can write the relation as follows:

$$\text{value (VarExp var) env h = get(env, var) h,}$$

$$\text{where var} \in \text{Identifier, env} \in \text{Env, h} \in \text{Heap}$$

The variable expression is another expression that does not affect heap.

7.6.2 Semantics of Expressions That Indirectly Affect Heap

Most compound expressions can affect heap if their subexpressions can affect heap. For these expressions, the most important consideration is the order in which a side effect of one expression is visible to the next expression. To illustrate this point, consider the case for addition expression:

$$\text{value (AddExp } e_0 \ldots e_n) \text{ env h = } v_0 + \ldots + v_n, h_n$$

$$\text{if value } e_0 \text{ env h = } v_0 \text{ } h_0, \ldots, \text{ value } e_n \text{ env } h_{n-1} = v_n \text{ } h_n$$
$$\text{where } e_0, \ldots, e_n \in \text{Exp, env} \in \text{Env, h, } h_0, \ldots h_n \in \text{Heap}$$

Since an addition expression has no effect on the environment, all its subexpressions are evaluated in the same environment. However, each subexpression of the addition may affect the heap. Therefore, a left-to-right order is used in the relation given here for side-effect visibility.

In defining such semantic relations for memory-related operations, the order in which side effects from one subexpression are visible to the next subexpression has significant implications on the semantics of the defined programming language. For instance, consider an alternate semantics of the addition expression, in which each subexpression, exp_0 to exp_n, is evaluated using the heap h. Such a model would offer different trade-offs.

7.6.3 Semantics of Heap-Related Expressions

Three expressions in Reflang directly affect heap. These are reference expression, assignment, and free expression. The dereference expression reads memory locations in the heap but doesn't change them. The value relation for the dereference expression is defined as

$$\text{value (RefExp e) env h} = \text{l, } h_2$$

$$\text{if value e env h} = v_0\ h_1$$
$$h_2 = h_1 \cup \{\ \text{l} \mapsto v_0\ \}\qquad \text{l} \notin \text{dom}(h_1)$$
$$\text{where e} \in \text{Exp}\quad \text{env} \in \text{Env}\quad h, h_1, h_2 \in \text{Heap}\quad \text{l} \in \text{RefVal}$$

The relation given here says that to evaluate the value of a reference expression (RefExp e), we must first find the value of the subexpression e, and if that value is v_0, allocate a new location l in the heap and store value v_0 at that location. The value of the reference expression is the reference value l, and the modified heap h_2 contains a mapping from this new location to value. Also, notice that this new heap reflects all the side effects (i.e., memory read/write) performed during the evaluation of the subexpression exp.

The value relation for the assignment expression is defined as

$$\text{value (AssignExp } e_0\ e_1\text{) env h} = v_0, h_3$$

$$\text{if value } e_1 \text{ env h} = v_0\ h_1 \qquad \text{value } e_0 \text{ env } h_1 = \text{l } h_2$$
$$h_3 = \{\ \text{l} \mapsto v_0\ \} \cup (h_2 \setminus \{\ \text{l} \mapsto \_\ \}) \qquad \text{l} \in \text{dom}(h_2)$$
$$\text{where e} \in \text{Exp}\quad \text{env} \in \text{Env}\quad h, h_1, h_2, h_3 \in \text{Heap}\quad \text{l} \in \text{RefVal}$$

Like reference expression, the first subexpressions are evaluated. The order of the evaluation is RHS e_1 and then LHS e_0 (i.e., the side effects produced by e_1) will be visible to e_0. The notation $h_2 \setminus \{\ \text{l} \mapsto \_\ \}$ means subtracting mappings for l from the set h_2.

Several variations of the assignment expression can be conceived (e.g., the value relation given here defines an assignment expression whose value is that of RHS). This semantics allows us to write statements like x = y = z in some programming languages, but it also causes one of the most common logical errors, if (x = y) { ... }, when the programmer actually means a comparison instead of an assignment. A programming language can prevent such errors by taking the value of an assignment expression to be unit (or void, as it is known in some languages).

The value relation for the free expression is defined as

$$\text{value (FreeExp e) env h} = \text{unit, } h_2$$

$$\text{if value e env h} = \text{l } h_1 \qquad \text{l} \in \text{dom}(h_1)$$
$$h_2 = h_1 \setminus \{\ \text{l} \mapsto \_\ \}$$
$$\text{where e} \in \text{Exp}\quad \text{env} \in \text{Env}\quad h, h_1, h_2 \in \text{Heap}\quad \text{l} \in \text{RefVal}\quad \text{unit} \in \text{Unit}$$

The relation here insists that the location to be freed, 1, is actually present in the heap h_1. This may cause dynamic errors in the program. Although freeing a memory location twice does reflect logical problems in the program, in some domains, it may not be considered a critical flaw. So a variation of this semantics may omit this check.

The value relation for the dereference expression is defined as

$$\text{value (DerefExp e) env h = v, } h_1$$

$$\text{if value e env h = 1 } h_1 \qquad \text{1} \in \text{dom(}h_1\text{)}$$
$$\{ \text{ 1 } \mapsto \text{ v } \} \subseteq h_1$$
$$\text{where e} \in \text{Exp} \quad \text{env} \in \text{Env} \quad \text{h,}h_1 \in \text{Heap} \quad \text{1} \in \text{RefVal} \quad \text{v} \in \text{Value}$$

7.7 Realizing Heap

Given the semantic relations that define Reflang, we can now begin to implement the programming language. To that end, figure 7.3 shows a realization of the heap abstraction. This implementation uses an array as back-end storage to implement the heap. So references (RefVal) encapsulate the index of the location in the back-end storage. The listing in figure 7.4 shows the concrete implementation of RefVal. The realization intentionally makes objects of this class immutable.

Several enhancements to the implementation of RefVal are possible. For example, this class can maintain information about whether the encapsulated location has been accessed and with what frequency. This class can also be extended to be able to refer to a larger heap. Currently, the maximum heap size that can be accessed is determined by the maximum value of int. The class can also be extended to maintain information about the type of value found by dereferencing this reference value.

The realization of heap in figure 7.3 provides implementation of each of the four methods, ref, deref, setref, and free.

The ref method is like malloc in languages like C and C++, in that it allocates a new memory location. It is, however, different because it requires a value that is to be stored in that memory location. Traditional malloc requires the size of the memory that is to be allocated. The allocation procedure is relatively simple. The method takes the next available location in the internal representation, _rep, and adjusts index. If the heap is full, a DynamicError is returned, signaling that we have run out of memory.

The deref method is similar to its counterpart in other languages. It returns the value stored at a given reference. This method raises another kind of DynamicError, signaling that an attempt to access a memory location outside the legal heap has been made. In some language implementations, for the sake of efficiency, such checks are not performed. In the absence of such checks, malicious programs may read arbitrary memory locations that may be storing data from other programs. Fortunately, modern operating systems provide checks against malicious usage. However, such checks do not guard multiple threads of execution within a single process from each other.

The setref method changes the value at a given reference. It also raises another kind of DynamicError, signaling that an attempt to access a memory location outside the legal heap has been made.

```
1 class Heap16Bit implements Heap {
2   static final int HEAP_SIZE = 65_536;

4   Value[] _rep = new Value[HEAP_SIZE];
5   int index = 0;

7   Value ref (Value value) {
8     if (index >= HEAP_SIZE)
9       return new Value.DynamicError("Out of memory error");
10    Value.RefVal new_loc = new Value.RefVal(index);
11    _rep[index++] = value;
12    return new_loc;
13  }
14  Value deref (RefVal loc) {
15    try {
16      if (_rep[loc.loc()] == null)
17        return new Value.DynamicError("Null pointer at " + loc.tostring());
18      return _rep[loc.loc()];
19    } catch (ArrayIndexOutOfBoundsException e) {
20      return new DynamicError("Segmentation fault at access " + loc.tostring());
21    }
22  }
23  Value setref (RefVal loc, Value value) {
24    try {
25      if (_rep[loc.loc()] == null)
26        return new Value.DynamicError("Null pointer at " + loc.tostring());
27      return _rep[loc.loc()] = value;
28    } catch (ArrayIndexOutOfBoundsException e) {
29      return new DynamicError("Segmentation fault at access " + loc.tostring());
30    }
31  }
32  Value free (RefVal loc) {
33    try {
34      _rep[loc.loc()] = null;
35      return loc;
36    } catch (ArrayIndexOutOfBoundsException e) {
37      return new DynamicError("Segmentation fault at access " + loc.tostring());
38    }
39  }

41  Heap16Bit(){}
42 }
```

Figure 7.3
An implementation of the heap abstraction in Reflang

The `free` method removes the value stored at a given reference. This method also raises another kind of `DynamicError`, signaling that an attempt to access a memory location outside the legal heap has been made. The current implementation of this method does not consider freeing an already free or unallocated location as an error. The reader may attempt to enhance the semantics of the interpreter to identify freeing an already free or unallocated location as an error. Also, notice that the free method sets the memory location being freed to `null`, thereby removing the older value from that memory location. In some language implementations, to foster efficiency, memory location is not erased by the implementation of free expressions. In such languages, malicious programs may allocate large chunks of memory simply to read data left over by previous programs.

```
1 class RefVal implements Value { //New in the reflang
2     private int _loc = -1;
3     RefVal(int loc) { _loc = loc; }
4     String tostring () {
5         return "loc:" + this._loc;
6     }
7     int loc() { return _loc; }
8 }
```

Figure 7.4
An implementation of the `RefVal` abstraction

The implementation of heap in figure 7.3 makes no attempt to compact the memory locations that are freed. The implementation also does not attempt to recycle memory locations that have recently been deallocated. Those enhancements are the subject of some of the problems in this chapter.

7.8 Evaluator with References

The implementation of new expressions related to references in the evaluator closely models the semantic relations discussed previously. As figure 7.5 shows, every program is evaluated in a fresh heap.

The methods in figure 7.6 implement semantic relations for reference, dereference, assignment, and free expressions. Notice that unlike mathematical relations that are defined using heaps that are immutable sets, in the actual implementation, the global heap of the evaluator is modified in each of the reference, assignment, and free expressions. This realization of these reference-related expressions heavily relies on the semantics provided by the operations of the heap abstraction.

Evaluation of the reference expression `RefExp` proceeds by evaluating its subexpression and then using the heap's helper function `ref` to store that value in a memory location. The value of this expression is the reference value. Notice that this expression does not attempt to stop error values from being stored in the heap. The reader may choose to enhance the interpreter to implement an alternative semantics, in which dynamic errors are not stored in the heap.

```
class Evaluator implements Visitor<Value> {
    Heap heap = null; //New for reflang

    Value valueOf(Program p) {
        heap = new Heap16Bit();
        return (Value) p.accept(this, initEnv) ;
    }

    ...
}
```

Figure 7.5
Evaluator with reference expressions

Evaluation of the dereference expression DerefExp also proceeds by evaluating the subexpression and directly building on the helper method deref, provided by the heap abstraction.

Evaluation of the assignment expression AssignExp proceeds by evaluating the RHS expression, followed by the LHS expression. This order of evaluation ensures that the changes in the heap made by the RHS expression are visible to the LHS expression. The implemented semantics says that the value of an assignment expression is the value of the RHS. An alternative semantics is to take the value of an assignment expression to be a unit value (like the free expression). The reader is encouraged to think about the trade-off between these two semantic choices, especially from the point of view of chaining multiple assignments.

Evaluation of the free expression FreeExp evaluates its subexpression to a reference value and uses the helper method free to remove the stored value at that location in the heap.

7.9   Problems with Manual Memory Management

In this section, we will review two common memory-related problems.

7.9.1   Referencing an Invalid Reference

What is the value of the following Reflang program?

```
( let                                                              1
    ((x  (ref  342)))                                             2
    (                                                             3
        (lambda (x y)                                            4
            (deref x)                                            5
        )                                                        6
        x (free  x)                                              7
    )                                                            8
)                                                                9
```

```
class Evaluator implements Visitor<Value> {
    ...
    Value visit (RefExp e, Env env) {
        Exp value_exp = e.value_exp();
        Value value = (Value) value_exp.accept(this, env);
        return heap.ref(value);
    }

    Value visit (DerefExp e, Env env) {
        Exp loc_exp = e.loc_exp();
        Value.RefVal loc = (Value.RefVal) loc_exp.accept(this, env);
        return heap.deref(loc);
    }

    Value visit (AssignExp e, Env env) {
        Exp rhs = e.rhs_exp();
        Exp lhs = e.lhs_exp();
        // Note the order of evaluation below.
        Value rhs_val = (Value) rhs.accept(this, env);
        Value.RefVal loc = (Value.RefVal) lhs.accept(this, env);
        Value assign_val = heap.setref(loc, rhs_val);
        return assign_val;
    }

    Value visit (FreeExp e, Env env) {
        Exp value_exp = e.value_exp();
        Value.RefVal loc = (Value.RefVal) value_exp.accept(this, env);
        heap.free(loc);
        return new Value.UnitVal();
    }

}
```

Figure 7.6
Evaluator with reference expressions

The program dereferences an already freed location! Thus, it produces a dynamic error as a value with the error message "Null pointer at loc:0." For the source of this error message, see line 17 in figure 7.3. The dereference expression that produces this error is at line 5, and the expression that frees the memory location is at line 7. In this case, an inadvertent free expression causes the program to produce an error.

In programming languages that require programmers to manage memory themselves, dereferencing an already freed location is one of the most common errors, leading to a *null pointer error*. In most modern programming languages, the language runtime manages the memory automatically, thus relieving programmers of this task. There are several potential upsides to the programming language runtime managing the memory for the programmers—the decrease in memory-related errors being the most important. As we will read later, the task of automatically freeing memory has to ensure that no memory location that could still be used by the remainder execution of the program is inadvertently freed. Computing the set of memory locations that are not going to be used is a complex task that often requires using sound upper bounds. Thus, some memory locations that might not be used by the remainder execution might still not be freed by automatic memory management techniques. Thus, in applications where the program needs to operate on a tightly constrained hardware platform and every memory cell is important, automatic memory management techniques are typically not employed, although recent research has made significant progress on improving these techniques, making them more precise.

7.9.2 Running Out of Memory

What does the following interaction with the Reflang interpreter produce? For the purpose of this discussion, assume that the size of the heap is 10:

```
$ (define mref (lambda (x) (if (> (deref (ref x)) 0) (mref (- x 1)) (ref x))))
$ (mref 3)
loc:4
$ (mref 2)
loc:8
$ (mref 0)
```

If no other programs have run already, running the last program produces an out-of-memory error. Note that this error is raised in the semantics of the reference expression when the heap doesn't have any space left. Astute readers might argue that it might make sense to reset the heap between each program so that the program doesn't run out of memory after allocating 10 memory locations. Indeed, that fix in the semantics of the Reflang interpreter will help fix the out-of-memory error for the previous interaction. Next, consider the interaction here, starting with a fresh interpreter:

```
$ (define mref (lambda (x) (if (> (deref (ref x)) 0) (mref (- x 1)) (ref x))))
$ (mref 9)
Out of memory error
```

This program also produces an out-of-memory error. The function `mref` will make nine recursive calls, allocating a memory cell during each call. During the call `(mref 0)`, the program will allocate the 10th memory cell, and because x is zero, the false branch of the conditional expression is evaluated. The false branch attempts to allocate the 11th memory cell, leading to the out-of-memory error because the heap size is 10.

This all seems fairly reasonable. The heap size is 10 cells, and the program ran out of memory after allocating 10 memory cells. This is not the most optimum use of limited memory available to the interpreter. You may notice that after allocating the memory location in the expression `(deref (ref x))`, the program immediately dereferences that memory location, but it doesn't store the reference in any local or global variable, nor does it pass the memory location as an argument to other functions. In other words, after the expression `(deref (ref x))` has completed evaluation, the program does not have a way to refer to the memory cell allocated by the expression `(ref x)`. Such objects that are not accessible to the program are referred to as the *garbage memory*. The program shown previously produces 10 garbage memory cells and runs out of memory when allocating the 11th memory cell. It would be desirable for the program not to waste 10 memory cells.

Most modern programming languages provide a mechanism to detect and remove this wasteful memory. These techniques are called *garbage collection*. In essence, a garbage collection technique identifies those memory locations that are guaranteed to be inaccessible from the remainder of the program and automatically frees them. A garbage collection technique relies on the concept of *reachability*. Given a name, the set of reachable memory locations includes those that can be accessed directly or indirectly using that name. For instance, for the expression here, the reachable memory location for name c is `loc:0`:

```
( let ((c (ref 342))) ... )
```

Similarly, for the expression here, the reachable memory locations for name c are `loc:0`, `loc:1`, and `loc:2`.

```
( let ((c (ref ( list (ref 342) (ref 541))))) ... )
```

Here, value `342` is stored at `loc:0`, value `541` is stored at `loc:1`, and the list value is stored at `loc:2`. The notion of reachability is used to determine which memory locations might still be accessible by the remainder of the program. Then, those memory locations that are not accessible are removed from the heap, since they are garbage.

Summary

In this chapter, we introduced language features that can manipulate memory locations. While previous language features, such as variable definitions and global definitions, also allow multiple parts of a program to share information, memory cells allow multiple names to refer to the same memory locations. Additionally, memory cells can be freed, whereas variables cannot be freed.

We also learned about the heap abstraction and references that point to a memory cell within the heap. Heaps are areas in the physical memory that are reserved for dynamic memory allocation, and references are locations with the heap. We reviewed the memory-related operations `ref`, `deref`, and `free` expressions. To support reference-related operations, we extended the interpreter to have a shared heap. The reference expression creates new locations within that heap, the dereference expressions accesses memory locations pointed to by the reference, and the free expression removes the memory location. We also reviewed how error conditions such as out-of-memory errors are handled by the language semantics. Finally, we reviewed some limitations of manual memory management, which are the driving force behind the development of automatic memory management techniques.

Exercises

7.9.1. The goal of this question is to understand the semantics of the Reflang expressions. Perform the following operations on your implementation of Reflang and explain the output.

```
(deref (ref 1))                                                 1
(free (ref 1))                                                  2
(let ((loc (ref 1))) (set! loc 2))                              3
(let ((loc (ref 3))) (set! loc (deref loc)))                    4
```

7.9.2. Write three Reflang programs that use aliases. Recall that an alias is created when two variables refer to the same memory location.

7.9.3. *[Memory-mapped I/O]* Modify the Reflang language so that the locations 0, 1, and 2 are treated specially as standard input, standard output, and standard error, respectively. Take the following steps to implement this functionality:

1. Modify the heap abstraction so that it allocates memory starting with location 3.
2. Modify the initial environment so that the names `stdin`, `stdout`, and `stderr` are mapped to reference values `loc:0`, `loc:1`, and `loc:2`, respectively.
3. Modify the semantics of a free expression so that attempts to free the locations 1, 2 and 3 result in a dynamic error with the messages, "`Illegal attempt to free stdin,`" "`Illegal attempt to free stdout,`" and "`Illegal attempt to free stderr,`" respectively.
4. Modify the semantics of a dereference expression so that attempts to dereference locations 1 and 2 result in a dynamic error with the messages "`Illegal read from stdout`" and "`Illegal read from stderr,`" respectively. Further, modify the semantics of dereference expression so that attempts to dereference location 0 result in a call to internal read from standard input in your defining language and return the line read from the standard input as a string value. If reading from input causes an input exception, the result should be a dynamic error with the message, "`Read from stdout failed.`"
5. Modify the semantics of an assign expression so that attempts to assign to location 0 result in a dynamic error with the message, "`Illegal write to stdin.`" Further, modify the semantics of an assign expression so that attempts to assign to locations 0 and 1 result in printing the value being assigned (RHS) on `System.out` and `System.err`, respectively. The value of the assign expression in those cases should be a unit value.

The following interaction log illustrates the properties of the resulting language:

```
$ (ref 342)
loc:3
$ stdin
```

```
loc:0
$ stdout
loc:1
$ stderr
loc:2
$ (free stdin)
 Illegal attempt to deallocate stdin (free stdin)
$ (free stdout)
 Illegal attempt to deallocate stdout (free stdout)
$ (free stderr)
 Illegal attempt to deallocate stderr (free stderr)
$ (deref stdout)
 Illegal read from stdout (deref stdout)
$ (deref stderr)
 Illegal read from stderr (deref stderr)
$ (deref stdin)
Memory mapped I/O is cool!
Memory mapped I/O is cool!
$ (set! stdout "Hello World!")
Hello World!
$ (set! stderr "Hello World!")
$ Hello World!
```

7.9.4. *[Versioned heap]* Modify the semantics of Reflang to implement a heap abstraction that implements versions of a heap. In a versioned heap, writing to an existing memory location does not overwrite the old value; rather, it creates a new version of that memory location that contains the new value.

7.9.5. *[Alias notification]* This problem is about references and aliasing. In Reflang, an expression like the following creates two aliases (`class` and `course`) to the memory cell storing the value `342`:

```
(let ((class (ref 342))) (let ((course class)) (deref course)))
```

Modify the Reflang interpreter so it prints a message when an alias is created. An example appears here:

```
$ (let ((class (ref 342))) (let ((course class)) (deref course)))
Alias created: name class ref value loc:0.
Alias created: name course ref value loc:0.
342
```

7.9.6. *[Typed heap]* This question is about a semantic variation of the heap abstraction.

A typed heap enforces the property that in a memory location, only values of compatible types can be stored. Two types are compatible if one is the subtype of the other. Extend the Reflang interpreter to support a typed heap.

Modify the semantics of the assign expression `assignexp` to check that upon setting the value of a location, the type of the new value is compatible with the type of the old value already stored in that location. Otherwise, raise a dynamic error.

Hint: in Java, you can use `isAssignableFrom` to check for compatibility of types.

The following log interaction illustrates the semantics of a typed heap:

```
$(let ((x (ref 0))) (set! x 12))
12

$(let ((x (ref 0))) (set! x #t))
Assigning a value of an incompatible type to the location in  (set! x #t)

$(let ((x (ref (ref 0)))) (set! x (ref(ref(ref 5)))))
loc:4
```

7.9.7. *[Hot locations]* This question is about a semantic variation of reference-related expressions.

A hot heap location is one that is accessed more often by a program. Extend Reflang to support hot store locations.

- The first step in keeping track of hot store locations is to augment the store locations to have an addition integer field, `access-count`.
- The second step is to enhance the logic of accessing a store location to increment `access-count` on both reads and writes of memory locations.

To achieve this semantics, modify the Reflang interpreter as follows:

1. Modify the heap so that each location is a pair of the value and a number (from now on, we will call this number `access_count`). You can also use a separate list to keep track of `access_count` for locations. Initially, the value of `access_count` for each location is 0.
2. Modify the interpreter so that, for every read of a location and assignment to the location, the field `access_count` of the location is incremented up 1.
3. Add a `frequency` expression to Reflang with the following syntax that takes a location and evaluates to the `access_count` of that location:

   freqexp: '(' 'frequency' exp ')' ;

7.9.8. *[Strict free]* This problem is about memory deallocation. In Reflang, the `free` expression deallocates memory. The current semantics of `free` expression is permissive, in that it allows a memory location to be deallocated even if it has been deallocated previously.

Change the semantics of the `free` expression such that attempts to deallo-cate a value that is already allocated result in a dynamic error with the message, "`Illegal deallocation of ref value loc:0`." For example,

```
$ (let ((c (ref 342))) (let ((d (free c))) (free c)))
Illegal deallocation of ref value loc:0
```

7.9.9. *[Reference arithmetic]* This problem is about explicit references. In current realization of the Reflang language, arithmetic operations are not permitted on a reference value.

1. Modify the semantics of a dereference expression such that it can dereference locations specified as explicit natural numbers. See the interaction log here for an example:

```
$ (let ((class (ref 342))) (deref 0))
342
```

2. Modify the semantics of an assignment expression such that it can assign loca-tions specified as explicit natural numbers. See the interaction log here for an example:

```
$ (let ((class (ref 342))) (set! 0 541))
541
```

3. Modify the semantics of addition and subtraction expressions such that addition and subtraction are permitted on reference values.

   In this resulting language, adding one or more numeric values to a reference value creates a reference value. See the interaction log here for an example:

```
$ (+ 1 (ref 342) )
loc:1
$ (+ 1 (ref 342) 1)
loc:2
```

In this language, subtracting one or more numeric values from a reference value results in a reference value. See the interaction log here for an example:

```
$ (– (+ 1 (ref 342)) 1)
loc:0
```

7.9.10. *[Uses reference arithmetic]* This problem is about explicit references.

1. In the previous problem, we enhanced the Reflang language to allow reference arithmetic. Add a new predicate expression, `rarith?`, to check if an expression uses reference arithmetic during its evaluation.
   The expression `rarith?` follows the grammar shown here:

```
rarithexp : '(' rarith ? exp ')';
```

The following interaction log illustrates the semantics of this expression:

```
$ ( rarith ? (+ 1 2))
#f
$ ( rarith ? (+ 1 (ref 342)))
#t

$ (define raddn (lambda (n r) (+ n r)))
$ ( rarith ? (raddn 1 (ref 342)))
#t
```

2. Write an example Reflang program that has reference arithmetic as its subexpression, but that subexpression is not executed during its evaluation. Your program must use at least one lambda expression.

7.9.11. *[Reachability]* This problem is about reachability, which is an important concept for automatic memory management. Given a name, the set of reachable memory locations includes those that can be accessed directly or indirectly using that name. For instance, for the following expression, the reachable memory location for name c is loc:0:

```
$ ( let ((c (ref 342))) (reachable c))
{ loc:0 }
```

Similarly, for the expression here, the reachable memory locations for name c are

```
$ ( let ((c (ref (list (ref 342) (ref 541))))) (reachable c))
{ loc:0, loc:1, loc:2 }
```

Here, value 342 is stored at loc:0, value 541 is stored at loc:1, and the list value is stored at loc:2.

Add an expression reachable that follows the grammar shown here:

```
reachableexp: '(' reachable Identifier ');
```

The value of the reachable expression is a string value that starts with an open brace `{` and ends with a close brace `}`. The string value contains a comma-separated list of reachable locations. Some examples appeared previously.

8 Forklang: A Language with Concurrency and Parallelism

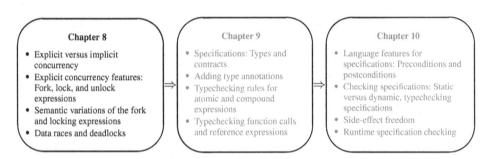

Chapter 8
- Explicit versus implicit concurrency
- Explicit concurrency features: Fork, lock, and unlock expressions
- Semantic variations of the fork and locking expressions
- Data races and deadlocks

Chapter 9
- Specifications: Types and contracts
- Adding type annotations
- Typechecking rules for atomic and compound expressions
- Typechecking function calls and reference expressions

Chapter 10
- Language features for specifications: Preconditions and postconditions
- Checking specifications: Static versus dynamic, typechecking specifications
- Side-effect freedom
- Runtime specification checking

Concurrency is a vital requirement for most modern software systems. It is the ability of a programming model or a programming language to allow running two or more simultaneous activities or *threads of control* during the execution of a software system. Concurrency is important for the following:

- *Building responsive software systems.* For example, imagine that a single thread of control was available for a software system with a user interface. Such a system would perhaps run a loop that will first read a response from the user and then process it. For the duration during which a response is being processed, the software would be unable to accept user responses. This could cause user input to be lost, and at the very minimum it would lead to an unsatisfactory experience typical of sluggish user interfaces.

- *Introducing parallelism in software.* Many software systems perform expensive (i.e., computationally heavy) tasks that can benefit, if the task can be decomposed into subtasks, subtasks can be performed simultaneously, and the result of the subtasks can be combined to determine the result of the original expensive task.

- *Modeling and simulation.* Another large class of software systems is designed to perform modeling and simulation of real-world systems (e.g., the stock market, weather system, astronomical systems, plant physiology, and social networks, etc.). These systems naturally involve entities that are concurrent. Although it is possible to use a single thread of control to model concurrent entities,[1] such modeling introduces complications and often does not naturally encode the domain of simulation.

It is for those reasons that most modern programming languages provide one or more features for concurrency and parallelism.

---

1. Consider a system with n concurrent entities. One methodology to model these entities using a single thread of control is to run an entity for a time slice and then schedule the next entity. The scheduler for an operating system typically performs such time slice–based scheduling.

8.1 Explicit versus Implicit Concurrency

A programming language feature for concurrency can be *explicit* or *implicit*. Explicit features for concurrency provide programmers with greater control over concurrency in their software; concurrent tasks can be started and stopped programmatically. The programming language provides mechanisms for controlling the number and lifetime of concurrent tasks.

An example of an explicit feature for concurrency is `thread`, in the Java programming language. A programmer can create and start a thread.[2]

Implicit features for concurrency provide programmers with mechanisms to identify potential concurrency in their software. The use of these mechanisms by the programmer is then provided as a hint by the programming language implementation. The language implementation itself manages the number and lifetime of concurrent threads during the execution of the software.

An example of an implicit feature for concurrency is the idea of parallel arrays. Applying an operation on the array may implicitly create n parallel tasks, where n is the number of elements in the array.[3]

Another example of an implicit feature for concurrency is an *actor*. Actors are a programming abstraction to model independently acting entities that can communicate with each other by exchanging messages. By describing a computation in terms of a collection of actors, a programmer provides hints to the programming language implementation. The language implementation then manages the number and lifetime of concurrent threads.

8.2 Explicit Concurrency Features

In this chapter, we will first discuss the design, semantics, and implementation of explicit features for concurrency. At the most basic level, a language requires support for both of the following:

- Creating a collection of concurrent tasks
- Mutually exclusive access to memory location

Often, facilities for synchronizing between concurrent tasks are also needed, but they can be easily modeled using facilities for obtaining mutually exclusive access to memory locations.

For simplicity, we can start with an expression to create two concurrent tasks. An example usage of such expression appears here:

```
(fork
  (+ 1 2) (+ 2 1)
)
```

2. To be precise, threads in Java are available as part of the standard library. Similar to Java, threads in C and C++ are available as standard libraries. However, the realization of these capabilities requires special treatment, at least in the runtime library, so in that sense they are not exactly on a par with regular libraries in chapter 6.
3. It would be useful to compare this facility with the `map` higher-order functions discussed in the context of our functional language in chapter 6.

Here, our intent is to run two additions (+ 1 2) and (+ 2 1) as concurrent tasks.

To obtain mutually exclusive access to a memory location, we can devise a lock expression:

```
(let
  ((var (ref 0)))
  (lock var)
)
```

Here, our intent is to obtain mutually exclusive access to the memory location that is pointed to by var.

To release mutually exclusive access to a memory location, we can devise an unlock expression:

```
(let
  ((var (ref 0)))
  (let
    ((val (lock var)))
    (unlock var)
  )
)
```

Here, the intent of the newly added code is to release mutually exclusive access to the memory location that is pointed to by var.

8.3 Semantic Variations of Fork

In designing a programming language feature for creating concurrent tasks, such as the fork expression, several design decisions need to be considered. Next, we discuss these decisions using the fork expression as an example:

- *Value.* What is the value of the fork expression (fork exp exp')? Some languages take the value of a fork expression to be unit (void). In such languages, concurrent tasks (children) created by a task (parent) communicate results to the parent task by writing to some previously decided heap location. In other languages, the value of a fork expression is a task identifier that can be used to uniquely identify a forked task. When a fork expression can fork multiple children tasks as once, such as (fork exp exp'), the value of fork is a set of task identifiers. In other languages, the value of a fork expression is the value of subexpressions as computed by children tasks.

  The manner in which the value of a fork expression is communicated to the parent task has implications on reasoning about the interaction of the parent task and the children. For example, if a heap location is used to communicate value, then the parent might have to implement logic to periodically check that heap location.

- *Join semantics.* What is the join semantics of the fork expression? Several variations may also exist with regard to this aspect. For example, when a task evaluates a fork expression (fork exp exp'), does the evaluation of the parent task goes on? Or does it suspend until the children evaluating exp and exp' complete their work, either normally or abnormally? Alternatively, is it the case that the parent task creates a concurrent task to evaluate `exp`, its own thread evaluates `exp'`, and the evaluation in the parent task's thread waits until the child task evaluating `exp` is done?

- *Sharing semantics.* What is the heap-sharing semantics of the fork expression? For example, when a fork expression (`fork exp exp'`) evaluates, is the heap shared between the parent task and the concurrent tasks that evaluate `exp` and `exp'`? In languages like C, in which the fork construct creates a new process, no heap locations are shared between the parent process and the children, except perhaps those created using shared memory primitives. On the other hand, in languages like Java and C#, in which a forklike construct thread creates a new thread of control, the parent and children may share the entire heap. Besides these extremes, there are also models in which the children tasks and the parent share parts of the heap.

  The sharing semantics also has implications on program design and reasoning. For example, for writing programs in which parent and children tasks collaborate very closely on shared data structures, it would be more efficient to allow sharing of heap locations. On the other hand, allowing such sharing significantly increases the burden of reasoning about programs because programmers now have to reason about interleaving of concurrent tasks with regard to shared memory locations.

8.4   Semantic Variations of Lock Expressions

Similar to the fork expression, in designing mechanisms for providing mutually exclusive access to certain resources, there are several design decisions of interest. Next, we examine these design decisions using the lock and unlock expressions as examples:

- *Blocking versus nonblocking.* The first question is: does evaluating (`lock exp`) block the execution of the current thread if the lock is not available? In some cases, it is preferable to return a Boolean value representing whether a lock acquisition attempt was successful or not. However, the most prevalent semantics is one in which execution of the current thread is blocked if the lock is not available. In some languages, such as Java, alternative primitives for "trying lock" are also available that attempt to acquire a lock and fail if that attempt is unsuccessful, instead of blocking the entire thread.

- *Reentrant semantics.* What happens when a task attempts to acquire a lock that it holds already? Does the lock acquisition attempt go through and have no effect? Another alternative in some languages is to raise an error, treating an attempt to acquire a lock again as a logical error. Yet another alternative in some languages is to treat the second attempt to acquire as a fresh attempt, thereby implicitly releasing the previously acquired lock. Implicitly relinquishing a previously acquired lock may have the effect of allowing other tasks that are waiting for the same lock to acquire it.

- *Memory consistency.* Modern processors consist of a number of cores, each of which is capable of running an independent thread of control. Each core may maintain its local memory known as the *cache*, and every core will share the same main memory. In the design of these processors, to optimize for efficiency cores, do not attempt to maintain an *always consistent* memory model (i.e., it is possible for the same memory location to have different values in the cache of two or more cores of the same processor at the same instant). Rather, the processor design attempts to follow an *eventually consistent* memory model (i.e., values are eventually updated so that they are the same in the cache of all cores).

In designing the semantics of a lock expression, the decision to incorporate memory consistency plays a big role in terms of usefulness of the lock feature, as well as on the performance efficiency of realizing this feature. If locking implies memory consistency, then a concurrent task can rely on locking to safely read or update a memory location and be sure that the value that is read or written is the latest value at that location. That is, the new value updated by the concurrent task will be visible to every other task. On the other hand, having a consistency requirement would mean that the locked value ought to be evicted from the local cache of other cores.

- *Timeout.* What happens when a task attempts to acquire a lock, that lock is held by another task, and the language provides a blocking semantics (i.e., the task that is attempting to acquire the lock is blocked)? Will this task stay blocked forever? This situation is problematic when the other task that holds the lock in question may be either blocked or dead. In such situations, a deadlock may occur. To prevent such deadlocks, some languages provide a timeout feature (i.e., an attempt to acquire a lock blocks the current task for a certain time). After that time, if the lock is still not available, an error is raised and the lock acquisition attempt fails.

Against this background on design and decisions, we now begin a discussion of *Forklang*, a language with explicit features for concurrency and mutually exclusive locks. The Forklang language builds upon the Reflang language discussed in chapter 7, which integrated a model of heap, as well as explicit features for memory allocation, dereference, assignment, and deallocation. We use a language with references as a basis for Forklang to illustrate the behavior of shared memory concurrent programs and their challenges.

8.5   New Expressions for Concurrency

The grammar for newly added expressions is shown in figure 8.1.

```
Expression  ::=  ...                              Expressions
            |   (fork Expression Expression)      Fork Expression
            |   (lock Expression)                 Lock Expression
            |   (unlock Expression)               Unlock Expression
```

Figure 8.1
New expressions for explicit concurrency

For simplicity, we limit the fork expression to creating two concurrent tasks, but being able to create an arbitrary number of concurrent tasks doesn't pose any significant additional challenges.

As usual, to realize these new expressions, new abstract syntax tree (AST) nodes are needed to store their kind and subexpressions. We do not define them here, but the interpreter corresponding to this chapter implements these new AST nodes as the classes ForkExp, LockExp, and UnlockExp.

8.6   Semantics of a Fork Expression

Earlier in this chapter, we discussed several semantic variations of the fork expression. In the rest of this chapter, we will assume a variation in which the value of a fork expression is a pair containing the value of two subexpressions, the join semantics is such that the parent task suspends execution waiting for children to finish, and execution of the parent resumes when both children evaluate to a value.

```
$ (fork 342 342)
(342 342)
```

The sharing semantics that we adopt is one in which the parents and two children tasks share the same heap. Therefore, writes to memory location by one would be seen by the other.

```
$ (let ((var (ref 0))) (fork (set! var 342) (deref var)))
(342 342)
```

To run the subexpressions of a fork expression, we create a data structure that builds on the thread primitive in the defining language:[4]

```
class EvalThread extends Thread {
  Env env;
  Exp exp;
  Evaluator evaluator;
  private volatile Value value;

  protected EvalThread(Env env, Exp exp, Evaluator evaluator){
    this.env = env;
    this.exp = exp;
    this.evaluator = evaluator;
  }

  public void run(){
    value = (Value) exp.accept(evaluator, env);
  }
    ...
}
```

Since the underlying data structure for threads does not allow for passing parameters when a thread is created, the `EvalThread` class is designed to hold the starting environment of the concurrent task, the expression, and the evaluator that is to be used. When this `EvalThread` is started, it simply evaluates the `exp` expression in the current environment. Note that since the heap is stored as part of the evaluator, this concurrent task may share the heap with other tasks.

---

4. This realization strategy is very similar to the realization strategy for the `Thread` class in the defining language Java, which is defined in terms of the operating systems thread primitive (e.g., `PThreads` on Linux systems).

```
public Value value(){
  try {
    this. join () ;
  } catch (InterruptedException e) {
    return new Value.DynamicError(e.getMessage());
  }
  return value;
}
```

To find the result of the subexpression evaluation, the `EvalThread` class also provides a value method, which attempts to join the thread. The attempt to join may cause the calling thread to be blocked until evaluation of the subexpression is done or an exception is thrown.

Using this data structure, we can easily implement the semantics of the fork expression in the evaluator as follows:

```
class Evaluator implements Visitor<Value> {
    ...
    Value  visit (ForkExp e, Env env) {
        Exp fst = e.fst_exp() ;
        Exp snd = e.snd_exp();
        EvalThread fst_thread = new EvalThread(env, fst, this);
        EvalThread snd_thread = new EvalThread(env, snd, this);
        fst_thread. start () ;
        snd_thread.start() ;
        Value fst_val = fst_thread.value() ;
        Value snd_val = snd_thread.value();
      return new Value.PairVal(fst_val, snd_val);
  }
    ...
}
```

This implementation creates and starts two threads to evaluate both subexpressions of the fork expression (constructor call and start calls), finds the resulting value of both expressions, and returns these values as a pair. From the implementation, it is intuitive to see that the fork expression can be generalized to run two or more expressions concurrently.

8.7 Semantics of a Lock-Related Expression

For lock and unlock expressions, recall that we have already discussed several semantic variations. For this chapter, we adopt the blocking semantics for locks (i.e., an attempt to acquire a lock is blocked until the lock is available). Our locks are also reentrant (i.e., the locking succeeds if the current task already holds the lock, as in the example here):

```
(let
  ((var (ref 0)))
```

```
( let
   (( val  (lock var)))
   (lock var)
 )
)
```

To realize lock-related expressions, we also rely upon the synchronization facilities provided by the defining language. We implement the model by extending reference values with locking capabilities:

static class RefVal **implements** Value {

   ...

  /* Locking a memory location */
  int _lockCount = 0;
  Thread _lockingThread = **null**;
  boolean _locked = **false**;

  public synchronized void lock() {
    Thread currentThread = Thread.currentThread();
    wait: **while** (_locked && _lockingThread != currentThread)
      try {
        wait () ;
      } **catch** (InterruptedException e) {
        continue wait;
      }
    _locked = **true**;
    _lockCount++;
    _lockingThread = currentThread;
  }

  public synchronized void unlock() {
    Thread currentThread = Thread.currentThread();
    if (_lockingThread == currentThread) {
    _lockCount—;
    if (_lockCount == 0) {
     _locked = **false**;
      notify () ;
    }
    }
  }
}

The Forklang version of `RefVal` implements two standard utility functions for locking and unlocking a location. The effect of doing so is that each reference value can potentially be locked as originally intended. The `lock` function implements waiting until other threads have released the lock. The call to `wait` is blocked until the lock is available. The `wait` method in Java blocks the current thread until some other thread calls the `notify` method on the same object. If the lock count is zero, then the thread waiting for the lock is notified.

With this semantic change in place, we can implement lock and unlock expressions as follows:

```
Value visit (LockExp e, Env env) {
  Exp value_exp = e.value_exp();
  Object result = value_exp.accept(this, env);
  if (!( result instanceof Value.RefVal))
    return new Value.DynamicError("Locking non–ref val");
  Value.RefVal loc = (Value.RefVal) result ;
  loc.lock();
  return loc;
}
```

Here, the evaluation of the lock expression evaluates the subexpression, checks whether the result is a reference value, and then uses the facilities of the underlying reentrant lock to acquire a lock on that location. The call `loc.lock()` may block if the underlying lock is not available:

```
Value visit (UnlockExp e, Env env) {
    Exp value_exp = e.value_exp();
    Object result = value_exp.accept(this, env);
  if (!( result instanceof Value.RefVal))
    return new Value.DynamicError("Unlocking non–ref val");
    Value.RefVal loc = (Value.RefVal) result ;
    try{
      loc.unlock();
    } catch(IllegalMonitorStateException ex){
      return new Value.DynamicError("Lock held by another thread");
    }
  return loc;
}
```

Our realization of the unlock expression also utilizes the underlying facilities of the reentrant lock to release a previously acquired lock.

8.8 Data Races in Forklang Programs

Data races are one of the most notorious problems of concurrent programs, and they are difficult to detect and reproduce. A data race happens when two or more threads share a memory location and access it without synchronization, and one of these accesses writes to the memory location. A data race can result in different results for the same program. Accesses to shared memory locations can be synchronized by requiring that a lock be acquired before accessing the shared location and be released after the access is done.

To illustrate this point, consider the program here:

```
(let
  ((x (ref 0)))
  (fork
    (set! x (+ 1 (deref x))) (set! x (+ 1 (deref x)))
  )
)
```

In this program, two threads share a memory location x, and both these threads write into x by increasing its value. According to the definition given here, such a program has a data race on location x, and depending on scheduling of the threads, the value of location x can be either 1 or 2. That is, if thread 1 evaluates (deref x) and then the scheduler switches to thread 2 to evaluate its (deref x), and then both threads have the value of x as 0. Then each thread increases the value 0 of x by 1, resulting in the value 1 for x. However, in a different scheduling, the first thread can run and finishes, setting x to 1, and then the second thread can run, setting x to 2. As can be seen, without proper synchronization among accesses to x in these two threads, the program can evaluate to value 1 or 2.

8.9 Deadlocks in Forklang Programs

Deadlocks are another key problem with concurrent programs that prevent the programs from making progress. To illustrate deadlocks, consider the following Forklang program:

```
(let
  ((x (ref 0)))
  (fork
    (lock x) (lock x)
  )
)
```

In this program, two children tasks of a fork expression share a lock x. In the evaluation of this program, one of the threads locks x without unlocking it later. This in turn means that the other thread can never lock x, and thus cannot finish its evaluation. Thus, the second task will be blocked. In some programming languages, once a task finishes, all its acquired resources are automatically released. In such a programming language, the other concurrent task may be temporally blocked, but it will be unblocked as soon as the concurrent task holding the lock finishes executing.

Deadlocks may not necessarily arise due to a single lock. To illustrate deadlocks using more than one resource, consider the following Forklang program:

```
(let
  ((x (ref 0)) (y (ref 0)))
  (fork
    (let ((val (lock x))) (lock y))
    (let ((val (lock y))) (lock x))
  )
)
```

In this program, two children tasks of a fork expression acquire the locks in a different order. The first task acquires the lock on x and then on y, whereas the second task does the reverse. As a result, neither of these tasks may succeed because each will be waiting for the other to relinquish the lock, which will not happen.

Let us look at another famous example in computer science that models philosophers sitting around a table, with a single fork between each philosopher. The example illustrates a deadlock scenario involving multiple concurrent processes:

```
(define fork0 (ref 42))
(define fork1 (ref 42))
(define fork2 (ref 42))

(define philosopher0
  (lambda (f)
    (let
      ((f0 (lock fork0))
       (f1 (lock fork1))
       (result (f (deref fork0)))
       (f1 (unlock fork1))
       (f0 (unlock fork0)))
      result
    )
  )
)

(define philosopher1
  (lambda (f)
    (let
      ((f1 (lock fork1))
       (f2 (lock fork2))
       (result (f (deref fork1)))
       (f2 (unlock fork2))
       (f1 (unlock fork1)))
      result
    )
  )
)

(define philosopher2
  (lambda (f)
    (let
      ((f2 (lock fork2))
       (f0 (lock fork0))
       (result (f (deref fork2)))
       (f0 (unlock fork0))
       (f2 (unlock fork2)))
```

```
      result
    )
  )
)

(define factorial
   (lambda (n)
    ( if (= n 0) 1
      (* n ( factorial (– n 1)))
    )
   )
)

(define philosophers
  (lambda ()
    (fork
      (philosopher0 factorial )
      (fork
        (philosopher1 factorial )
        (philosopher2 factorial )
      )
    )
  )
)
```

Each philosopher attempts to eat by acquiring two forks, one on the left and another on the right. So, the first philosopher, `philosopher0`, will acquire `fork0` and `fork1`, eat (modeled here by solving a function), and then put the forks down (modeled here by unlocking the `fork` variables). Similarly, the second philosopher, `philosopher1`, will acquire `fork1` and `fork2`, eat, and then put the forks down. And the third philosopher, `philosopher2`, will acquire `fork1` and `fork2`, eat, and then put the forks down in turn. In this program, a deadlock can occur when each philosopher has acquired one fork and is waiting for the second fork, held by the neighbor philosopher.

We will not cover deadlock removal strategy in great detail in this chapter, but most strategies rely on establishing a global order on acquiring locks. Then, each process uses that same order to acquire and release the resource. For instance, for our dining philosophers example, if we were to establish an order on the forks from 0–2, and ensured that each philosopher attempted to acquire the lower-number fork before acquiring a higher-number fork, the ordering will prevent deadlocks from occurring. In the program here, `philosopher2` will first acquire `fork 0` and then acquire `fork 2`. As of this writing, deadlock detection and removal algorithms constitute an active subarea of research within the programming languages and software engineering research areas.

Summary

Support for concurrency and parallelism is critical in modern programming languages. This support is available in a variety of forms. At the highest level, the features for concurrency and parallelism either require the programmer to manage concurrency and parallelism explicitly (explicit concurrency and parallelism features) or the language runtime handles the details of the parallelism and concurrency freeing programmers from that burden (implicit concurrency and parallelism features). In this chapter, we focused on introducing explicit features for concurrency and parallelism, as well as features for acquiring mutually exclusive access to memory locations. We reviewed the design and semantics of representative language features for explicit concurrency. The `fork` expression created concurrent tasks. The `lock` expression acquired mutually exclusive access to a memory location for the purposes of a single concurrent task. The `unlock` expression relinquished this access. We also saw some semantic variations of the `fork` and the `lock` expressions. Finally, we reviewed two common error conditions in concurrent programs: data races and deadlocks. A data race occurs when two concurrent tasks access a shared memory location and at least one of those accesses is to perform a write operation. Depending on the order of access, the program may produce different results. A deadlock occurs when two or more concurrent tasks hold mutually exclusive access to a resource while waiting to obtain mutually exclusive access to the resource held by the other concurrent task.

Exercises

8.9.1. *[Join]* Our concurrency model includes facilities for creating a collection of tasks and mutually exclusive access to memory locations. These facilities can be used to model synchronization between two tasks, typically known as *join*. For example, consider *join*, an expression that allows a current task to wait for another task specified by the join expression. This can be easily modeled by assigning a lock to each task. Then, a task `t` waiting for another task `t'` to finish can be modeled as trying to acquire a lock `l'`, at the join point in task `t`, which is acquired at the beginning of the task `t'` and released at the end of the task `t'`. Write an example program in Forklang that illustrates this pattern for two and three tasks created using the `fork` expression.

8.9.2. *[Fork many]* Extend the `fork` expression in the language of this chapter to be able to create two or more concurrent tasks, instead of exactly two concurrent tasks.

8.9.3. *[Protected access]* In the Forklang language, it is possible for a task to access a memory location without acquiring a lock first. This makes it possible for a task to introduce errors in the execution of another task, even if that other task properly acquires and releases locks. Modify the semantics of heap read and write operations in Forklang such that they enforce locking discipline.

8.9.4. *[Data races]* The following problems relate to data races in Forklang programs.

1. Write a Forklang function that creates a location in the heap, stores an empty list at that location, and assigns the name "buffer." Following this, the program forks two concurrent tasks: the first task replaces the value stored at the location "buffer" with a list containing '342', the second task reads the list value stored at the location "buffer." The value of this program is the value of these two concurrent tasks. Can this programs produce different values on different runs?

2. Write two Forklang programs that have exactly one data race. Each program must share only one location among its threads and must use `deref`, `set!`, and `call` expressions and must evaluate to two different values for different schedules.

3. Modify your programs in the first part by adding sufficient synchronization using `lock` and `unlock` expressions, such that these programs no longer have data races (i.e., they are data race free).

4. Modify your programs in the first part by adding sufficient synchronization using synchronized expressions, such that these programs no longer have data races.

8.9.5. *[Deadlock]* The following problems are about deadlocks in Forklang programs:

1. Write a Forklang function that creates three references and assigns them the name 'a', 'b', and 'c'. After creating these three references, the program forks three concurrent tasks: the first task acquires a lock on 'a' and then a lock on 'b', the second task acquires a lock on 'b' and then a lock on 'c', and the third task acquires a lock on 'c' and then a lock on 'a'. Will this program always terminate?

2. Write two Forklang programs that have a deadlock. Each program must share two locks among its threads and must use `call`, `lock`, or `unlock` expressions.

3. Modify your programs in the previous part such that these programs do not have deadlocks anymore.

8.9.6. *[Synchronized blocks]* Forklang supports the locking and unlocking of locks to synchronize accesses (read and write) to memory.

Languages like Java provide higher-level synchronization mechanisms such as synchronized methods or blocks. A synchronized method of an object locks the object at the beginning of the execution of the method and unlocks it before returning from the method. Similarly, a synchronized block locks the object upon entering the block and unlocks it when exiting the block.

Extend Forklang with a synchronized expression.

The syntax of a synchronized expression follows the following grammar:

syncexp: '(' 'synchronized' exp exp ')' ;

Semantically, a synchronized expression (synchronized exp1 exp2) treats exp1 as a lock. Similar to the lock expression, it evaluates exp1 to a location and acquires the lock. Then the synchronization expression evaluates exp2 while the lock is acquired. And finally, the lock is released when the evaluation of exp2 is done.

The following interaction log illustrates the semantics of synchronized expression:

```
$ (let ((x (ref 0))) (synchronized x (set! x (+ 1 (deref x)))) (
    synchronized x (set! x (+ 1 (deref x)))) )
2
```

Whereas the same program without synchronization could evaluate to 1 or 2:

```
$ (let ((x (ref 0))) (set! x (+ 1 (deref x))) (set! x (+ 1 (deref x))))
1
```

8.9.7. *[Heap-passing Interpreter]* Our realization of the Forklang language maintained a shared heap. Those program expressions that assess heap directly manipulated this shared heap. This design had the advantage that it avoided having to pass around the heap object (similar to environments). The main disadvantage of this design was that it was difficult to implement variations of heap semantics where parts of the program may potentially use a variation of the original heap.

Modify the Forklang interpreter so that an expression can explicitly control the heap that is available during evaluation of its subexpressions.

8.9.8. *[Fork Processes]* Our realization of the Forklang language creates two threads. In some programming languages, fork creates a separate process (i.e., the forked task and the original task do not share memory). In this exercise, you will gradually modify the Forklang interpreter to implement processes.

- *[Heap clone]* Extend the heap abstraction with a cloning functionality. The clone of a heap has all the locations that are present in the original heap. For each valid location (i.e., a location that contains a stored value), the value stored in the heap clone is the same as the value stored in the original heap. Is it essential to clone each value stored in the original heap?
- *[Process]* Modify the semantics of a fork, such that the two new concurrent subtasks utilize a heap that is a clone of the original heap.

IV TYPES AND SPECIFICATIONS

9 Typelang: A Language with Types

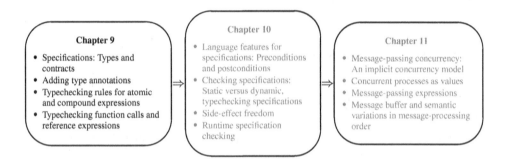

In this chapter, you will learn about types, type-system, type checking, and related concepts. If you have programmed in languages like C, C++, Java, and C#, you have already enjoyed the benefits of types in your programs. This chapter presents a systematic study of the foundation behind types and related facilities.

We will study these concepts by exploring a programming language called Typelang. The complete implementation of Typelang is available with the book code, hosted at https://github.com/hridesh/typelang.

9.1 Why Types?

To explore the motivation of using types, let us consider the procedure f here:

```
(let ((f (lambda (x) (x 2))))
    ...
)
```

For this program, it is natural to ask, *does the procedure f always run correctly?* After some deduction, we may conclude that the answer is no. The procedure f may not always run correctly due to one or more of the following reasons:

– Its argument x may *not* be a procedure.
– x may *not* take one argument.
– x's first argument may *not* be a numeric value.

For example, a programmer may inadvertently write the following call expression:

```
(f 2)
```

in the body of the `let` expression causing a runtime error. Runtime errors are better than the alternative (incorrect output) because they help us identify when a program has failed to perform as desired, but they can still lead to user dissatisfaction, and in some cases critical failure.[1] Ideally, we would like to detect and prevent as many runtime errors as we can.

In this setting, if we wanted to prevent all such runtime errors in the use of procedure `f`, we can't just look at procedure `f` by itself and understand what it is doing. Rather, we must analyze every usage of `f` to figure out if it will work correctly. For example, in the listing here, we might consider `f` to be incorrect, the usage of `f` to be incorrect, or the entire program to be incorrect (depending on our personal preference):

```
( let  (( f  (lambda (x) (x 2))))
  (f 2)
)
```

What is basically wrong about this program?

1. The procedure expects data from its clients to satisfy a certain contract. *Code that calls the procedure is a client of the procedure.*
2. The contract between clients and the procedure is missing, or at least implicit. Since the contract is implicit or missing, we cannot reliably answer the question: *who is to blame for the entire program going wrong?*
3. The contract of the procedure is not satisfied by its clients.

9.2   Kinds of Specifications

We will discuss the notion of specifications in detail in later chapters, but at the moment, let us focus on contracts for procedures. What do we mean by a contract of procedure `f`? Our meaning is identical to the use of the phrase "contract between two parties" in a non-programming setting. The main purpose of a procedure's contract in a program is to do the following:

- Allow one to divide the labor. (What is this procedure's responsibility and what is the client's responsibility?)
- Allow developers to understand a procedure by looking at the procedure code and its contract.
- Allow the assignment of blame. (When is the client or the procedure to blame?)

In our example, the two parties are (1) the procedure `f`, and (2) a client of the procedure `f`. We are concerned about two aspects:

---

1. The reader is encouraged to think about the impact of runtime errors in software that goes in systems like the pacemaker, radiation therapy machines, and rockets.
   - Leveson, Nancy G., and Turner, Clark S., "An Investigation of the Therac-25 Accidents," IEEE Computer, July 1993.
   - Lions, J. L. et al., "ARIANE 5: Flight 501 Failure, A Report by the Inquiry Board," July 1996. Excerpts: *The internal SRI* software exception was caused during execution of a data conversion from 64-bit floating point to 16-bit signed integer value. The floating point number which was converted had a value greater than what could be represented by a 16-bit signed integer.*

1. The procedure's expectations from the client
2. Its promise to the client

What are the expectations of procedure f in our example from any of its clients?

1. Clients must pass a procedure as an argument.
2. Furthermore, that procedure must be applicable to a number.

What is the promise of procedure f to clients?

If invoked properly using a procedure x as an argument, it will return the same value returned by procedure x passed as an argument when invoked with 2 as a parameter.

This is still not completely concrete, but we have made progress.

In the previous example, if the programmer who wrote the code for f had written the code of the procedure as follows (i.e., added a comment), then they can clearly blame the client of f for not calling the procedure properly:

```
( let
  (
    ( f
      (lambda (x /* x shall be a procedure that takes 1 numeric argument. */)
        (x 2)
      )
    )
  )
  (f 2)
)
```

The newly added comment is a kind of *informal contract* between the client and the procedure. You will often hear the terms "contract" and "specification" used interchangeably. Specifications help eliminate unsafe computation, such as runtime errors that were discussed previously, but they also help elucidate what is desired of a computation. There are several kinds of specification:

1. Ultra-lightweight specifications: *Types.* Most types are stated by the programmer by writing program annotations and associating them with pieces of code that produce values. These will be the subject of much of the discussion in this chapter.
2. Lightweight specifications: These allow mixing mathematical and programmatic specifications. For example, in Eiffel language, JML for Java, Spec# for C#, and CodeContracts for C#, are behavioral interface specification languages.
3. Fully mathematical specification: These are precise mathematical descriptions of programs. Examples include the Z language and its object-oriented extension, Z++, Object-Z, and the Alloy language.

Typically, the expressiveness of specifications goes up when we shift from types to fully mathematical specification languages (i.e., more complex properties of programs can be represented). The cost is related in that the cost of specifying programs also goes up from types to fully mathematical specification languages.

9.3 Types

In a nutshell, types divide values manipulated by programs into kinds,[2] such as all values of
the numeric kind, Boolean kind, or string kind. When written out explicitly as annotations,
types can also be thought of as lightweight specification of the contracts between producers
and consumers of values in a program. When we say that "a certain value has type T," we
are implicitly stating that any operation that is considered valid for type T is also valid for
that value. When we say that "certain expression has type T," we also are implicitly stating
that all values produced by the expression would have type T.

This division of program values into types provides several new opportunities:

- *Abstraction.* Instead of thinking in terms of concrete values, we can think in terms of
types, which hides the concrete details of values.
- *Performance.* The explicit division of values into types allows language implementations
to utilize type information for selecting the proper routines to handle a set of values.
- *Documentation.* When used as program annotations, types also serve as excellent
sources of documentation.[3] For example, writing x : num (read as "x has type num")
is much more descriptive than writing just x.
- *Verification.* Types can also be utilized to declare certain programs as illegal without
observing concrete runtime errors in those programs. For example, we can declare the
program (+ n s) as illegal by determining that n:num, s:String and + accepts
two numeric values.

In the rest of this chapter, we will build support for types. We will create an extension of
the Reflang programming language called *Typelang*. It will be built as an explicitly typed
language (i.e., types will appear as syntactic annotations in user programs). Contrast this
with implicitly typed languages, in which types do not appear as syntactic annotations in
user programs such as Python.

9.4 Adding Type Annotations

The core set of features in Typelang are presented in figure 9.1. In previous chapters, we
did not discuss the full grammar, but for Typelang, since some of the top-level elements
will also change, we will review the full grammar to observe all syntactic changes. Notice
the type annotations, represented as T, that now appear in the syntax.

The first change appears in the syntax of the define declarations, where a new
nonterminal *T* (representing types) is added. This nonterminal is defined in figure 9.2.

According to the grammar displayed in figure 9.2, there are four kinds of types: unit
types, number types, Boolean types, function types, and reference types. The unit, number,

---

2. There is much controversy surrounding the definitions of types, so we will not venture into providing yet
another definition, but we do encourage you to look at some previous attempts, such as the following:

- Benjamin Pierce, *Types and Programming Languages*, MIT Press (2002).
- John C. Reynolds, *Fable on Types*, 1983.

3. However, they still need to be supplemented by proper source code comments and other more detailed
documentation.

```
Program      ::=  DefineDecl* Exp?                        Program
DefineDecl   ::=  (define Identifier:T Exp)               Define
Exp          ::=                                          Expressions
                  Number                                  NumExp
             |    (+ Exp Exp⁺)                            AddExp
             |    (- Exp Exp⁺)                            SubExp
             |    (* Exp Exp⁺)                            MultExp
             |    (/ Exp Exp⁺)                            DivExp
             |    Identifier                              VarExp
             |    (let ((Identifier:T Exp)⁺) Exp)         LetExp
             |    ( Exp Exp⁺)                             CallExp
             |    (lambda (Identifier:T⁺) Exp)            LambdaExp
             |    (ref:T Exp)                             RefExp
             |    (deref Exp)                             DerefExp
             |    (set! Exp Exp)                          AssignExp
             |    (free Exp)                              FreeExp
```

Figure 9.1
Grammar for the Typelang language. All of the type annotations (":T") in the syntax are new to the language. Nonterminals that are not defined in this grammar are exactly the same as those in Reflang.

and Boolean types are *base types* (i.e., their definition does not consist of other types). The unit type is like `void` in Java. The function and reference types are defined in terms of other types. The function type is also referred to as the *arrow type*.

```
T  ::=                                                    Types
   |  unit                                                Unit Type
   |  num                                                 Number Type
   |  bool                                                Boolean Type
   |  ( T* -> T )                                         Function Type
   |  Ref T                                               Reference Type
```

Figure 9.2
Basic types in Typelang

The following listing shows some example define declarations that use each of these types. These examples also introduce new syntax for other expressions, but for the moment, let us focus on the syntax of define declarations and new types:

```
$ (define pi : num 3.14159265359)
$ (define r : Ref num (ref : num 2))
$ (define u : unit (free (ref : num 2)))
```

The first line says that the programmer's intent is to define `pi` as a variable of type `num`. Similarly, the second line says that `r` is a variable of type `Ref num` (i.e., reference to a number), and the third line says that `u` is a variable of the `unit` type.

Given these definitions, we can clearly observe the difference between the earlier define form (define pi 3.14159265359) and this new form. For instance, in the new form, the annotation num on the first line acts as a contract between the consumers of the definition pi and the expression to its right (3.14159265359). If the consumers of pi expect this variable to have a value other than num, that is their mistake. If the expression in the define declaration provides a nonnumeric value for pi, that expression is to blame.

The following listing shows other examples of incorrect programs:

```
$ (define fi : num "Hello")
$ (define f : Ref num (ref : bool #f))
$ (define t : unit (free (ref : bool #t)))
```

A function value also has function types. The following listing shows examples of function types:

```
$ (define iden : (num –> num) (lambda (x : num) x))
$ (define fls : (num –> bool) (lambda (x : num) #f))
```

The first line says that iden is a variable of function type (num->num); that is, a function that accepts a number as an argument and returns a number as the result. The second line says that fls is a function that accepts a number as an argument and returns a Boolean as the result. In previous chapters, we talked about higher-order functions. The function type is able to represent types of such functions as well. The following listing shows examples of some function types for higher-order functions:

```
$ (define nconst : (num –> (num –> num)) (lambda (x : num) (lambda (y : num)
    x)))
$ (define bconst : (bool –> (num –> bool)) (lambda (b : bool) (lambda (x : num
    ) b)))
```

The blame assignment for function types work very similar to that of the base types. For instance, consider the function f here, whose declared type is num->num:

```
$ (define f : (num –> num) (lambda (x : bool) x))
```

The name f is being assigned a function value that is of type bool->bool. Thus, the producer of the value, the lambda expression, is to blame. As another example, in the following listing, id is declared to be a variable of the function type (num->num) (i.e., a function that accepts a number as argument and returns a number as the result), but it is being assigned a function value that is of the function type ((num->num)->(num->num)). Therefore, the lambda expression is incorrect:

```
$ (define id : (num –> num) (lambda (x : (num –> num)) x))
```

Since Typelang extends Reflang, it has all the standard expressions shown in figure 9.1. Among these expressions, the syntax for varexp, numexp, addexp, subexp, multexp, and divexp does not change to include type annotations. The syntax for numexp, addexp, subexp, multexp, and divexp doesn't change because the intended semantics of these expressions makes clear that they produce numeric values; therefore, additional type annotations would be superfluous.

The syntax for `varexp` does not include a type annotation because the variable expression by itself cannot offer any guarantees about its valuation. The value of a variable depends on the environment, as we have seen in previous chapters.

9.5 Checking Types

As mentioned in section 9.3 earlier in this chapter, one of the important benefits of types comes with checking programs—essentially identifying those programs that this particular notion of types says could lead to runtime errors.

9.5.1 Typechecking, Type-System, Well-Typed, and Ill-Typed

The process of verifying a program using types is often referred to as *typechecking*. This process is aided by a logical system of rules known as the *type-system*. Since types can be thought of as lightweight contracts between producers and consumers of values, the rules of a type system specify how that contract works for different language features. Similar to legal contracts, the system of rules must cover all eventualities.

Given a type-system, a program is said to be *well typed* if it does not report any type error. An *ill-typed* program is one that fails typechecking. A *type error* is a situation where one of the rules of the type-system cannot be satisfied by the program.

In this section, we will gradually build a type-system for Typelang. The goal of this system is to prevent certain kinds of dynamic errors from showing up at runtime; rather, we will detect and remove such errors during typechecking.

9.5.2 Rules in a Type System

A *type-system* is a collection of rules. Informally, like any logic system, there are two kinds of rules: those that unequivocally assert a fact and those that imply a fact if some other assertion holds.

In the rest of this discussion, we will use the following notation to represent the first kind of rules. These are like axioms in mathematics:

$$(\text{Fact A})$$
$$A$$

We will use the following notation to represent the second kind of rules:

$$(\text{B if A})$$
$$\frac{A}{B}$$

This form is read as, "the assertion below the line will hold if the assertion above the line hold." The assertions above the line are called *premises*, and the assertions below the line are called *conclusions*.

Sometimes we will also use the following notation to represent the second kind of rule:

$$(\text{C if A and B})$$
$$\frac{A \quad B}{C}$$

This form is read as, "assertion C below the line will hold if the assertions A and B above the line hold." The premises above the line are implicitly joined using a conjunction.

9.6 Typechecking Rules for Constants

We will now begin developing the type-system of Typelang. This system must be capable of handling any arbitrary Typelang program. The completeness is ensured by giving a rule for each feature in the language. Programs can be formed only using features, and for each feature, there is a rule. For example, the type-system of Typelang could unequivocally assert that all numeric values (constants) have type **num**. In the following code, n is a **NumVal**:

(NUM)

n : **num**

This assertion says that all numbers will be thought of as having type **num**. Recall that (Num) represents the name of the rule, the term before ':' can be an expression, value, or program, and the term after ':' is the type of the expression, value, or program.

The notation $term : T$ should be read as the *term* has type T.

Similarly, the type-system of Typelang could unequivocally assert that all Boolean values (constants) have type **bool**. In the following code b, is a **BoolVal**:

(BOOL)

b : **bool**

We could have easily enumerated the set of Boolean values in the definition here. If we have other kinds of constants, such as, Strings, the type-system needs to be enhanced to add support for those constants. For the moment, let us focus on this smaller set for ease of presentation.

9.7 Typechecking Rules for Atomic Expressions

Next, we will introduce typechecking rules for atomic expressions (i.e., expressions that do not have subexpressions). In the subset of Typelang that we are considering at the moment, the only such expression is a numeric expression (*NumExp n*). The type-system of Typelang asserts that all numeric expressions (NumExp) have type **num**. In the following code n is a number:

(NUMEXP)

(*NumExp n*) : **num**

This assertion says that the type **num** is a contract between a producer, which in this case is an expression of kind NumExp, and consumers of that expression. This contract says that the producer always promises to produce values of type **num**, and no consumer should expect any other value besides a **num**.

In the case of (*NumExp n*), it is easy to see that the producer expression will never violate the contract. Also, notice that the assertion that (*NumExp n*) has type **num** isn't dependent on any other premise (besides the fact that n is a number that is already checked by the parser). By applying this rule, we can say that (*NumExp 0*) has type **num**, so does (*NumExp 1*), and so on.

9.8 Typechecking Rules for Compound Expressions

The typechecking rules that we have seen so far are unconditional assertions. Now, consider an addition expression that adds the value of arbitrary subexpressions. Can we say that this addition expression will always produce values of type **num**? Clearly, we will not be able to assert that without knowing what the subexpressions are. We might be able to make a different *conditional* assertion: if subexpressions of the addition expression always produce values of type **num**, then the addition expression also will produce a value of type **num**. The typechecking rule shown here models this intent:

(ADDEXP)

$$\frac{e_i : \textbf{num}, \forall i \in 0..n}{(AddExp\ e_0\ e_1\ \ldots\ e_n) : \textbf{num}}$$

This rule can be read as, "if the subexpressions e_0 to e_n have type **num**, then the expression $(AddExp\ e_0, e_1, \ldots, e_n)$ will have type **num** as well." This typechecking rule establishes a contract between producers of values in this context (expressions $e_0, e_1, \ldots, e_n$) and the consumer of these values (the addition expression). It also clearly states the conditions under which the addition expression is going to produce a numerical value. Notice that the rule does not mention situations where expressions $e_0, e_1, \ldots, e_n$ might produce a dynamic error. Such situations are implicitly covered and produce type errors. If the expressions $e_0, e_1, \ldots, e_n$ fail to produce a numerical value, then the addition expression offers no guarantees.

Using this rule, we can state that $(AddExp\ (NumExp\ 0), (NumExp\ 1))$ will have type **num** since $(NumExp\ 0)$ has type **num**, and so does $(NumExp\ 1)$. Similarly, we can say that $(AddExp\ (AddExp\ (NumExp\ 0),\ (NumExp\ 1)), (AddExp\ (NumExp\ 2),\ (NumExp\ 3)))$ has type **num** since, as expected, both the subexpressions $(AddExp\ (NumExp\ 0), (NumExp\ 1))$ and $(AddExp\ (NumExp\ 2), (NumExp\ 3))$ have type **num**.

We can similarly state the typechecking rules for the multiplication expressions:

(MULTEXP)

$$\frac{e_i : \textbf{num}, \forall i \in 0..n}{(MultExp\ e_0\ e_1\ \ldots\ e_n) : \textbf{num}}$$

The typechecking rule for multiplication can be read similarly; for instance, if the subexpressions e_0 to e_n have type **num**, then the multiplication expression $(MultExp\ e_0, e_1, \ldots, e_n)$ will have type **num** as well. The rules for subtraction and division are similarly stated here:

(SUBEXP)

$$\frac{e_i : \textbf{num}, \forall i \in 0..n}{(SubExp\ e_0\ e_1\ \ldots\ e_n) : \textbf{num}}$$

(DIVEXP)

$$\frac{e_i : \textbf{num}, \forall i \in 0..n}{(DivExp\ e_0\ e_1\ \ldots\ e_n) : \textbf{num}}$$

The rule for division deserves special mention because division expressions can produce divide-by-zero errors. The rule given here does not account for divide-by-zero errors. This is an example of a situation where the type-system being developed is insufficient to detect and remove certain classes of errors. The reader is encouraged to think about mechanisms to check whether a subexpression of the division expression can evaluate to zero without evaluating the subexpression.

Exercises

9.8.1. *[Practice]* Write five examples of well-typed and ill-typed programs that use all the arithmetic expressions.

9.8.2. *[Eliminate Simple Divide-By-Zero Errors]* For some expressions such as (/ x 0), where 0 appears as an immediate subexpression, it is easy to check for and eliminate divide-by-zero errors. Enhance the typechecking rule for the division expression so that the type-system is able to detect and remove such errors, where 0 is an immediate subexpression of the division expression.

9.9 Types for Variables

The typechecking rules that we have seen so far are about expressions that do not directly define and use variables. For our very first language, Arithlang, these rules worked well, but all of our later languages support variable definition and usage. Therefore, it is important to enhance these rules to account for that.

9.9.1 Type Environments
What should be the type of a variable expression x? What should be a typechecking rule for a variable expression?

In the context of Varlang, we asked a similar question: what should be the value of a variable expression x? The answer was: it depends on what the surrounding context of x says. We then modeled that surrounding context as a data-type *environment*. An environment is a map that provides an operation to look up the value of a variable. We saw both functional and object-oriented implementation of environments in previous chapters. Going forward, we will refer to the environments in which values are stored as *value environments*, to distinguish them from another kind of environment that we will introduce shortly.

For types, we can use a similar strategy. The type of a variable expression x is dependent on the surrounding context of x. The surrounding context is modeled as a data-type type environment. A *type environment* is a map that provides an operation to look up the type of a variable. The definition given here models this intent:

$$\mathtt{get(tenv, \ v')} = \begin{cases} Error & tenv = (\mathtt{EmptyEnv}) \\ t & tenv = (\mathtt{ExtendEnv \ v \ t \ tenv'}) \\ & \text{and } v = v' \\ \mathtt{get(tenv', \ v')} & \text{Otherwise.} \end{cases}$$

Here, v, $v' \in \mathtt{Identifier}$, the set of the identifier, $t \in T$, the set of types in the Typelang language, and $\mathtt{tenv}$, $\mathtt{tenv'} \in \mathtt{TEnv}$, the set of type environments. As before, take the notation $(\mathtt{EmptyEnv})$ to mean a type environment created using a constructor of type $\mathtt{EmptyEnv}$, and take $\mathtt{EmptyEnv}$ to mean all such elements (i.e., the entire set). Similarly, $(\mathtt{ExtendEnv \ v \ t \ tenv})$ is a type environment created using a constructor of type $\mathtt{ExtendEnv}$, with $\mathtt{var}$, t, and $\mathtt{tenv}$ being the values used to construct this type environment.

This definition provides a single operation $\mathtt{get}$ to look up the type of a variable from a type environment. It says that looking up any variable in an empty type environment leads to error. Furthermore, it says that looking up a variable in an extended type environment constructed using $\mathtt{var}$, t, and $\mathtt{tenv}$ is type t if the variable being searched is the same as $\mathtt{var}$. Otherwise it is the same as looking up the variable in $\mathtt{tenv}$.

To illustrate the idea of a type environment, consider a type environment $tenv_0$, which is empty:

$$tenv_0 = (\mathtt{EmptyEnv})$$

We can extend this type environment to add a new name-to-type binding that says that the name x has type **num**. Looking up x in that type environment would yield **num**:

$$tenv_1 = (\mathtt{ExtendEnv \ x \ \textbf{num} \ } tenv_0)$$

We can further extend this type environment to add a new name-to-type binding that says that the name y has type **bool** respectively:

$$tenv_2 = (\mathtt{ExtendEnv \ y \ \textbf{bool} \ } tenv_1)$$

Looking up x in this type environment would yield **num**, and looking up y would yield **bool**. The type bindings added previously are preserved in the new type environment.

We can further extend this type environment to add a new name-to-type binding that says that the name x has type **bool**:

$$tenv_3 = (\mathtt{ExtendEnv \ x \ \textbf{bool} \ } tenv_2)$$

Looking up x in this type environment would yield **bool**, and looking up y would yield **bool**. The type bindings for x added previously is overridden in this new type environment.

9.9.2 Typechecking Rule for Variables

With the notion of a type environment in place, we are now ready to state the rule for typechecking the usage of a variable:

(VAREXP)

$$\frac{get(tenv, var) = t}{tenv \vdash (VarExp\ var) : t}$$

This rule uses a new notation $tenv \vdash e : t$. This should be read as follows: assuming the type environment `tenv`, expression `e` has type `t`. The overall rule here says that in the context of the type environment `tenv`, the variable expression with variable `var` has type `t`, if looking up the name `var` in the type environment `tenv` gives the result `t`.

Since our previous typechecking rules did not use the type environment, we will also need to enhance them accordingly. These enhanced versions are presented here:

(NUM)

$$tenv \vdash n : \textbf{num}$$

(NUM)

$$tenv \vdash b : \textbf{bool}$$

(NUMEXP)

$$tenv \vdash (NumExp\ n) : \textbf{num}$$

For the three rules given here, the type environment doesn't play a major role because the values produced by (and thus the types of) these expressions are not dependent on the context:

(ADDEXP)

$$\frac{tenv \vdash e_i : \textbf{num}, \forall i \in 0..n}{tenv \vdash (AddExp\ e_0\ e_1\ \dots\ e_n) : \textbf{num}}$$

For the addition expression, the only noteworthy aspect of the typechecking rule is that the type environment used to perform typechecking of subexpressions is the same as that of the addition expression. In other words, variables and their types stored in the type environment are not affected by the addition expression:[4]

(MULTEXP)

$$\frac{tenv \vdash e_i : \textbf{num}, \forall i \in 0..n}{tenv \vdash (MultExp\ e_0\ e_1\ \dots\ e_n) : \textbf{num}}$$

(SUBEXP)

$$\frac{tenv \vdash e_i : \textbf{num}, \forall i \in 0..n}{tenv \vdash (SubExp\ e_0\ e_1\ \dots\ e_n) : \textbf{num}}$$

(DIVEXP)

$$\frac{tenv \vdash e_i : \textbf{num}, \forall i \in 0..n}{tenv \vdash (DivExp\ e_0\ e_1\ \dots\ e_n) : \textbf{num}}$$

The typechecking rules for multiplication, subtraction, and division are also similar and pass around the typing environment to rules that typecheck their subexpressions without inserting or removing any variables.

---

4. The reader is encouraged to consider whether the type environment would remain the same while checking subexpressions of e_i.

9.9.3 Type Annotations for Let Expressions

Typelang requires a programmer to specify the types of identifiers of a `let` expression, as shown in the syntax given here. In a later section, we will look at variations in which some of these types can be omitted. In a `let` expression, each declared identifier has a type, as shown in figure 9.3. To illustrate this point, consider the following `let` expression, which declares a variable x of a type number with value 2:

```
( let  ((x : num 2))  x)
```

letexp   ::=   (**let** ((*Identifier* : *T* exp)⁺) *exp*)   *Let expression*

Figure 9.3
Syntax of the `let` expression in Typelang

The type annotation `: num` establishes a contract between the producer and the consumer of the value x. In the case of let, the consumer is the body of the `let` expression x, and the producer is the expression 2.

Similarly, in the following listing, the `let` expression declares two variables x and y, both of type **num** with values 2 and 5, thereby establishing a contract between producers of those values and their consumers (i.e., the addition expression). The consumer expression in this case relies on this contract to show that (+ x y) produces a numeric value by applying the typechecking rule for addition described previously:

```
( let
  ((x : num 2)
   (y : num 5))
  (+ x y)
)
```

However, a variation of the previous `let` expression shown in the listing here fails to typecheck:

```
( let
  ((x : num 2)
   (y : bool #t))
  (+ x y)
)
```

Clearly, an addition expression cannot add a number and a Boolean. More precisely, this `let` expression fails to typecheck because the `let` expression can guarantee to the addition expression only that x will be a **num** and y will be a **bool**, but the typechecking rule for the addition expression expects that the type of both x and y will be **num**. This mismatch results in a type error thrown by the (AddExp) rule.

To summarize, just like the define form, in a `let` expression, the type annotation on the identifier, such as `num` in the previous two examples, acts as a contract between the consumers of this variable definition (the body of the `let` expression) and the expression to its right. If the consumers of x expect this variable to have a value other than `num`, they are in error. If the expression in the `let` expression provides a nonnumeric value for x, that expression is to blame. The type-system can detect and prevent these runtime errors.

9.9.4 Typechecking Rules for Let Expressions

Checking a `let` expression can be thought of as a two step process:

1. Check whether variables are being assigned a compatible value. The following code
   has an example error that would be caught during this check:

```
(let
  ((x : num #t))
    ...
)
```

   The type annotation claims that x is a **num**, and therefore assigning a value of **bool**
   is illegal.

2. Assuming that the variables have their declared type, check whether the usage of those
   variables in the body of the `let` expression is compatible with their declared types.
   The following code presents an example error that would be caught during this check:

```
(let
  ((x : num 2)
   (y : bool #t))
    (+ x y)
)
```

The typechecking rule for the `let` expression stated here includes both of these checks:

(LETEXP)

$$\frac{\begin{array}{c} tenv \vdash e_i : t_i, \forall i \in 0..n \\ tenv_i = (ExtendEnv\ var_i\ t_i\ tenv_{i-1}), \forall i \in 1..n \\ tenv_0 = (ExtendEnv\ var_0\ t_0\ tenv) \\ tenv_n \vdash e_{body} : t \end{array}}{tenv \vdash (LetExp\ var_0\ ...\ var_n\ t_0\ ...\ t_n\ e_0\ ...\ e_n\ e_{body}) : t}$$

This rule also uses the new notation $tenv \vdash e : t$. Recall that this notation should be read
as, "assuming the type environment `tenv`, expression e has type t." Informally, the rule
says that a `let` expression that is defining *n* variables (var_0 ... var_n), giving them types
(t_0 ... t_n), and assigning them values of certain expressions (e_0 ... e_n) has type *t* if both
of the following are true:

- Each value expression (e_i) has the same type as the declared type (t_i) of corresponding
  variable (var_i).
- In the context of a new type environment that extends the type environment *tenv* with
  new bindings from variables (var_i) to their types (t_i), the body of the `let` expression has
  type *t*.

9.10   Types for Functions and Calls

Function definitions and calls are two language features where the idea of *type as contract*
is more explicit. The type for a function is a contract between the body of the function (the

lambdaexp ::= (**lambda** (*{identifier : T}**) *exp*)   *Lambda*

Figure 9.4
Syntax of the lambda expression in Typelang

consumers of the argument values and the producers of the result value) and the callers of
the function (the producers of argument values and the consumers of the result value). The
duality in this notion of contracts naturally leads to two components of the function type
(T^* -> T). The first part, T^*, represents the types of zero or more arguments, and the
second part, T, represents the type of result.

9.10.1   Type Annotations for Lambda and Call Expressions

Typelang requires a programmer to specify the type of arguments in a lambda expression.
The type of an argument in a lambda expression is specified after ':' in its declaration,
as shown in the syntax here:

A lambda expression must be of a function type, as specified in the syntax in figure 9.4.
A function type specifies the types of a function's arguments, as well as the return type of
the function. In a function type (t_a->t_r), t_a is the argument type and t_r is the return
type. The cardinality of the arguments of a lambda expression must match the cardinality
of the argument types in the function type. In other words, each argument of a lambda
expression must have a corresponding type in the function's type.

To illustrate this point, consider the following lambda expression, which declares a
function with three arguments, x, y and z, and returns their sum:

```
(lambda
  (
    x : num      // Argument 1
    y : num      // Argument 2
    z : num      // Argument 3
  )
  (+ x (+ y z))
)
```

The type of this lambda expression is (*num num num -> num*), which specifies the types
of arguments x, y, and z as the numeric type num and the function's return type as num as
well. This lambda expression is well typed in Typelang.

As another example, the following call expression declares the same function given previously and then calls it by passing the integer parameters 1, 2, and 3 for arguments x, y,
and z:

```
(
  (lambda
    (
      x : num      // Argument 1
      y : num      // Argument 2
      z : num      // Argument 3
    )
```

```
    (+ x (+ y z))
  )
  1 2 3
)
```

To typecheck a call expression, we have to typecheck the function being called, to check the number and types of actual parameters, and check the correspondence between the types of the formal parameters and the corresponding type of each actual parameter. The type for the lambda expression in this call expression is (*num num num −> num*), and the function is being invoked on three actual parameters, each with **num** type. Since the number of type of the actual parameters and formal parameters agree, this call expression type-checks in Typelang, and the type of the overall call expression is the return type of the function (**num**). However, a variation of the call expression shown here would not typecheck because #t is of type bool, not of type number, which the function expects for z:

```
(
  (lambda
    (
      x : num      // Argument 1
      y : num      // Argument 2
      z : num      // Argument 3
    )
    (+ x (+ y z))
  )
  1 2 #t
)
```

More precisely, this call expression is ill typed because the type for the lambda expression in this call expression is (*num num num −> num*), and the function is being invoked on three actual parameters with type **num**, **num**, and **bool**, respectively.

9.10.2 Typechecking Rules for Lambda and Call Expressions
The rule for checking lambda expressions and calls is similar to that for checking the let expresssion:

(LAMBDAEXP)
$$tenv_0 = (ExtendEnv\ var_0\ t_0\ tenv)$$
$$tenv_i = (ExtendEnv\ var_i\ t_i\ tenv_{i-1}), \forall i \in 1..n$$
$$tenv_n \vdash e_{body} : t$$
$$\overline{tenv \vdash (LambdaExp\ var_0\ \ldots\ var_n\ t_0\ \ldots\ t_n\ e_{body}) : (t_0\ \ldots\ t_n{-}{>}t)}$$

This rule also uses a new notation $tenv \vdash e : t$. Recall that this notation should be read as, "assuming the type environment tenv, expression e has type t." Informally, this rule says that a lambda expression that is defining a function with n formal parameters ($var_0 \ldots var_n$) and giving them types ($t_0 \ldots t_n$) has type $t_0 \ldots t_n{-}{>}t$ if the following is the case.

In the context of a new type environment that extends the type environment *tenv* with new bindings from variables (var_i) to their types (t_i), the body of the lambda expression has type t.

The rule for the call expression is the consumer of a function type:

$$(\text{CALLEXP})$$
$$\frac{tenv \vdash e_f : (t_0 \ \ldots \ t_n \text{->} t) \qquad tenv \vdash e_i : t_i, \forall i \in 0..n}{tenv \vdash (CallExp \ e_f \ e_0 \ \ldots \ e_n) : t}$$

This rule says that a call expression that is calling a function with n formal parameters of types ($t_0 \ \ldots \ t_n$) and return type (t) typechecks if each expression e_i whose value is an actual parameter has the corresponding type t_i. Notice that in this rule, we are not creating a new type environment, as the type of the function (e_f) and actual parameters are computed in the same scope.

9.10.3 Illustrating Typechecking Rules
To illustrate typechecking rules, let us consider an example program in Typelang:

```
((lambda (x : num y  :  num)
   (let  ((z:num) 3) (+ x (+ y z))
 )
 1 2)
```

The process of applying the typechecking rules will proceed as follows.

1. First, since the outermost expression is a call expression, the rule for that expression applies. That rule says that a call expression is well typed if the first expression after the starting parenthesis (operator) has a function type and the types of the remaining expression (operands) are compatible with that function type.

2. Second, since the operand is a lambda expression, the rule for the lambda expression will apply to checking if the expression (lambda (x : num y : num)(let ((z:num)3) (+ x (+ y z)))) is well typed and has a function type. The rule for a lambda expression says that the expression has a function type if, in an extended typing environment with two new bindings from formal parameter names to their types, the body of the function is well typed. Assuming that the program would run in an empty environment, this extended type environment (let us call it *tenv'*), would have two bindings, x to num and y to num.

3. Third, the body of the lambda expression will be checked assuming the typing environment *tenv'*. Here, the rule for the let expression will apply, which says that such an expression is well typed if (1) in the typing environment *tenv'*, the initializer expression 3 has the type num; and (2) in the typing environment that extends *tenv'* to add a new binding from name z to type num, the body of the let expression (+ x (+ y z)) is well typed. Let us call the new type environment *tenv''*; it extends *tenv'* to add a binding from z to num.

4. Fourth, the addition expression (+ x (+ y z)) will be checked assuming the typing environment *tenv''*. By applying the rule for addition, we have that an addition is well typed if its operands are well typed and have the type num.

5. Fifth, the variable expression x will be checked to determine if it is well typed and has the type num, assuming the typing environment *tenv''*. Since the typing environment *tenv''* maps x to num, this holds.

6. Sixth, the addition expression (+ y z) will be checked to determine if it is well typed and has the type num, assuming the typing environment *tenv″*. By applying the rule for addition expression, we have that this expression is well typed if its operands are well typed and have the type num.

7. Seventh, the variable expression y will be checked to determine if it is well typed and has the type num, assuming the typing environment *tenv″*. Since the typing environment *tenv″* maps y to num, this holds.

8. Eighth, the variable expression z will be checked to determine if it is well typed and has the type num assuming the typing environment *tenv″*. Since the typing environment *tenv″* maps z to num, this holds.

Exercises

9.10.1. More practice with types in Typelang:

1. Check this let expression, explain why it is well typed, and write its type.

   (let ((x : num 2)) (let ((y : num 5)) (+ x y)))

2. Check this let expression, explain why it is well typed, and write its type.

   (let ((x : num 2))
      (let ((z : (num –> num)
        (lambda (y : num) (+ x y))))
      (z 5)
)
)

3. Check this lambda expression, explain why it is well typed, and write its type.

   (lambda (x : num y : num z : num)
     (+ x (+ y z))
)

4. Check this lambda expression, explain why it is well typed, and write its type.

   ((lambda (x : num y : num z : num)
     (+ x (+ y z)))
     1 2 3
)

5. Check this let expression, explain why it is well typed, and write its type.

   (let ((f : (num –> (num –> num))
     (lambda (x : num)
       (lambda (y : num)
         (+ x y)))))
   f)

9.10.2. Explain the following typechecking errors in Typelang programs:

1. Check this `let` expression, explain why it is ill typed, and specify the typechecking rule that will detect the error.

   (let ((b : bool #t)) (let ((y : num 5)) (+ y b)))

   What did the typechecking rule expect, and what did it find?

2. Check this `let` expression, explain why it is ill typed, and specify the typechecking rule that will detect the error.

   ```
   (let ((x : num 2))
     (let ((z : (num –> num)
       (lambda (y : num) (+ x y))))
       (z #f)
     )
   )
   ```

   What did the typechecking rule expect, and what did it find?

3. Check this lambda expression, explain why it is ill typed, and specify the typechecking rule that will detect the error.

   ```
   (lambda (x : num y : bool z : num)
     (+ x (+ y z))
   )
   ```

   What did the typechecking rule expect, and what did it find?

4. Check this lambda expression, explain why it is ill typed, and specify the typechecking rule that will detect the error.

   ```
   ((lambda (x : num y : num z : num)
     (+ x (+ y z)))
     1 2 #f
   )
   ```

   What did the typechecking rule expect, and what did it find?

5. Check this `let` expression, explain why it is ill typed, and specify the typechecking rule that will detect the error.

   ```
   (let ((f : (num –> (bool –> num))
     (lambda (x : num)
       (lambda (y : num)
         (+ x y)))))
     f)
   ```

   What did the typechecking rule expect, and what did it find?

9.11   Types for Reference Expressions

We will now discuss how to typecheck reference-related expressions. The type of a reference is the reference type **Ref** T, as shown in figure 9.5.

refexp   ::=   (**ref** :*T exp*)   *Ref expression*

Figure 9.5
Syntax of the `ref` expression in Typelang

9.11.1   Type Annotations for Reference-Related Expressions
Typelang requires a `ref` expression to specify the type of content of the memory location that it refers to, as shown in the following syntax.

To illustrate this point, the following expression allocates a memory location of type **num** with value 2:

(ref : num 2)

Similarly, the following reference expression allocates two memory locations: the first of type **num** and the second of type **Ref num**:

(ref : Ref num
  (ref : num 2)
)

The type **Ref num** is different from base types like **num** and **bool**, and similar to the function types in that it can help construct other types. Examples include **Ref num**, which is a reference to a number; and **Ref Ref num**, which is a reference to a reference to a number.

As another example, the following expression declares r as a reference to a reference with value number 5, and evaluation of the program returns 5:

(let
  (
    (r : Ref Ref num (ref : Ref num (ref : num 5)))
)
  (deref (deref r))
)

9.11.2   Typechecking Rules for Reference Expressions
The rule for checking reference-related expressions are similar to previous rules. Let us first consider the rule for reference expressions used to allocate memory:

(REFEXP)
$$\frac{tenv \vdash e : t}{tenv \vdash (RefExp\ t\ e) : \textbf{Ref}\ t}$$

The rule says, "assuming the type environment `tenv`, a reference expression has type **Ref** t if its subexpression e has type t." A reference expression cannot hope to produce a memory location that has a value of type t if its subexpression e did not produce a value of type t. Notice that the type environment used to check the subexpression is $tenv$ as well, because the reference expression does not define any new names.

The rule for dereference expresses this expression's dependence on its subexpression producing a reference:

(DEREFEXP)
$$\frac{tenv \vdash e : \textbf{Ref}\ t}{tenv \vdash (DerefExp\ e) : t}$$

The rule says, "assuming the type environment $tenv$, a dereference expression has type t if its subexpression e has type $\textbf{Ref}\ t$." A dereference expression cannot hope to look up a memory location to obtain a value of type t if its subexpression e did not produce a value of type $\textbf{Ref}\ t$. This rule catches malformed programs where an attempt is made to dereference other types of values, such as a number. So, it prevents some programming errors in the use of references. The reader is encouraged to think about other kinds of programming errors with references that this rule doesn't prevent, such as attempts to dereference a reference that has already been freed. Preventing such errors are beyond the scope of this type-system.

The rule for an assignment establishes the contract between the right-hand side (RHS) and the left-hand side (LHS) of an assignment:

(ASSIGNEXP)
$$\frac{\begin{array}{c} tenv \vdash e_1 : t \\ tenv \vdash e_0 : \textbf{Ref}\ t \end{array}}{tenv \vdash (AssignExp\ e_0\ e_1) : t}$$

The rule says, "assuming the type environment $tenv$, an assignment expression has type t if its subexpression e_1 representing the RHS of an assignment has type t, and if its subexpression e_0 representing the LHS of an assignment has type $\textbf{Ref}\ t$." Notice that the overall expression is given the same type as the RHS because the value produced by assignment expression in Typelang are the same as the value of the RHS.

The rule for the free expression establishes that it is being applied to deallocate references, not other kinds of values such as a number:

(FREEEXP)
$$\frac{tenv \vdash e : \textbf{Ref}\ t}{tenv \vdash (FreeExp\ e) : \texttt{unit}}$$

The rule says, "assuming the type environment $tenv$, a free expression has type $\texttt{unit}$ if its subexpression e representing the reference being freed has type $\textbf{Ref}\ t$"; that is, it is actually a reference. Notice that this rule doesn't prevent a free expression from being applied to values that are already freed. Removing such malformed programs is beyond the capabilities of this type-system.

Summary

In this chapter, we reviewed the notion of types and typechecking. Types are a form of lightweight specifications designed to prevent errors in programs. Types can be explicitly added to programs to aid the underlying logical system that checks the program for consistency. Typechecking rules state how to check types of atomic elements and how to combine types for subexpressions to check the types of compound expressions. In the statement of typechecking rules, we also introduced a new data structure type environment. A type environment is like a value environment except it maps names to types.

10 Speclang: A Language with Specifications

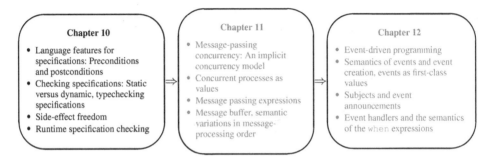

Chapter 10	Chapter 11	Chapter 12
• Language features for specifications: Preconditions and postconditions • Checking specifications: Static versus dynamic, typechecking specifications • Side-effect freedom • Runtime specification checking	• Message-passing concurrency: An implicit concurrency model • Concurrent processes as values • Message passing expressions • Message buffer, semantic variations in message-processing order	• Event-driven programming • Semantics of events and event creation, events as first-class values • Subjects and event announcements • Event handlers and the semantics of the when expressions

In this chapter, we will learn more about specifications. We will become familiar with the idea of precondition, postcondition, specification cases, invariants, and other related concepts. If you have programmed in languages like Eiffel, JML, and Spec#, you have already enjoyed the benefits of specifications in your programs. This chapter presents a systematic study of the foundation behind specifications and related facilities.

In previous chapters, we have discussed that in programming systems on a large scale, it is beneficial to have a contract between the producers and consumers of values. The kind of types that we have seen so far provide a notion of contracts between producers and consumers of values. Specifications are important because they provide a richer set of guarantees.

We will study these concepts by discussing a programming language called Speclang. The complete implementation of Speclang is available with the book code, hosted at https://github.com/hridesh/speclang. We will build Speclang by extending Typelang, which was developed in chapter 9.

10.1 Motivation

To motivate the need for specifications, let us consider the procedure f here:

```
(let ((f (lambda (x) (/ 342 x))))
  ...
)
```

Procedure f works correctly when (1) x's value is a number, and (2) x's value is not 0. Otherwise, the expression (/ 342 x) is not defined, and therefore the procedure will not produce output.

In previous chapters, we have learned about using types to enforce such specifications between producer and consumers of values. For instance, by adding the type annotation num to specify the type of input x, we could specify the first constraint on its value. This modified version is shown in the following listing. Recall from the previous chapter that the notation (num -> num) means that f is a function that accepts a value of type num as an argument and produces a value of type num as the result:

```
(let ((f : (num -> num)
       (lambda (x : num) (/ 342 x))))

  ...
)
```

This modified function definition, while better compared to the previous version, is still insufficient. For example, it would prevent erroneous invocations of the function f like (f "hello") and raise a type error blaming the client code (f "hello") for incorrectly using the function. However, we are not quite there yet. In particular, if the following program fails, who is to blame?

```
(let ((f : (num -> num)
       (lambda (x : num) (/ 342 x))))
      (f 0)
)
```

Should f be blamed, or should it be the client code (f 0)? Technically, f would be blamed because it doesn't put any constraints on the value of x beyond saying that it must be a value of type num. Here, 0 is a value of type num, and therefore f should have provided an answer. If we would like the blame of this error to be assigned to the client of f, then constraints on the value of x must be made stronger. In this chapter, we will see language features of Speclang that allow us to do exactly that.

10.2 Language Features for Specifications

To begin, let us reconsider the example given previously. To do a proper blame assignment, the function f must ensure that the value of x is greater than zero. The code here adds a specification to the code of function f to check this property:

```
1 (let
2    ((f : (num -> num)
3      (lambda
4        (x:num | (> x 0) -> (> result 0))
5        (/ 342 x)
6      )
7  ))
8    (f 0)  // Precondition violation here.
9 )
```

The code at lines 1–3 and 5–9 is the same as before, but this code will raise the following error when evaluated using the Speclang interpreter due to the change at line 4:

Precondition violation in call (f 0)

The code at line 4 adds the specification to the function f using the syntax of Speclang. The new code after | [i.e., (> x 0) -> (> result 0)] is the specification.

Speclang supports a kind of specification known as *behavioral specifications*. Behavioral specifications document the behavior of a function. What should be true before the function is called? What should hold after the function has completed evaluating? Behavioral specifications consist of two parts: preconditions and postconditions. *Preconditions* are obligations on the clients of the function; that is, conditions that must hold before a function can be called. *Postconditions* are obligations on the function. If the precondition of the function is met and the function is called, then the postconditions must hold. In the example here, the Boolean condition before the -> is the precondition and the Boolean condition after the -> is the postcondition. The precondition says that the argument x must be greater than zero. The postcondition says that if the precondition of the function holds and the function f is called, then the result of the function will be greater than zero.

What if the function doesn't require anything from the client and doesn't provide any assurances? While that is not recommended, it can be stated by leaving the precondition and postcondition as the value #t that always holds. An example of that appears here:

```
$ ((lambda (x: num | #t -> #t) (+ 3 (+ 4 x))) 2)
9
```

We could strengthen the precondition by requiring that x is greater than zero. The listing here adds that precondition to the function, which is still met by the call:

```
$ ((lambda (x: num | (> x 0) -> #t) (+ 3 (+ 4 x))) 2)
9
```

Another example, given here, shows a different precondition that now requires that x is greater than 3. This precondition is not met by the client, so a precondition violation is raised:

```
$ ((lambda (x: num | (> x 3) -> #t) (+ 3 (+ 4 x))) 2)
Precondition violation in call ((lambda ( x ) (+ 3.0 (+ 4.0 x ) )) 2.0 )
```

Similarly, we can strengthen the postcondition. In the listing here, the postcondition states that the result of the function is equal to 342, which doesn't hold, and so we see a postcondition violation:

```
$ ((lambda (x: num | (> x 0) -> (= result 342)) (+ 3 (+ 4 x))) 2)
Postcondition violation in call ((lambda ( x ) (+ 3.0 (+ 4.0 x ) )) 2.0 )
```

Clearly, the postcondition of the function didn't match the implementation. In the example here, the postcondition is made more accurate:

```
$ ((lambda (x: num | (> x 0) -> (= result 9)) (+ 3 (+ 4 x))) 2)
9
```

Now, both the precondition and postcondition are met, so no specification errors are raised.

What is the specification of the function in the listing shown here?

```
$ ((lambda (x: num) (+ 3 (+ 4 x))) 2)
9
```

When no specifications are provided, most specification languages assume a default specification (i.e., the precondition is true and the postcondition is true). For the listing given previously, the specification would be considered the same as if the function were written like the following listing:

```
$ ((lambda (x: num | #t –> #t) (+ 3 (+ 4 x))) 2)
9
```

The explicitly specified default method specification is not different from this code.

The postconditions of a function can help document expected results of the function, but just stating the postconditions is often not enough. To illustrate, consider the new postcondition for the function here, which says that the result would be greater than 7. The default precondition is used:

```
$ ((lambda (x: num | #t –> (> result 7)) (+ 3 (+ 4 x))) 2)
9
```

For the client given here, the postcondition holds; however, consider a different client that calls the function with an argument –1:

```
$ ((lambda (x: num | #t –> (> result 7)) (+ 3 (+ 4 x))) –1)
Postcondition violation in call ((lambda ( x ) (+ 3.0 (+ 4.0 x ) )) –1.0 )
```

This function call results in a postcondition violation. What is wrong? In this case, the function can't provide assurances that the result would be greater than 7 without requiring some assurances from the client. The listing that follows fixes that problem. The function now states that if the argument is greater than zero and the function is invoked, then the result would be greater than 7:

```
$ ((lambda (x: num | (> x 0) –> (> result 7)) (+ 3 (+ 4 x))) –1)
Precondition violation in call ((lambda ( x ) (+ 3.0 (+ 4.0 x ) )) –1.0 )
```

Now, this specification is able to do proper blame assignment. The problem really was the failure of the client code, as it didn't satisfy the precondition. The listing here fixes the client:

```
$ ((lambda (x: num | (> x 0) –> (> result 7)) (+ 3 (+ 4 x))) 2)
9
```

Now we have satisfied both the precondition and the postcondition for the function.

As another example, let us consider the function natsum here, which computes the sum of natural numbers using recursion. For clarity, we have added line breaks between the types of the function, the precondition, and the postcondition:

```
1 (define natsum : (num -> num)
2   (lambda (n : num
3     | (>= n 0)
4       -> (= result (/ (* n (+ n 1)) 2)))
5   (if (= 0 n) n
6     (+ n (natsum (- n 1)))
7   )
8 )
9 )
```

The precondition of this function at line 3 states that the input can be greater than or equal to zero. The postcondition of this function at line 4 states that the result of the function must equal $(n*n+1)/2$.

10.3 Example Specifications for List Functions

Let us look at some more examples of specification, beginning with specifications for some functions over lists. You might remember the `length` and `append` functions from the previous chapter, each of which computes the length of the list and concatenates two lists, respectively. The listings here adds specifications to these functions:

```
1 (define length : (List<num> -> num)
2   (lambda (l : List<num>
3     | #t -> (>= result 0))
4   (if (null? l) 0
5     (+ 1 (length (cdr l)))
6   )
7 )
8 )
```

The specification for `length` appears on line 3. The precondition for `length` is #t. It might be tempting to say that l is a list, but that is already ensured by the type l. The postcondition for this function says that the result of this function will be greater than or equal to zero (in the case of an empty list).

This specification for `length` is a good start, but still fairly weak. When we say that the specification is weak, we mean that the specification is unable to disallow a nonconforming implementation or the specification doesn't provide enough information to the client of the function. The specification for `length` shown previously can be satisfied by an implementation of `length` that simply returns a random positive number. We can further strengthen the specification by stating that the the function would evaluate to zero if the list is empty. When the list is not empty, the result is 1 more than the length of the sublist, given by (cdr l). The following listing shows this stronger specification for the `length` function:

```
1 (define length : (List<num> -> num)
2   (lambda (l : List<num>
3     | (null? l) -> (= result 0)
```

```
4          || (not (null? l)) -> (= result (+ 1 (length (cdr l)))))
5       ( if (null? l) 0
6           (+ 1 (length (cdr l)))
7        )
8     )
9 )
```

First, note the syntax `specification || specification'` at lines 3 and 4. Unlike the previous specification for the function `length`, which had only one case, in this modified specification we have two cases: when the list is empty and otherwise. Both cases have the form `pre -> post`. The first (in lexical order) specification whose precondition holds is used to check the postcondition. In other words, if the function call satisfied `pre` and the function were evaluated, then `post` must hold. Similarly, if the function call satisfied `pre'` and the function were evaluated, then `post'` must hold. For our example here, if the precondition `(null? l)` held and the function `length` were run, then the postcondition `(= result 0)` must hold, and if the precondition `(not (null? l))` held and the function `length` were run, then the postcondition `(= result (+ 1 (length (cdr l))))` must hold. The next listing shows the code for the function `append` with specifications.

```
1 (define append : (List<num> List<num> -> List<num>)
2    (lambda (lst1: List<num> lst2: List<num> |
3        #t -> (= (length result) (+ (length lst1) (length lst2))))
4      ( if (null? lst1) lst2
5         ( if (null? lst2) lst1
6            (cons (car lst1) (append (cdr lst1) lst2))
7         )
8       )
9    )
10 )
```

The specification for `append` appears on line 11. The precondition for `append` is `#t`, since the types `lst1` and `lst2` already ensure that these arguments are lists. The precondition for `append` says that the length of the appended list is the sum of the lengths of the two argument lists.

Notice that it is possible to call other helper functions to help write preconditions and postconditions. In some specification languages, these are special functions called *predicate functions*. In Speclang, we are not distinguishing these functions. It is useful to note that these helper functions must not change the reference values in the program. Otherwise, checking the precondition or postcondition might change the result of the program that is undesirable. We will revisit this property in section 10.7.1.

It might be desirable to make richer assertions about the function `append`, such as that every element in the `result` is either in `lst1` or in `lst2`. The listing here builds a few helper functions to add this assertion to the postcondition of the function `append`:

```
1 (define or : (bool bool -> bool)
2    (lambda (b1 : bool b2: bool)
```

```
 3    ( if  b1 #t b2)
 4   )
 5 )

 7 (define and : (bool bool –> bool)
 8   (lambda (b1 : bool b2: bool)
 9     ( if  b1
10       ( if  b2 #t #f)
11       #f
12     )
13   )
14 )

16 (define contains :  ( List<num> num –> bool)
17   (lambda (l :  List<num> n:num)
18     ( if  (null?  l) #f
19       ( if  (= (car  l) n) #t
20         (contains (cdr  l) n)
21       )
22     )
23   )
24 )
```

The definitions of and and or are fairly straightforward. The contains function checks if an element is in a list. Next, we build a function that, given a list and a predicate function, checks that predicate on each element of the list and returns true if it holds on all elements:

```
1 (define forall  :  ( List<num> (num –> bool) –> bool)
2   (lambda (l :  List<num> f: (num–>bool))
3     ( if  (null?  l) #t
4       ( if  (f (car  l)) ( forall  (cdr  l) f)
5         #f
6       )
7     )
8   )
9 )
```

The function forall is akin to the universal quantifier (∀) in mathematics and logic but specialized here for list of numbers and assertions over a number.

Now, since we have all the ingredients of the postcondition, we can build the key logic of the postcondition as the higher-order function post shown here. Given two lists, post returns a predicate function that takes a number and checks whether that number is in either list:

```
1 (define post :  ( List<num> List<num> –> (num –> bool))
2     (lambda (lst1 :  List<num> lst2 :  List<num>)
```

```
3       (lambda (n : num)
4          (or (contains lst1 n) (contains lst2 n))
5       )
6    )
7  )
```

Using the function `post`, we can write a revised postcondition of the function `append` that also asserts that all elements in the result are either in the first list or in the second list:

```
1  (define append : (List<num> List<num> -> List<num>)
2    (lambda (lst1: List<num> lst2: List<num>
3      | #t ->
4         (and
5           (= (length result) (+ (length lst1) (length lst2)))
6           (forall result (post lst1 lst2))
7         ))
8      (if (null? lst1) lst2
9        (if (null? lst2) lst1
10          (cons (car lst1) (append (cdr lst1) lst2))
11        )
12      )
13    )
14 )
```

The modified postcondition is given at lines 4–7. The condition on the length of the list is the same as before. The additional postcondition is placed at line 6, which checks the condition implemented by `post`; that is, whether each element of `result` is in either `lst1` or `lst2`.

The example illustrates that while some effort might be necessary to build predicate functions to check desired specifications, the ability to use the full power of the programming language to write specifications is very powerful. These predicate functions written for specifying specifications could be utilized for programming, as well as for specifying other related functions (e.g., the and, or, `contains`, and `forall` functions). Some of the general-purpose functions (e.g., and, or, `memberof`, and `forall`) are also frequently supported by full-fledged specification languages as built-in features.

In the rest of this chapter, we will understand different aspects of specifications and specification checking by building an implementation of Speclang. This implementation helps clearly understand the key idea like precondition, postcondition, side-effect freedom, and specification checking. This interpreter will build on the Typelang interpreter.

10.4 Syntax of New Features for Writing Specifications

The main changes in the grammar for Speclang are highlighted in figure 10.1. This grammar builds on the grammar for the Typelang language.

The grammar shows the new specification feature added to the lambda expression. The specifications are marked as optional ({ } ?). When no specifications are provided, then the

```
Program     ::=  DefineDecl* Exp?                           Program
DefineDecl  ::=  (define Identifier:T Exp)                    Define
Exp         ::=                                          Expressions
                 Number                                       NumExp
            |    (+ Exp Exp+)                                 AddExp
            |    (- Exp Exp+)                                 SubExp
            |    (* Exp Exp+)                                MultExp
            |    (/ Exp Exp+)                                 DivExp
            |    Identifier                                   VarExp
            |    (let ((Identifier:T Exp)+) Exp)              LetExp
            |    ( Exp Exp+)                                  CallExp
            |    (lambda (Identifier:T+ {| Spec}?) Exp)    LambdaExp
            |    (ref:T Exp)                                  RefExp
            |    (deref Exp)                                 DerefExp
            |    (set! Exp Exp)                             AssignExp
            |    (free Exp)                                  FreeExp
Spec        ::=                                        Specifications
                 Exp* -> Exp*                                SpecCase
            |    Spec {|| Spec }*                            FuncSpec
```

Figure 10.1
Grammar for the Speclang language. All the type annotations (":T") in the syntax are new to
the language. Nonterminals that are not defined in this grammar are exactly the same as those in
Typelang.

default precondition and postcondition of the lambda expression is true. The specification
of the function `FunSpec` allows one or more specification cases, separated by ||. Each
specification case takes the form of a list of preconditions followed by an arrow (similar to
function types), followed by a list of postconditions. If multiple precondition expressions
are given in a specification case, all of them must hold. Similarly, if multiple postcondition
expressions are given in a specification case, all of them must hold.

At the syntactic level, the Speclang language does allow the use of those expressions
that change the heap of the program, such as `RefExp` and `AssignExp`. As we will see
later in this chapter, the type system of Speclang disallows the use of such specifications.

10.4.1 Modifications to AST Nodes and the AST Visitor
To store these new expressions, we also need to introduce two new abstract syntax tree
(AST) nodes: `FuncSpec` and `SpecCase`. As usual, adding new AST nodes requires
extensions to other parts of the interpreter that must process each kind of expression (e.g.,
the `Visitor` interface, and expression formatter).

10.5 Checking Specifications: Static versus Dynamic

Writing a specification as part of the function definition can serve to document the functions' behavior precisely and help clients of the function use it properly. While this

property alone makes writing specifications worthwhile, most languages provide additional value from the specification by checking it against usage to prevent accident violation of preconditions by the client and postconditions by the function implementation.

This check to validate a specification against implementation and usage can happen without running the program, similar to how the type checker was implemented in the previous chapter, or it can happen at runtime. The first kind of checking is called *static verification*, and the second kind of checking is called *dynamic verification*, or often *runtime assertion checking*. Typically, static verification techniques employ methods to abstractly run or interpret the function for all possible input values, and verify the specification for these abstract runs. Since the method abstractly tackles all possible input values, a guarantee is provided that the implementation of the function is valid with regard to the specified specifications. No further checking of the function's implementation is necessary unless it changes, in which case static verification needs to be conducted again. We will not be discussing these methods in detail here, but we will note that effective static verification techniques are a subject area of great importance for programming language research because they have the potential to significantly reduce the number of errors in programs.

In contrast, runtime assertion checking techniques check the specification for the actual invocation of the function. For that particular run of the function, preconditions are checked over arguments to determine if they hold. If the preconditions hold, then the function body is run. Once the function body completes execution, then the postcondition is checked. If the postconditions hold, then the client receives the result of the function. Otherwise, a specification violation error is raised. Due to the nature of runtime assertion checking techniques, they can provide assurances that the function satisfies its specification for the arguments that were used during runtime assertion checking. This is typically a weaker assurance compared to static verification techniques that provide guarantees about all possible inputs.

To illustrate the difference, let us reconsider the function nat sum as given here, which computes the sum of natural numbers using recursion:

```
1 (define natsum : (num -> num)
2   (lambda (n : num | (>= n 0) -> (= result  (/  (* n (+ n 1)) 2)))
3     ( if (= 0 n) n
4         (+ n (natsum (- n 1)))
5     )
6   )
7 )
8 (natsum 3)
```

A static verification technique would attempt to prove that the specification at line 2 holds for all values of n, whereas a dynamic verification technique would check whether the specification holds for the number 3, as shown on the function call at line 8. While dynamic verification might appear limited at first, it is often very effective because logical errors do tend to manifest themselves in simpler examples. In the example given here, the specification is checked for inputs 3, 2, 1, and 0. The first is an explicit input to the function nat sum; the rest are inputs for the recursive call.

In the design of Speclang, for the sake of simplicity, we will focus on incorporating a runtime assertion checking mechanism in the programming language.

10.6   Typechecking Specifications

We have added specifications to the lambda expression. Thus, the rule for checking lambda expressions should also be modified as follows to account for these specifications:

(LAMBDAEXP)

$$tenv_0 = (ExtendEnv\ var_0\ t_0\ tenv)$$
$$tenv_i = (ExtendEnv\ var_i\ t_i\ tenv_{i-1}), \forall i \in 1..n$$
$$tenv_{sp} = (ExtendEnv\ result\ t\ tenv_n)$$
$$sp_j = spre_j\!-\!>spost_j, \forall j \in 0..m$$
$$tenv_n \vdash spre_j : \textbf{bool}, \forall j \in 0..m$$
$$tenv_{sp} \vdash spost_j : \textbf{bool}, \forall j \in 0..m$$
$$tenv_n \vdash e_{body} : t$$

$$\overline{tenv \vdash (LambdaExp\ var_0\ \ldots\ var_n\ t_0\ \ldots\ t_n\ sp_0\ \ldots\ sp_m\ e_{body}) : (t_0\ \ldots\ t_n\!-\!>t)}$$

The rule given here also uses the typing rule notation $tenv \vdash e : t$ from chapter 9. Recall that this notation should be read as, "assuming the type environment `tenv`, expression `e` has type `t`." The new meaning due to specifications are *emphasized* in the following text with italics. Informally, the rule says that a lambda expression that is defining a function with *n* formal parameters ($var_0\ \ldots\ var_n$), giving them types ($t_0\ \ldots\ t_n$) and *has* m *specification cases ($sp_0\ \ldots\ sp_m$)* with type $t_0\ \ldots\ t_n\!-\!>t$ if the following are true:

- In the context of a new type environment that extends the type environment *tenv* with new bindings from variables (var_i) to their types (t_i), the body of the lambda expression has type *t*.
- *In the context of the type environment* t_n *each precondition* $spre_j$ *of each specification case is well typed and has type* ***bool***.
- *In the context of a new type environment that extends the type environment* $tenv_n$ *with new bindings from a special variable (result) to its type (t), each postcondition* $spost_j$ *of each specification case is well typed and has type* ***bool***.

Let us consider the second and third new conditions in the itemized list in detail. They specify that to typecheck the specification case (sp_j), all the formal parameters of the lambda expressions must be defined (which is ensured by passing the type environment $tenv_n$, which has all of these names defined) and a special variable (*result*) must be defined that has the same type as the result type of the lambda expression (which is ensured by extending the type environment $tenv_n$ to add a binding from *result* to *t*). In this type environment, the specification case ought to be well typed.

10.7   Side-Effect Freedom

Notice that the type rule described in the previous section only limits a precondition and a postcondition to being an expression of type **bool**. Does that suffice?

Let us consider the code here, which is similar to our previous example except that x is passed as a reference in the function. The function has a default precondition and postcondition:

```
$ ((lambda (x: Ref num | #t –> #t) (+ 3 (+ 4 (deref x)))) (ref: num 2))
9
```

Now, let us consider a variation of the function, given here with a specification. The specification is similar to before—if x is greater than 0, then the result will be greater than 7. This specification is only reading the value of x:

```
$ ((lambda (x: Ref num | (> (deref x) 0) –> (> result 7)) (+ 3 (+ 4 (deref x))))
    (ref: num 2))
9
```

Next, consider another variation of the example:

```
$ ((lambda (x: Ref num | (> (deref x) (set! x 0)) –> (> result 7)) (+ 3 (+ 4 (
    deref x)))) (ref: num 2))
Postcondition violation in call ((lambda ( x ) (+ 3.0 (+ 4.0 (deref x) ) )) (ref
    2.0) )
```

In this version, the literal 0 is replaced by the assign expression (set! x 0), which, according to our semantics of the assignment expression, evaluates to 0. So, in fact, this new expression also checks that the precondition x is greater than 0; however, the function fails to meet its postcondition. This is because in the process of performing the precondition check, the value of x was changed to 0, which caused the postcondition to be violated. Such specifications, which change the meaning of the program, are not desirable. In fact, a program that passes all specification check ought to produce the same result, even when all specifications are removed from that program. In other words, besides checking for correctness, specifications ought not to change the behavior of the program.

In chapter 7, we studied the side effects of an expression, such as writing memory locations. In order for an expression in the specification to not change the behavior of the program, it must not have any side effects. This property is known as *side-effect freedom* of expressions. An expression that does not have a side effect is called a *pure expression*. All expressions that are used within the precondition and postcondition must be pure expressions. Our typechecking rule so far doesn't check for side-effect freedom. That subject will be discussed next.

10.7.1 Implementing Side-Effect Freedom

In the previous subsection, we discussed the need for expressions in specifications to be free of side effects. If these expressions have side effects, observing the state of the program can actually change its state. We will now implement this check in the Speclang interpreter. We will add this check to the type system of Speclang. This check is implemented as a separate module in the purity checker.

What are the side effects of atomic expressions like NumExp, StrExp, BoolExp, and UnitExp? Clearly, these expressions can't change any memory locations. Therefore, these expressions by themselves are pure.

What about arithmetic expressions that combine two or more other expressions? These expressions themselves do not have side effects, but their subexpressions might. Therefore, these arithmetic expressions are pure if their subexpressions are pure:

```
Boolean visitCompoundArithExp(CompoundArithExp e, Env<Type> env) {
  List<Exp> operands = e.all();

  boolean purity = true;
  for (Exp exp : operands) {
    purity &= (Boolean) exp.accept(this, env);
  }

  return purity ;
}
```

Similarly, binary comparator expressions like greater, less, and equal do not have side effects themselves, but their subexpressions might. Therefore, these comparison expressions are pure if their subexpressions are pure:

```
Boolean visitBinaryComparator(BinaryComparator e, Env<Type> env) {
  Exp first_exp = e. first_exp () ;
  Exp second_exp = e.second_exp();

  return (Boolean) first_exp.accept(this, env)
            && (Boolean) second_exp.accept(this, env);
}
```

Computing the side effects of list functions is similar to binary and arithmetic expressions. These expressions have side effects, if their subexpressions do. We illustrate using `ConsExp` here, but other expressions are similar:

```
public Boolean visit(ConsExp e, Env<Type> env) {
  Exp fst = e. fst () ;
  Exp snd = e.snd();
  return (Boolean) fst.accept(this, env) && (Boolean) snd.accept(this, env);
}
```

Computing the side effects of expressions that define variables is similar. A define declaration has side effects, if the right-hand-side (RHS) expressions (the values of defined variables) do:

```
public Boolean visit(DefineDecl d, Env<Type> env) {
  return (Boolean) d._value_exp.accept(this, env);
}

public Boolean visit(LetExp e, Env<Type> env) {
  List<Exp> value_exps = e.value_exps();
  boolean purity = true;
```

```
  for (Exp exp : value_exps) {
    purity = purity && (boolean) exp.accept(this, env);
  }


  return purity && (Boolean) e.body().accept(this, env);
}
```

A `let` expression has side effects, if the RHS expressions and the body have side effects. The memory-related expressions produce as well. For instance, consider the following code:

```
 1  (let
 2    ((f: (Ref num -> num)
 3      (lambda
 4        (x: Ref num
 5          | (> (deref x) (set! x 0)) -> (> result 7))
 6          (+ 3 (+ 4 (deref x)))
 7        )
 8      )
 9    )
10    (f (ref: num 2))
11  )
```

In this code, the specification at line 5 has side effects, so evaluating the code produces the following error:

Type error: The precondition must be a pure expression found (> (deref x) (set! x 0.0)) in (> (deref x) (set! x 0.0)) ->(> result 7.0)

For the assignment expression and the free expression, it is clear that they may change the state of the heap, and therefore checking the specification will produce side effects that would be visible to the program:

```
public Boolean visit(DerefExp e, Env<Type> env) {
  Exp exp = e.loc_exp();
  return (Boolean) exp.accept(this, env);
}
```

Even though the dereference expression is a memory-related expression, it just reads the contents of the memory, and thus a dereference expression has side effects only if its subexpression does:

```
public Boolean visit(RefExp e, Env<Type> env) {
  Exp value = e.value_exp();
  return (Boolean) value.accept(this, env);
}
```

What about reference expressions that allocate memory? Allocating a new memory location doesn't have side effects on existing memory locations that the program accesses. So, a reference expression produces side effects only if its subexpression does. There are other expressions, such as reading a file and printing a value, that produce side effects and therefore can't be included in specifications.

10.8 Runtime Specification Checking

So far, we have discussed the syntax of writing specifications, typechecking to validate types used in the specification, and checking for side-effect freedom. In this section, we will look at runtime checking of specifications.

Adding specifications changes the semantics of the call expression. Before the function is called, preconditions must be checked, and after the function finishes running, postconditions must be checked. In the listing here, we will discuss these semantic changes:

```
public Value visit (CallExp e, Env<Value> env) {
    ...  // Elided code that evaluates the operator to value and raises dynamic
    // error, if the operator does not evaluate to a function value.

    ...  // Elided code that evaluates actual arguments, raises dynamic
    // error if there is an argument mismatch, and extends env to create
    // an environment fun_env for the function body to run

    FuncSpec spec = (FuncSpec) operator.spec();
    int speccase = (int)((Value.NumVal) evalSpecCases(spec, fun_env)).v();
    if (speccase < 0)
        throw new ProgramError("Precondition violation in call:"+ts. visit (e, null));
```

First, the specification cases are evaluated. Using the environment `fun_env` to evaluate these specification cases ensures that the evaluation has access to all the formal parameter names. Recall from before that the first specification case whose precondition holds is checked for that function call. Here, the specification cases evaluate to the lexical order of specification case whose precondition holds, and it gives a negative value if the precondition of neither of the specification cases holds. A precondition violation is reported if none of the specifications cases have a precondition that was found to hold:

```
    Value fresult = (Value) operator.body().accept(this, fun_env);
    Env<Value> post_env = new ExtendEnv<>(fun_env, "result", fresult);
    SpecCase post = spec.speccases().get(speccase);
    BoolVal postcondition = (Value.BoolVal) evalPostConditions(post, post_env);
    if (postcondition.v()) // Postcondition is true
        return fresult ;
    throw new ProgramError("Postcondition violation in call:"+ts. visit (e, null));
```

If the precondition for one of the specification cases holds, then the body of the function is evaluated. Next, the result of the function is bound to the built-in variable, `result`. We also need to find the specification case among those that will be used during this evaluation. In the environment that binds `result` to the value produced by the function body, postconditions are checked. If the postcondition holds, then the value of the function call is the value produced by the function body. Otherwise, a postcondition violation error is reported.

The helper functions `evalSpecCases`, `evalPreConditions`, and `evalPostConditions` are shown in the following listings:

```
private Value evalSpecCases(FuncSpec s, Env<Value> env) {
  List<SpecCase> speccases = s.speccases();
  for(int i=0; i< speccases.size(); i++) {
    Value speccase_value = evalPreConditions(speccases.get(i), env);
    if (!( speccase_value instanceof Value.BoolVal))
      throw new ProgramError("Condition not a boolean in expression");
    Value.BoolVal condition = (Value.BoolVal) speccase_value;
    if (condition.v()) return new Value.NumVal(i);
  }
  return new Value.NumVal(-1);
}
```

The preconditions for each specification case are evaluated until the first set of preconditions all hold, which is the result of the specification case:

```
Value evalPreConditions(SpecCase s, Env<Value> env) {
  for (Exp precondition : s.preconditions()) {
    Value precond_value = precondition.accept(this, env);
    if (!( precond_value instanceof Value.BoolVal))
      throw new ProgramError("Condition not a boolean in expression");
    Value.BoolVal condition = (Value.BoolVal) precond_value;
    if (!condition.v())
      return condition;
  }
  return new Value.BoolVal(true);
}
```

Each precondition of the specification case must hold in order for the entire specification case to hold. Similarly, each postcondition of the specification case must hold. As soon as a precondition or a postcondition evaluates to `false`, evaluation of the remainder of the expressions is skipped:

```
Value evalPostConditions(SpecCase s, Env<Value> env) {
  for (Exp postcondition : s.postconditions()) {
    Value postcond_value = postcondition.accept(this, env);
    if (!( postcond_value instanceof Value.BoolVal))
      throw new ProgramError("Condition not a boolean in expression");
    Value.BoolVal condition = (Value.BoolVal) postcond_value;
    if (!condition.v())
      return condition;
  }
  return new Value.BoolVal(true);
}
```

In summary, the addition of behavioral specifications primarily affects the semantics of the call expression. Before a call, the preconditions are evaluated, and after the call, the postconditions are evaluated. If the function specification contains multiple specification cases, the first (in lexical order) specification case whose preconditions are met is used to check postconditions.

In this chapter, we have not covered other features of specification languages, such as being able to refer to the value in the precondition state, specifying function invariants, and specifying memory locations that could be changed by the function. These interesting features are given as exercises to the reader. The design and implementation of specification languages constitute an active area of research in programming languages.

Summary

In this chapter, we learned about specifications that convey the expectations that a code can rely upon (preconditions) and the guarantees that it will provide (postconditions). We also learned about the role of specifications toward blame assignment when something goes wrong in a program. We investigated language features for writing simplified specifications for functions. We also looked over several example specifications, including those for list functions. Specifications can be verified statically or dynamically. In this chapter, we focused on dynamically validating specifications, also referred to as *runtime assertion checking*. For runtime assertion checking, as well as for static verification, it is important that expressions that are used within the specifications do not modify references. In other words, the specification expressions should be free of side effects, and so we also reviewed the process of checking for side-effect freedom.

Exercises

10.8.1. *[Sum of Cubes]* Write a specification for the sumcubes function, as shown here:

```
(define sumcubes : (num -> num)
  (lambda (n : num | #t -> #t )
    ( if (= 0 n) n
        (+ (* n n n) (sumcubes (- n 1)))
    )
  )
)

(sumcubes 3)
```

10.8.2. *[Find]* Write a specification for the function `find` shown here:

```
(define find : ( List<string> num -> string)
  (lambda (l : List<string> index : num
      | #t -> #t)
    ( if (null? l) "error"
      ( if (= 0 index) (car l)
          (find (cdr l) (- index 1))
      )
    )
  )
)

(find ( list : string   "contracts" "are" "important") 2)
```

10.8.3. *[Cases of Append]* Write a more detailed specification for the function `append` shown here, which uses specification cases to make four separate instances of the function explicit in the specification: when `lst1` is empty and `lst2` is empty, when `lst1` is empty and `lst2` is nonempty, when `lst1` is nonempty and `lst2` is empty, and when `lst1` is nonempty and `lst2` is nonempty:

```
(define append : (List<num> List<num> -> List<num>)
  (lambda (lst1: List<num> lst2: List<num>)
    ( if (null? lst1 ) lst2
      ( if (null? lst2 ) lst1
        (cons (car lst1 ) (append (cdr lst1) lst2 ))
      )
    )
  )
)
```

10.8.4. *[Prestate values]* When writing specifications, it is helpful to have access to the values of the variables in the precondition state (i.e., when the function body has not run). In some specification languages, the precondition state is also referred to as the *old state*. Extend Speclang to add the ability to access precondition states by adding an `old` expression. An `old` expression must be used only within postconditions in a specification. An example appears here:

```
(lambda
  (x: Ref num
    | #t -> (= (+ (deref x) 1) (deref (old x))) )
  (set! x (+ (deref x) 1))
)
```

In this example, the postcondition states that the new value of the variable x is 1 greater than the old value of the variable x.

10.8.5. *[Function Invariants]* Invariants are conditions that hold throughout a computation. Invariants are useful for specifying data structures since there are certain constraints that must always hold for the data structure. Such invariants are called *data structure invariants*. Invariants are also useful for loops in the program and hold across all interations of the loop. Such invariants are called *loop invariants*. An invariant for a function holds both before the function is called and after the function has completed running.

Add the function invariant feature to Speclang. One or more function invariants could be specified at the beginning of specification cases:

```
(lambda
  (x: Ref num | (> (deref x) 0) | #t -> (= result 342))
  (+ 3 (+ 4 (deref x)))
)
```

In this example, the function invariant states that x will be greater than zero both before and after the function call.

10.8.6. *[Frame axioms]* It is often desirable to make assertions about the set of memory locations that a function is allowed to modify. Other memory locations remain unchanged. A specification language typically provides features to identify memory locations that might be modified by a function.

Add the `modifies` feature to Speclang, which allows programmers to specify which memory locations might be modified by a function, and by the corollary, that nothing else changes. An example appears here, where the function satisfies its `modifies` specification:

```
(lambda
  (x: Ref num
    | (modifies x) | #t -> #t)
  (set! x (+ (deref x) 1))
)
```

The syntax for the `modifies` feature is similar to the invariants features discussed in question 10.8.5. Indeed, both features have a similar flavor that specifies constraints that hold before and after the function call.

Another example appears here, where the function does not satisfies its `modifies` specification:

```
(lambda
  (x: Ref num y: Ref num
    | (modifies x) | #t -> #t)
  (set! y (+ (deref x) 1))
)
```

V ADVANCED FEATURES

11 Msglang: A Language with Message-Passing Concurrency

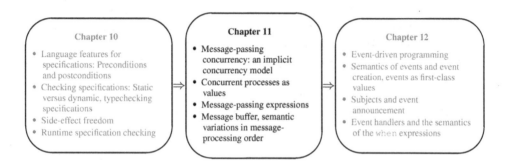

Chapter 10	Chapter 11	Chapter 12
• Language features for specifications: Preconditions and postconditions • Checking specifications: Static versus dynamic, typechecking specifications • Side-effect freedom • Runtime specification checking	• Message-passing concurrency: an implicit concurrency model • Concurrent processes as values • Message-passing expressions • Message buffer, semantic variations in message-processing order	• Event-driven programming • Semantics of events and event creation, events as first-class values • Subjects and event announcement • Event handlers and the semantics of the when expressions

In chapter 10, we learned that concurrency and parallelism are important requirements for modern software systems. We also examined explicit features for concurrency (namely, `fork` and `lock`). When we say that concurrency is explicit, we mean that the developer is responsible for creating threads of control, managing these threads, synchronizing between the threads and destroying them. The language provides a primitive to create a new thread of control (e.g., `fork`) for synchronization between threads and for stopping a thread. This is similar to explicit management of memory using the `ref` and `free` primitives in Reflang. In languages that provide explicit control over concurrency, programmers have more flexibility to create programming patterns. On the other hand, since the programmers have to manage threads themselves, there are more opportunities for making mistakes. We saw some examples of such concurrency mistakes in chapter 8.

When we say that concurrency is implicit, we mean that the developer is not responsible for creating threads of controls, managing these threads, synchronizing between the threads, and destroying them. Instead, the runtime of the programming language manages threads automatically behind the scene. As an analogy, in languages that have implicit memory management, such as Java, the programmer is not responsible for managing memory. Rather, new memory is allocated implicitly when the programmer creates a new object. The memory for an object is destroyed (or freed) automatically when the object is no longer in the lexical scope and there aren't any live references pointing to that object. We studied mechanisms such as garbage collection, which implement memory management in the runtime of the programming language in chapter 7. Similarly, in a language with implicit concurrency, programmers are not responsible for managing threads of control. Rather, the language runtime allocates a new thread of control if needed. If the thread is no longer needed, it can be relinquished. Programmers do not explicitly synchronize between threads. Instead, synchronization occurs behind the scene as needed. In programming languages that manage concurrency implicitly, programmers are freed from having to think about program concurrency and can focus on their task at hand. There are fewer possibilities of making mistakes. On the other hand, the language may support only certain patterns of concurrency and not others. Some programmers might find it difficult to adapt to the concurrency patterns supported by the programming language.

In this chapter, we will consider an implicit language model for concurrency based on *message passing*. Programming languages and programming frameworks that support message-passing concurrency generally have features to create entities, typically called *processes*, which interact with each other by exchanging messages. Message-passing concurrency has a long history, dating back to at least 1967 and the programming language Simula. Simula introduced the notion of a class that exchanged messages with other classes. This notion of class in Simula 67 inspired the development of monitors around 1973 by Per Brinch Hansen. Successive works on actors by Atkinson and Hewitt, and *Communicating Sequential Processes* by Tony Hoare, just to name a few, developed these ideas further.

In this chapter, we will learn about these ideas while developing a concurrent language called *Msglang*. The complete implementation of Msglang is available with the book code, hosted at https://github.com/hridesh/msglang.

11.1 Examples

To illustrate the idea of processes, consider the listing here:

```
1 (define hello
2   (process
3     (receive (message)
4       ( print "Hello")
5     )
6   )
7 )

9 (send hello "hi")
```

This listing defines a process in the language Msglang and sends it a message. The definition of the process is at lines 2–6. The process declaration includes an expression in its body, which will be run when the process is created. The syntax `receive` followed by `message` says that this process can receive messages sent to it that have one element. This is a simplified language. In practice, message-passing languages support processes that can receive different kinds of messages, but for now, we will just consider this simplified language, which can accept only one kind of message. The code at line 4 shows what this process will do when it receives a message. Here, this process's definition says that it will print the message "hello." Then, at line 1, we give this process the name `hello`. This name is like an address, and it can be used to refer to this process.

What will the process `hello` do, if it doesn't receive any messages? Nothing! This process will just sit there, waiting to receive a message.

At line 9, an example of the message sending is shown. The `send` expression at line 9 takes the name of the process as the first argument (here, `hello`) and sends the contents of the message to the process as the remaining parameters. When this program is run, the message "hi" is sent to the process `hello`, which prints the message "hello."

The listing here shows another example of a process:

```
1 (define sum
2   (process
3     (receive (num1 num2)
4       ( print (+ .num1 num2))
5     )
6   )
7 )

9 (send sum 300 42)
```

As in the previous example, here we are also defining a process at lines 2–6 and giving it the name `sum` at line 1. However, unlike the previous example, this process runs an expression as its body. This receive expression accepts messages containing two elements—two numbers, to be precise. When this process receives a message, it prints the sum of these two numbers as shown at line 4. At line 9, the `send` expression is sending a message to the `sum` process containing two numbers, `300` and `42`. After the process `sum` receives this number, it prints `342`. This example can also be rewritten to receive one number at a time:

```
1 (define seq (lambda (cmd1 cmd2) cmd1))

3 (define sum
4   (process
5     (receive (num1)
6       (receive (num2)
7         ( print (+ num1 num2))
8       )
9     )
10  )
11 )

13 (seq (send sum 300) (send sum 42))
```

The listing here shows another example that has multiple processes:

```
1 (define sum
2   (process
3     (receive (num1 num2)
4       ( print (+ num1 num2))
5     )
6   )
7 )

9 (define forward
10   (process
```

```
11     (receive (num1 num2)
12       (send sum num1 num2)
13     )
14   )
15 )
```

```
17 (send forward 300 42)
```

The process `sum` in this example is the same as in the previous example. It prints the sum of two numbers sent to it in a message. A new process, `forward`, is defined at lines 9–15. This process essentially acts as a repeater. It sends the messages that it receives to the process `sum`. The `send` expression at line 12 sends the two values `num1` and `num2` to the process `sum`. The `send` expression at line 17 is sending the two values `300` and `42` to the process `forward`, which in turn forwards those values to the process `sum`, which finally adds them together and prints `342`.

This example shows two kinds of processes: those that only receive messages and act on them, and those that both send and receive messages.

In all of the examples so far, the processes that we are defining run concurrently. Next, we will see an example that leverages this concurrency. This example leverages a trick that we saw in previous chapters to run two expressions in a sequence. The function `seq` at lines 1–3 takes two parameters:

```
1 (define seq
2   (lambda (cmd1 cmd2) cmd1)
3 )
```

```
5 (define sum
6   (process
7     (receive (num1 num2)
8       (print (+ num1 num2))
9     )
10  )
11 )
```

```
13 (define multforward
14   (process
15     (receive (num1 num2)
16       (seq
17         (send sum num1 num2)
18         (send sum (+1 num1) (+ 1 num2))
19       )
20     )
21   )
22 )
```

```
24 (send multforward 300 42)
```

The process sum defined at lines 5–11 in this example is the same as in the previous example. It prints the sum of two numbers sent to it in the message. The process multiforward, defined at lines 13–22, is different than the process forward defined in the previous example. When this process receives a message, it sends two messages in sequence. First, at line 17, this process sends the original numbers to the process sum. Then, at line 18, the multiforward process increments the original numbers num1 and num2 by 1 and sends these incremented numbers to the sum process again. Therefore, when the multiforward process is sent a message containing the numbers 300 and 42 at line 24, it sends a message containing the numbers 300 and 42 to the process sum.

This example illustrates concurrent computation by the processes sum and multiforward. While sum is busy computing and printing the sum of 300 and 42, multiforward concurrently computes the sum of 300 and 1 and 42 and 1 to prepare the next message to be sent to sum. In this example, the concurrency leads to parallelism between these two tasks, but that may not always be the sole purpose of concurrent computation.

A process can also send messages to itself, referred to as *self*. Next, we will look at an example of self-sending. This is similar to recursion, as discussed in previous chapters where a procedure was calling itself:

```
1 (define serieshelper
2   (process
3     (receive (num accumulator)
4       ( if (> num 0)
5         (send
6           ( self )
7           (- num 1)
8           (+ num accumulator)
9         )
10         ( print  accumulator)
11       )
12     )
13   )
14 )

16 (define series
17   (process
18     (receive (num)
19         (send serieshelper num 0)
20     )
21   )
22 )

24 (send series 342)
```

In this example, two processes are used to implement the sum or series function. Two processes, series and serieshelper, are cooperating to compute the sum of a simple series. The process series is like the forwarding process that we saw previously. When this process receives a message containing a number, it forwards that number and a starting value of the accumulator to serieshelper, which then prints the value of the accumulator if the number is less than zero at line 10. Otherwise, it decrements num by 1 at line 7 and computes the current term of the series (+ num accumulator) at line 8; and then it sends a message to itself to compute and add the next term of the series at lines 5–9.

To send a message to itself, the process needs to know its name or address. At line 6, the self expression is used to obtain the address of the current process. Most programming languages that support message passing have this or a similar mechanism for self-addressing. In object-oriented languages like Java, the this mechanism is inspired by the self mechanism for self-addressing in message-passing languages.

So far, we have seen examples where messages are exchanged in one way, such as from series to serieshelper. A request-response pattern is also useful in message-passing programs, as the example here illustrates. This example builds on a previous example, but with a change. Instead of simply printing the sum of the two numbers, the worker needs to send back the result to the client:

```
1 (define worker
2   (process
3     (receive ( client  num1 num2)
4       (send client #f (+ num1 num2) 0)
5     )
6   )
7 )

9 (define client
10   (process
11     (receive (request num1 num2)
12       ( if  request
13         (send worker (self) num1 num2)
14         ( print  num1)
15       )
16     )
17   )
18 )

20 (send client #t 300 42)
```

In this example, once the worker receives two numbers as part of a message, it computes the sum of these two numbers and sends it back to the client at line 4. The first parameter of the send expression is the address of the client. The second parameter marks that the message is a response. In this example, the client only needs to handle two kinds of messages. The third parameter is the result that is sent back to the client, and the fourth parameter is a placeholder value that is not used for response messages. To initiate work by the client at line 20, two numbers are sent to it. This message send operation supplies #t as the second parameter of the message send, marking that this is a request message. The client code checks if the incoming message is a request, and if it is, it forwards the request to worker. Otherwise, if it is a response, then that response is printed. Using a parameter to differentiate between the kinds of messages is a common pattern in message-passing languages.

To conclude the set of example message-passing programs, the next listing shows an example where two processes model the game of ping-pong by passing messages back and forth. This example also illustrates the process termination using the `stop` expression, which causes the process to complete execution. Once a process has completed execution, it can no longer receive or process any more messages:

```
1 (define seq (lambda (cmd1 cmd2) cmd1))

3 (define ping
4   (process
5     (receive (sender num)
6       ( if
7         (> num 0)
8         (seq
9           ( print  "ping")
10          (send sender (self) (– num 1))
11          )
12        (stop)
13        )
14      )
15    )
16 )

18 (define pong
19   (process
20     (receive (sender num)
21       ( if
22         (> num 0)
23         (seq
24           ( print  "pong")
25           (send sender (self) (– num 1))
26          )
27         (stop)
28        )
29      )
30    )
31 )

33 (send ping pong 42)
```

The first process, `ping`, accepts messages that have two parts: the sender's address and a number. The second process, `pong`, also accepts messages with two parts.

The body of the `ping process` processes this message containing two parts. If the number `num` received as the message is greater than zero, the process prints the message "`ping`" or "`pong`" and replies to the process address passed as `sender` with its own

address and num $-$ 1. The process obtains its own address using the expression (self).
If the number num received as the message is equal to or less than zero, then the process
stops (i.e., it dies). This is achieved using the (stop) expression.

Finally, the expression (send ping pong 42) triggers the ping process, sending
it the address of the pong process and the number 42.

So this program will exchange the following sequence of messages between two processes: the actor ping will send the message 41 to the actor pong; as a result, pong will
send the message 40 to ping; as a result, ping will send the message 39 to pong, and
the process continues. Finally, pong will send the message 0 to ping. On receiving the
message 0, the process ping will stop.

In the rest of this chapter, we will examine the various aspects of processes and message
passing by building an implementation of Msglang. This implementation helps clearly
understand key ideas like process creation and message queue, message send and receive,
and protocols for processing received messages. This interpreter will build on the Reflang.

11.2 New Expressions

The main changes in the grammar for Msglang are bolded in figure 11.1. This grammar
builds on the grammar for the Reflang language.

```
Program      ::=   DefineDecl* Exp?                       Program
DefineDecl   ::=   (define Identifier Exp)                Define
Exp          ::=                                          Expressions
                   Number                                 NumExp
               |   (+ Exp Exp⁺)                           AddExp
               |   (− Exp Exp⁺)                           SubExp
               |   (* Exp Exp⁺)                           MultExp
               |   (/ Exp Exp⁺)                           DivExp
               |   Identifier                             VarExp
               |   (let ((Identifier Exp)⁺) Exp)          LetExp
               |   ( Exp Exp⁺)                            CallExp
               |   (lambda (Identifier⁺) Exp)             LambdaExp
               |   (ref Exp)                              RefExp
               |   (deref Exp)                            DerefExp
               |   (set! Exp Exp)                         AssignExp
               |   (free Exp)                             FreeExp
               |   (process Exp)                          ProcessExp
               |   (send Exp Exp⁺)                        SendExp
               |   (receive (Identifier⁺) Exp)            ReceiveExp
               |   (self)                                 SelfExp
               |   (stop)                                 StopExp
```

Figure 11.1
Grammar for the Msglang language. The expressions in bold are new to the language. Nonterminals
that are not defined in this grammar are exactly the same as those in Reflang.

The grammar shows five new expressions added for Msglang: `process` expression, `send` expression, `receive` expression, `self` expression, and `stop` expression. These new expressions use a prefix form similar to the remainder of the expressions in the grammar. The process expression begins with the keyword `process`, followed by the expression that will serve as the body of the process. The `send` expression contains the first expression that evaluates to the address of the receiver and one or more expressions that evaluate to the fields of the message that is going to be sent to that receiver. The `receive` expression begins with the keyword `receive`, followed by one or more `Identifier` items that are names that will be bound to message fields when a message is sent to this process. We will refer to the number of fields in the message as the *cardinality* of the message. The `self` and the `stop` expressions don't have any components.

11.2.1 Modifications to AST Nodes and the AST Visitor

To store these new expressions, we also need to introduce five new abstract syntax tree (AST) nodes: `ProcessExp`, `SendExp`, `ReceiveExp`, `SelfExp`, and `StopExp`. As usual, adding new AST nodes requires extensions to other parts of the interpreter that must process each kind of expression (e.g., the `Visitor` interface and the expression formatter).

11.3 ProcessVal: A New Kind of Value

What should be the result of evaluating an expression `(process (print n) )`? In our language, the set of normal values is given by

```
Value : NumVal | BoolVal | StringVal | PairVal | FunVal

      | NullVal | RefVal | UnitVal | DynamicError
```

The set of values include normal values; unit and null values; `DynamicError`, which represents an abnormal state of programs; and `RefVal`, which supports memory-related operations. We have at least two choices here. We can choose to represent processes in the semantics using `FunVal`, the body of the process could be modeled as the body of the function, and the formal parameters of the function could model the fields of the message. Sending a message could be replaced by a procedure call. This scheme can certainly work, but it would not provide concurrency between the sender and the receiver processes. Alternatively, we can add a separate kind of value to the language. This new kind of value can represent a concurrent entity. Sending a message would be modeled as an operation on this value. In the design of Msglang, we choose the second alternative:

```
Value : ... | ProcessVal
```

A value of the `ProcessVal` kind has its own thread of concurrent execution. Alternatively, several values of `ProcessVal` can share their own threads of concurrent execution. For simplicity, in our design and implementation, we picked the straightforward alternative of assigning one thread of concurrent execution to each value of `ProcessVal`. Another design decision is about memory locations and heaps. Should different processes write to

```
1    class ProcessVal extends Thread implements Value {
2      private Env _env;
3      private Exp _body;
4      private Evaluator _evaluator;
5      private Heap _h;
6      private java. util .concurrent.LinkedBlockingDeque<List<Value>> _queue;
7      public ProcessVal(Env env, Exp body, Evaluator evaluator, Heap h) {
8        _env = env;
9        _body = body;
10       _evaluator = evaluator;
11       _h = h;
12       _queue = new java.util.concurrent.LinkedBlockingDeque<List<Value>>();
13       this. start () ;
14     }
15     public List<String> formals() { return _formals; }
16     volatile boolean _exit = false;
17     private synchronized boolean _exit() { return _exit; }
18     public synchronized void exit() { _exit = true; }
19     public String  tostring () {
20       return "process: " + this;
21     }
22     public boolean equals(Value v) {
23       if (v instanceof ProcessVal)
24         return super.equals(v);
25       return false;
26     }
```

Figure 11.2
Implementation of `ProcessVal` in the Msglang language

the same heap? Selecting this design has the advantage that sending a reference value from one process to another entails just sending the value because both processes share the heap. If each process have its own heap, then sending a reference value to another heap could entail copying the entire set of references that could be reached via the reference being sent from the heap of the sender process to the receiver process.

The decision to share a heap among processes comes with a major disadvantage though. When multiple concurrent processes share the same heap, the behavior of a process cannot be understood using just the code of that process. Rather, actions of other processes that share the heap must also be understood. For instance, if X and Y are references, a simple expression (+ (deref X) (deref Y)) evaluated within a process can evaluate to different values if X and Y are also accessible to other concurrent processes that might simultaneously write to those memory locations. This is an example of a data race between processes (we discussed data races in chapter 8). This design decision is also not reflective of some message-passing scenarios in which concurrent processes cannot share heap; for instance, they might be running on different physical computers.

An alternative is to prohibit sending reference values via messages altogether. If that design decision is adopted, then processes could have their own separate heaps and read and write to their own heaps, but when interacting with other processes, the values stored in a heap will need to be converted into values not stored in the heap and sent via messages. The idea of *serialization* and *deserialization* has its roots in passing messages among processes that don't share a heap.

We will begin with a simpler design of Msglang in which processes share a heap. So, sending a reference value between processes is simple, but at the same time, this design of Msglang suffers from data races between processes. This realization, shown in figure 11.2, extends the `Thread` class in Java, which means that it can run as an independent thread of execution. Every `Thread` must implement a `run` method, and we will look at `ProcessVal`'s implementation of that method shortly. To initialize a `ProcessVal`, a reference to an environment (`env`), a reference to the evaluator, and a reference to the shared heap `h` are supplied.

11.4 Receiving a Message

Next, we will discuss the message receive mechanism supported by Msglang. Each process can receive messages, as we saw in previous examples. There are several decisions that need to be made when designing the message receive mechanism in Msglang, and we will discuss those next.

11.4.1 Message Buffer

What if a process is busy serving a previous message when it receives a new message? In Msglang, we make the design decision to store the received message in a buffer so that the process doesn't lose incoming messages while it is busy processing. An alternative design decision could have been to discard incoming messages until the process has finished serving the previous message. This alternative has the advantage of not requiring any space to store incoming messages, but also the disadvantage that senders would need to continuously poll the receiver until it is ready to receive a message, and such "busy waiting" wastes significant computational cycles. Yet another design decision is to have a message buffer of finite size, and the process starts to lose messages if the buffer is full. This allows a form of message rate limiting to avoid overwhelming the process when multiple interchangeable processes that can serve the same purpose are available. For example, when multiple service counters that can serve clients are available, it might make sense to balance the queue so the load is balanced. This design will also require the senders to check if a message is received successfully. Most message-passing languages support a message buffer of finite size, where the size is generally large enough that in most practical circumstances, the process does not lose messages. The size of the message buffer is generally limited by the amount of available memory.

The semantics of Msglang uses a message buffer of finite size, where the size is limited by the available memory. In other words, for most practical purposes, Msglang processes likely will not drop incoming messages, but they will signal the sender process if they do.

```
27   public boolean sendhelper (List<Value> request) throws InterruptedException
        {
28     if (!_exit()) {
29       _queue.put(request);
30       return true;
31     }
32     return false;
33   }
```

Figure 11.3
The `sendhelper` method within `ProcessVal` in the Msglang language

11.4.2 Message Processing

Which message should be processed first? This is another design decision where semantic variations are possible. For example, should the process consume the messages in the order in which they are received? This strategy would allow requests that are waiting the longest to be served first, and that could be seen as a fair strategy. Should the process consume the latest message first? There are certain advantages to this strategy. Since the messages have data that must be read from the memory, processing a message that was recently sent enhances the chances that the message data could still be at a higher level of memory hierarchy, such as the cache of the central processing unit, and thus reading these data might be faster. Then, this strategy has the potential to starve messages that are waiting in the buffer. Should the process consume incoming messages in some priority-order? This strategy could allow urgent signals in the program to be processed faster by the processes, but it also has the potential to starve lower-priority messages waiting in the buffer. Should the process consume related messages at the same time? Each of these semantic variations is suitable for different circumstances. The First-In-First-Out (FIFO) strategy is similar to how requests are served in the real world. The semantics of Msglang uses the FIFO strategy, but readers will explore other strategies as exercises later in this chapter.

The implementation of `ProcessVal` realizes the two semantics choices, message buffer and message processing, by storing the incoming messages in a linked blocking queue, as shown at line 7 in figure 11.2. The semantics of linked blocking queues is such that an attempt to retrieve an item blocks a thread if there are no items in the queue. The helper function `sendhelper` in figure 11.3 shows the logic of inserting an incoming message into this queue. If the process has not already terminated, as indicated by the helper function `_exit`, and if the attempt to enqueue the message succeeds, then the caller receives `true` as the return value and `false` otherwise. As we will see later in this chapter, the evaluator utilizes this helper function to realize the semantics of the `send` expression in Msglang.

Previously, we learned that the semantics of `ProcessVal` views each value as an independently running thread. This semantics is realized using the `Thread` features in the defining language. The `ProcessVal` class inherits from the `Thread` class in the defining language, and thus inherits all its properties. A thread in Java needs to implement a Java method called `run`, which starts running when the `start` method is called. In the implementation of `ProcessVal`, the underlying thread is started as soon as the value is

```
34      public void run(){
35          Env body_env = new ExtendEnv(_env, "self", this);
36          while(!_exit()) {
37              _body.accept(_evaluator, body_env, _h);
38          }
39      }
40   }
```

Figure 11.4
The run procedure of `ProcessVal` in the Msglang language

fully constructed, and the message buffer is initialized at line 13 in figure 11.2. This causes the `run` method shown in figure 11.4 to start running. The body of the `run` method consists of a loop that runs until the process has not exited. The exit condition is tested using the helper function `_exit`. The `run` method creates an environment for running the body of the process by adding a mapping from the name `self` to the current `ProcessVal`, and then evaluates the body of the process in this modified environment and the shared heap `_h`.

11.5 Semantics of Msglang Expressions

Now, since we have defined two essential concepts, the process value and message buffer, we can give semantics to Msglang programs.

```
1    public Value visit (ProcExp e, Env env, Heap h) {
2        return new Value.ProcessVal(env, e.body(), this, h);
3    }
```

Figure 11.5
Semantics of `ProcessExp` in the Msglang language

The semantics of `ProcExp`, the process expression, is that evaluating it creates a process value. The realization in figure 11.5 models this semantics. Evaluating a `ProcExp` creates a `ProcessVal` with the current environment (`env`), the body of the process expression (`e.body()`), the current evaluator, and the current heap (`h`). We know from section 11.4 that creating a `ProcessVal` starts the computational thread of the process, and it is ready to receive messages. Besides starting itself and setting up the message buffer, the newly created process will also evaluate the expression that forms the body of the process. As discussed previously, in this design, all processes share the same heap. An exercise later in this chapter asks the reader to implement a variation where each process has its own heap. In this design, all the processes share the same evaluator. Therefore, the evaluator code must be thread safe since it can be accessed by multiple processes concurrently.

The semantics of `SendExp`, the `send` expression, is that evaluating it leads to evaluating its argument expressions to their values. The value of the first argument expression must be a process value, and the remaining argument expressions evaluate to the message that is to be sent. Then, if the receiver process accepts the message, the send succeeds. Otherwise, it fails with a DynamicError.

```
1    public Value visit (SendExp e, Env env, Heap h) {
2       Object result  = e.operator().accept(this, env, h);
3       if (!( result instanceof Value.ProcessVal))
4          return new Value.DynamicError("Operator not a process in send " + ts.
                visit (e, env, h));
5       Value.ProcessVal process = (Value.ProcessVal) result;

7       List<Exp> operands = e.operands();
8       List<Value> actuals = new ArrayList<Value>(operands.size());
9       for(Exp exp : operands)
10         actuals.add((Value) exp.accept(this, env, h));

12      try {
13         if (process.sendhelper(actuals)) {
14            return new Value.UnitVal();
15         }
16      } catch (InterruptedException e1) {
17         e1.printStackTrace();
18      }
19      return new Value.DynamicError("Message send to finished process in " + ts.
                visit(e, env, h));
20   }
```

Figure 11.6
Semantics of SendExp in the Msglang language

The realization of the send expression in figure 11.6 models this semantics. At lines 2–5, the first argument is evaluated to a value, and a check is performed to ensure that it is a process value. At lines 7–10, arguments are evaluated that will be part of the message that is to be delivered. At lines 12–19, an attempt is made to send a message to the receiver using the helper function sendhelper, as we discussed previously. If this helper function succeeds, then the value of the send expression is a UnitVal. It is certainly possible to consider other return values for the send expression (e.g., #t or #f, depending on whether the message transmission succeeded or failed). In the current design, if the message transmission failed, then the value of the send expression is a DynamicError.

In the current design of Msglang, a send expression transmits a message to the receiver and proceeds without waiting for a response from the recipient. This message delivery style is called *asynchronous message send* or *nonblocking send*. At a future time, the recipient might not receive the actual message or the message format might not match, as we will learn next. An alternative message delivery style is called *synchronous message send* or *blocking send*, in which the sender waits for the receiver to send a reply message. In another message delivery style, the receiver can acknowledge the successful receipt of the message, but the sender doesn't wait for an actual response.

The semantics of `ReceiveExp`, the receive expression, is that evaluating it leads to looking up the current context to ensure that the expression is evaluated within a process, an attempt to retrieve a message from the queue of the current process that matches the expected message. If there are no such messages, then this process is blocked until a message arrives. If the message is received and it matches with the expected cardinality of the receive expression, then the value of the `receive` expression is the value of its body in an environment where formal parameters are bound to actual message content.

```
1    public Value visit (ReceiveExp e, Env env, Heap h) {
2       Value result = env.get("self");
3       if (!( result instanceof Value.ProcessVal))
4         return new Value.DynamicError("Current computation not within a process
                 in " + ts. visit (e, env, h));
5       Value.ProcessVal process = (Value.ProcessVal) result;

7       List<Value> actuals = process.receivehelper();
8       List<String> formals = e.formals();
9       if (formals.size()!=actuals.size())
10        return new Value.DynamicError("Argument mismatch in receive " + ts.visit(
                 e, env, h));

12      Env receive_env = env;
13      for (int index = 0; index < formals.size(); index++)
14        receive_env = new ExtendEnv(receive_env, e._formals.get(index), actuals.
                 get(index));
15      return e._body.accept(this, receive_env, h);
16   }
```

Figure 11.7
Semantics of `ReceiveExp` in the Msglang language

The realization of the `receive` expression in figure 11.7 models this semantics. At lines 2–5, the name "self" is looked up. If the name is present in the environment, then a check is performed to ensure that it is a process value. At lines 7–10, an attempt is made to retrieve the message using the function `receivehelper` that was discussed previously. If the cardinality of the retrieved message doesn't match the expected cardinality, then the receive fails with a `dynamic error`, as shown at line 10. At lines 12–14, formal parameters of the `receive` expression are bound to the actual value received to create an environment for running the body of the `receive` expression. Finally, the value of the `body` expression is computed at line 15, which is also the value of the `receive` expression.

In our current semantics, the value of the `receive` expression is not transmitted back to the sender, but it is conceivable to consider a synchronous message delivery design in which the value of the `receive` expression is returned to the sender as the value of the `send` expression:

```
 1 (define seq (lambda (cmd1 cmd2) cmd2))

 3 (define ticktock
 4   (process
 5     (receive ( tick )
 6       (receive (tock num)
 7         (seq
 8           ( print  tick )
 9           ( print  tock)
10         )
11       )
12     )
13   )
14 )

16 (seq (send ticktock  "tick ") (send ticktock  "tock"  342))
```

This current semantics also doesn't support out-of-order receipt of messages. If there are two `receive` expressions in the body of a process (such as in the example here) expression and the first `receive` expression expecting a message with one field, and the second `receive` expression is expecting a message with two fields, then the receive message will fail if the sender who is sending a message with two fields is able to send its message before the sender who is sending a message with one field is able to dispatch its message. This is called an *out-of-order delivery* problem.

The semantics of the `self` expression looks up the value of the name "self" in the current environment. If the value stored in the environment is a process value, then that value is the value of the `self` expression. The realization of the `self` expression shown in figure 11.8 models this semantics.

```
1    public Value  visit (SelfExp e, Env env, Heap h) {
2      Value result  = env.get(" self ") ;
3      if (!( result  instanceof Value.ProcessVal))
4        return new Value.DynamicError("Self is not a process in " +  ts . visit (e,
            env, h)) ;
5      return result ;
6  }
```

Figure 11.8
Semantics of `SelfExp` in the Msglang language

Astute readers will observe that it is easy to subvert this self-lookup in the current example. For instance, if the `self` variable can be declared and assigned a value that is the address of another process, subsequent `receive` expressions would receive messages from the queue of that other process. In practice, one can prevent redefining "self" by removing the use of `self` as an identifier or as a variable definition within the `define` or `let` expressions. We will leave adding these guards as an exercise for the reader later in the chapter.

The semantics of the `stop` expression looks up the value of the name "self" in the current environment. If the value stored in the environment is a process value, then the helper function `exit` is utilized to stop the execution of that process. The realization of the `stop` expression shown in figure 11.9 models this semantics for `StopExp`.

```
1    public Value visit (StopExp e, Env env, Heap h) {
2      Value result = env.get("self");
3      if (!( result instanceof Value.ProcessVal))
4        return new Value.DynamicError("Self is not a process in " + ts. visit (e,
            env, h));
5      Value.ProcessVal process = (Value.ProcessVal) result;  // Dynamic checking
6      process.exit() ;
7      return new Value.UnitVal();
8    }
```

Figure 11.9
Semantics of `StopExp` in the Msglang language

Note that a process can be stopped only from within, but in the current realization, it might be possible to subvert this semantics as discussed previously in the context of the `self` expression. The current semantics also allows a process to be stopped multiple times, and guards can be introduced to raise error if this semantics is considered undesirable.

Summary

In this chapter, we built a message-passing programming language called Msglang. A message-passing programming language is beneficial for both concurrency and parallelism and makes it easier to model real-world objects and their interactions. In fact, early object-oriented languages were modeled as message-passing languages, which is the main reason that the object on which a method is invoked is referred to as the *receiver*. We also studied semantic variations of the message-passing style. The language introduced a new concept, process as a value, and five new expressions for five actions: to create a new process, to send a message to the process, to receive a message within a process, to find the identity of the current process, and to stop a process. We also introduced the semantic word variation of a shared heap between processes that has the potential to introduce data races between processes.

Exercises

11.5.1. *[Count Down]* Write a Msglang program that declares a process that, when sent a number n as a message, prints n, and then sends itself n−1 as a message. This countdown terminates when n is 0.

11.5.2. *[State Machine]* Write a Msglang program that models a state machine. If the process receives an message containing number 0 followed by another message containing number 1, it prints "accept." Otherwise, it prints "reject."

11.5.3. *[Process Sort]* Using Msglang features, define a process-based sorting structure for positive and negative numbers. This structure will consist of four bins represented as global references (posevenbin, posoddbin, negevenbin, negoddbin), each of which holds a list of numbers. Each bin is initially an empty list. The sorting structure itself consists of seven processes organized as a perfect binary tree. The first process, named main, accepts the input number and forwards the number and its own address to either of its two children, pos and neg, based on whether the number is positive or negative. Both pos and neg have two children of their own, poseven and posodd, and negeven and negodd, and they forward the number that they receive to _even if it is even, and _odd if it odd. Along with the number, each process also receives the address of the main process.

Once the poseven process receives a number, it adds it to the global reference posevenbin and sends the message "poseven" to the main process using the address that it received. The processes posodd, negeven, and negodd behave similarly; that is, once the posodd process receives a number, it adds it to the global reference posoddbin and sends the message "posodd" to the main process using the address that it received, and so on. Care should be exercised in the design of the main process to allow it to accept messages from external entities, as well as from the leaf processes poseven, posodd, negeven, and negodd.

11.5.4. *[Wider Messages]* In the current design of Msglang, the receive expression fails if the cardinality of the received message doesn't match with the expected cardinality of the sent message. That might seem overly restrictive to some. If the sender sends more values then the receiver needs, known as *wider messages*, then another design might discard the extra values that are received and proceed to evaluate the body of the receive expression. In other words, receiving few values might surprise the receiver, but receiving more values might not, although it does have a "smell." Design and implement a variation of Msglang in which receive expressions accept and process wider messages, and illustrate your variation using examples.

11.5.5. *[Out-of-order Delivery]* If there are two receive expressions in the body of a process expression, and the first receive expression is expecting a message with two fields and the second `receive` expression is expecting a message with three fields, then the receive message will fail if the sender that is sending a message with three fields is able to send its message before the sender that is sending a message with two fields does so. As described previously, this is called an *out-of-order delivery* problem. Design and implement a variation of Msglang that supports out-of-order receipt of messages.

11.5.6. *[Priority Message Processing]* Design and implement a variation of `ProcExp` and `SendExp` that supports prioritized message processing. Each message includes priority as its first field, a positive integer, where lower numbers mean higher priority. Each process consumes its incoming messages in the order of priority (i.e., higher-priority messages are processed first). All messages at the same priority level are processes in a FIFO order.

11.5.7. *[Strongly Typed Receive]* In the current design of Msglang, the `receive` expression fails if the cardinality of the received message doesn't match with the expected cardinality of the sent message. In practice, stronger guarantees might be necessary. Design and implement a typed variation of the `receive` expression in which the `receive` expression is extended to specify the expected type of the message. If the cardinality of the sent message matches with the expected cardinality, then the type of the sent message is matched with the type expected by the `receive` expression.

11.5.8. *[Synchronous Delivery]* In the current design of Msglang, a `send` expression transmits a message to the receiver and proceeds without waiting for a response from the recipient. This message-delivery style is called *asynchronous message send* or *nonblocking send*. At a future time, the recipient might not receive the actual message or the message format might not match. An alternative message delivery style is called *synchronous message send* or *blocking send*, where the sender waits for the receiver to send a reply message. Design and implement a variation of Msglang in which sending a message blocks a process until a response is received from the recipient. The value of the `receive` expression is the response received by the sender, as well as the value of the `send` expression.

11.5.9. *[Isolated Processes]* Design and implement a variation of Msglang in which each process has its own heap. Creating a process creates the heap of that process. Then, implement two variations of the `send` expression, as follows:

- In the first variation, prohibit the `send` expression from sending any reference values, whether directly or indirectly. Only numerical values, Boolean values, string values, unit value, dynamic errors, and pairs of these values may be sent from one process to another.
- In the second (much more involved) variation, allow processes to send reference values directly or indirectly. When a reference value is sent, copy the tree rooted

at that reference from the heap of the sender to the heap of the receiver process, adjusting the references as necessary. Note: It might not be possible for references to have the same location in the heap of the recipient, as that location might already be allocated by the recipient.

11.5.10. *[Garbage Collection for Processes]* A process is a *garbage process* if it is not performing independent computation, it is blocked to receive a message from another process, and there are no other processes that can send the process a message to unblock it. Such processes can consume resources without performing any meaningful work. Design and implement a variation of Msglang in which such processes are identified and killed in order to reclaim resources.

12 Eventlang: A Language with Events

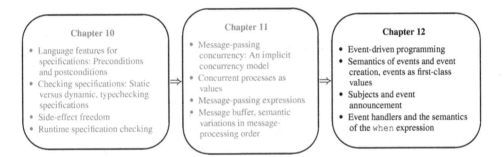

Chapter 10
- Language features for specifications: Preconditions and postconditions
- Checking specifications: Static versus dynamic, typechecking specifications
- Side-effect freedom
- Runtime specification checking

Chapter 11
- Message-passing concurrency: An implicit concurrency model
- Concurrent processes as values
- Message-passing expressions
- Message buffer, semantic variations in message-processing order

Chapter 12
- Event-driven programming
- Semantics of events and event creation, events as first-class values
- Subjects and event announcement
- Event handlers and the semantics of the when expression

In this chapter, you will learn about programming language features for event-driven programming. The idea of events (i.e., the occurrence of some phenomenon) is central to computer programming. It manifests itself in almost all layers of abstraction for computer programming. For example, computer hardware triggers events (interrupts) on occurrences such as a clock tick, a network packet arrival, or a disk read command completed. Operating systems and other higher layers of software abstractions, such as the virtual machine, and application frameworks trigger events on occurrences such as a mouse button click, a window resizing, or a dialog box click. As a concept, events are also used in representing and describing software architecture and design. In software architecture terms, systems that use events are called *implicit invocation systems* and sometimes *publish-subscribe systems*. In software design, the idea of an event appears as an *observer pattern*. Needless to say, event-driven programming is an integral part of the toolbox as a programmer.

We will study these concepts by realizing a programming language called Eventlang. The complete implementation of Eventlang is available with the book code, hosted at https://github.com/hridesh/eventlang. We will build Eventlang by extending Reflang, which was developed in chapter 7.

12.1 Event-Driven Programming

Event-driven programming involves three major concepts:

- *Event*, the notion in a programming language that models the occurrence of a certain phenomenon (e.g., mouse click, clock tick, network packet arrival, window resizing, timer expiring, task completion, or file being saved.
- *Subject*, the piece of computation in the program that triggers events. For some events, such as clock tick, that functionality may not be part of the user code.

- *Handler/observer*, the piece of computation in the program that runs when an event is triggered.

For simplicity, we will consider only programs in which the event, subject, and handler are all part of the same program. Let us begin by defining a simple event in Eventlang, as shown here:

```
$ (define hello (event (message)))
```

The event definition has two parts: the event keyword and the event information. Generally, it is not sufficient just to know that an event has occurred. It is also useful to understand some information about the event, such as where the mouse was clicked, which tick it is, the sender of the network packet, which window was resized, which timer expired, which timer was complete, or which file completed saving. For our event `hello`, the `message` represents that additional piece of information. This information must be provided by all subjects that trigger this event. This additional information is also referred to as the *event payload*.

The event definition appears like a function definition, except that no body has been defined that will be evaluated when the event is triggered:

```
$ (announce hello "Hello")
```

The listing here shows a piece of code for a subject that announces an event. Event announcement has three parts: the announce keyword, the name of the event that is being announced, and the value for the required event payload.

At first glance, event announcement might appear like a function call, except that no value is returned from an event, and from the definition of the event, we may not know what code will be run when the event is announced. At this point, the event announcement we have seen here will have no impact because no handlers are listening to the event `hello` yet. Next, we will see an example of attaching a handler to the event:

```
(when hello do (seq (print message) (print "World!")))
```

This listing shows a piece of code that attaches a piece of code with the event `hello` to run whenever that event is announced. The code has four parts: the keywords `when` and `do`, the name of the event (`hello`), and the code that is being attached to the event `(seq (print message) (print "World!"))`. This process is called *event registration*. Event registration doesn't run the code; rather, that code just waits until an event is announced. An event announcement such as the following will run the code:

```
$ (announce hello "Hello")
"Hello"
"World!"
```

The event announcement didn't explicitly call the code of the subject. Rather, the event acts as a mediator to dispatch the event invocation to the subject code. Event-driven programming is especially useful for these kind of programming patterns where a piece of code needs to invoke another piece of code without naming it. Naming another piece of code introduces *name dependence* between two pieces of code and couples them together. Event-driven programming facilitates decoupling.

Another benefit of event-driven programming is that it broadcasts an event to multiple subjects at the same time. To illustrate this point, consider the following event definition:

```
$ (define ev (event (a b)) )
```

This event expects two numbers, a and b, as the payloads.

The subject code here registers a piece of code to run when the event ev is announced that prints the sum of the two numbers.

```
$ (when ev do (print (+ a b)))
```

```
$ (announce ev 4 2)
6
```

When the event is announced, the single subject code runs printing the value 6.

The listing below registers another piece of code to run when the event ev is announced, which prints the multiplication of two numbers, a and b. This code has been registered after the code that prints the sum of the two numbers.

```
$ (when ev do (print (* a b)))
```

```
$ (announce ev 4 2)
6
8
```

Next, the announcement of the event ev runs both registered handlers, printing first the sum and then the product. These are printed in the order in which the handlers were registered. The event announcement didn't need to iterate through the list of registered handlers and didn't need to name them explicitly.

It is also possible to set up a chain of events and event handlers that trigger each other to form complex event sequences. This listing shows an example that triggers a chain of events inspired by the popular proverb "For Want of a Nail":

```
(define nail (event (nailed)))
(define shoe (event (attached)))
(define horse (event (canrun)))
(define rider (event (rode)))
(define message (event (delivered)))
(define battle (event (won)))
(define kingdom (event (saved)))

(seq
  (when nail do
    ( if  nailed
      (seq (print "Nail is nailed")
           (announce shoe #t))
      (seq (print "Nail is missing...")
           (announce shoe #f))
    )
  )
```

```
(when shoe do
  ( if attached
    (seq (print  "Shoe is attached")
         (announce horse #t))
    (seq (print  "For want of a nail, the shoe was lost.")
         (announce horse #f))
  )
)

(when horse do
  ( if canrun
    (seq (print  "Horse can run")
         (announce rider #t))
    (seq (print  "For want of a shoe, the horse was lost.")
         (announce rider #f))
  )
)

(when rider do
  ( if rode
    (seq (print  "Rider rode.")
         (announce message #t))
    (seq (print  "For want of a horse, the  rider  was lost.")
         (announce message #f))
  )
)

(when message do
  ( if delivered
    (seq (print  "Message was delivered.")
         (announce battle #t))
    (seq (print  "For want of a rider, the message was lost.")
         (announce battle #f))
  )
)

(when battle do
  ( if won
    (seq (print  "Battle  was won.")
         (announce kingdom #t))
    (seq (print  "For want of a message, the battle was lost.")
         (announce kingdom #f))
  )
)
```

```
(when kingdom do
  ( if  saved
    (seq ( print  "Kingdom was saved.")
         (announce kingdom #t))
    (seq ( print  "For want of a battle, the kingdom was lost.")
         ( print  "And all  for  the  want of a horseshoe nail.")))
  )
)

(announce nail #f)
)
```

Running this program prints the proverb as follows:

```
"Nail  is  missing ... "
"For want of a nail, the shoe was lost."
"For want of a shoe, the horse was lost."
"For want of a horse, the  rider  was lost. "
"For want of a rider, the message was lost."
"For want of a message, the battle was lost. "
"For want of a battle, the kingdom was lost."
"And all  for  the  want of a horseshoe nail."
```

Event-driven programming is very useful for setting up these complex rules for event propagation, which are often utilized in decision systems. In the rest of this section, we discuss the design and implementation of Eventlang features.

12.2 Syntax of New Features for Event-Driven Programming

The main changes in the grammar for Eventlang are highlighted in figure 12.1. This grammar builds on the grammar for the Reflang language.

The grammar shows three new expressions for Eventlang: the event expression, when expression, and announce expression. These new expressions use a prefix form similar to the rest of the expressions in the grammar. The event expression begins with the keyword event, followed by the set of identifiers that will serve as the payload of the event. The when expression contains the first expression that evaluates to an event and another expression that will be registered to run when that event is announced. The announce expression begins with the keyword announce, followed by an expression that is the event that will be announced and one or more expressions that will be evaluated and their values sent as the payload with the event announcement.

12.2.1 Modifications to AST Nodes and the AST Visitor

To store these new expressions, we also need to introduce three new abstract syntax tree (AST) nodes: EventExp, WhenExp, and AnnounceExp. As usual, adding new AST nodes requires extensions to other parts of the interpreter that must process each kind of expression, such as the Visitor interface and the expression formatter.

```
Program      ::=  DefineDecl* Exp?                    Program
DefineDecl   ::=  (define Identifier Exp)             Define
Exp          ::=                                       Expressions
                  Number                               NumExp
             |    (+ Exp Exp+)                          AddExp
             |    (- Exp Exp+)                          SubExp
             |    (* Exp Exp+)                          MultExp
             |    (/ Exp Exp+)                          DivExp
             |    Identifier                            VarExp
             |    (let ((Identifier Exp)+) Exp)         LetExp
             |    ( Exp Exp+)                           CallExp
             |    (lambda (Identifier+) Exp)            LambdaExp
             |    (ref Exp)                             RefExp
             |    (deref Exp)                           DerefExp
             |    (set! Exp Exp)                        AssignExp
             |    (free Exp)                            FreeExp
             |    (event Identifier+)                   EventExp
             |    (when Exp do Exp)                     WhenExp
             |    (announce Exp Exp+)                   AnnounceExp
```

Figure 12.1
Grammar for the Eventlang language. Expressions in bold are new to the language. Nonterminals that are not defined in this grammar are exactly the same as those in Reflang.

12.3 Semantics of Events and Event Creation

In the design of event-driven programming features, just like with function definitions and calls, naming is an important decision. In chapter 6, we learned that the decision to make function definitions (lambda expressions) anonymous has implications on recursive functional calls. Since the body of an event expression has no need to refer to the event definition, this concern doesn't arise in event expressions. Therefore, Eventlang supports anonymous event definitions. Event values could be given names using standard `let` or define expressions as we have seen in the previous examples in this chapter.

The next design decision has to do with whether event values are *first-class* values. Recall that a value is first class if it can be passed as parameters, returned as values, and stored in data structures. In our examples so far, we have seen the need to store event values in variables. It is also quite useful to be able to pass events as parameters or return events as values. The next listing shows an example where events are returned.

```
1 (define eveven (event (n)))
2 (define evodd (event (n)))

4 (define choose
5   (lambda (n)
6     ( if  (even n) eveven
7        evodd
```

```
 8   )
 9  )
10 )

12 (seq
13   (when eveven do (print "Even:" n))
14   (when evodd do (print "Odd:" n))
15   (announce (choose 4) 4)
16 )
```

This listing illustrates the benefits of first-class event values. Here, the function choose returns either eveven or evodd based on whether the argument n is even or odd. The event announcement expression at line 15 announces whichever event is returned by the function choose. Similar to higher-order functions, interesting programming patterns are enabled by treating events as first-class values.

To support events as first-class values, in Eventlang we extend the set of values supported by the language to add events as another kind of value, internally represented as EventVal, as shown here:

```
 1 static class EventVal implements Value {
 2    private List<String> _contexts;
 3    private List<Exp> _handlers;
 4    private List<Env<Value>> _handler_envs;
 5    public EventVal(List<String> contexts) {
 6     _contexts = contexts;
 7     _handlers = new ArrayList<Exp>();
 8     _handler_envs = new ArrayList<Env<Value>>();
 9    }
10    public List<String> contexts() { return _contexts; }
11    public List<Exp> handlers() { return _handlers; }
12    public List<Env<Value>> handler_envs() { return _handler_envs; }
13    public void register(Exp handler, Env<Value> handler_env){
14      _handlers.add(handler);
15      _handler_envs.add(handler_env);
16    }

18    public String tostring () {
19      String result = "(event ";
20      for(String context : _contexts)
21        result += context + " ";
22      result += ") ";
23      return result + ")";
24    }
25 }
```

This new kind of value keeps track of the set of handlers registered to receive that event announcement, as well as their original environments (i.e., at the time of handler

registration). By associating the set of handlers directly with the event values, the record keeping of handlers becomes easier. The event value also stores information
about the payload (context) that is necessary when announcing an event, so that during
event announcement, the set of actual parameters can be checked for conformance.

The semantics of the event expressions is fairly straightforward. It creates a value of type
EventVal and returns it.

As shown in the listing here, the context information from the event expression is used
to initialize the context information within the event value. The set of registered event
handlers is an empty set initially.

```
1    public Value visit (EventExp e, Env<Value> env) throws ProgramError {
2        return new Value.EventVal(e.contexts());
3    }
```

12.4   Semantics of Subjects and Event Announcements

Next, we discuss the semantics of event announcements. As usual, the set of argument
expressions are evaluated to find their values. A left-to-right evaluation order is utilized for
evaluating argument expressions, similar to most expressions that we have added so far:

```
1 public Value  visit (AnnounceExp e, Env<Value> env) throws ProgramError {
2    Exp event_exp = e.event();
3    Object result  = event_exp.accept(this, env);
4    if (!( result  instanceof Value.EventVal))
5       throw new ProgramError("Non–event value cannot be announced in
                expression " + ts.visit(e, null));
6    Value.EventVal event = (Value.EventVal) result ;
7    if (!( e.actuals() . size () == event.contexts() . size () ))
8       throw new ProgramError("Number of context variables do not match in
                announce expression " + ts.visit(e, null)) ;
```

While it is possible to add typing to the language, to prevent mismatch between the
context variables expected by the event and those provided during announce expressions,
in the Eventlang implementation, this check is performed at runtime. Such a mismatch is a
runtime error:

```
10     List<String> contexts = event.contexts() ;
11     List<Value> actuals = new ArrayList<Value>(contexts.size());
12     for(Exp exp : e.actuals() )
13         actuals.add((Value)exp.accept(this, env));
```

Next, each argument expression is evaluated to find its value. To run each handler expression, an environment needs to be created. This environment ought to map context variables
to the actual value provided during event announcement. There are three choices for the
initial environment: the initial environment used by the interpreter, the environment at
the event announcement, and the environment at registration time. In the design of Eventlang, the environment at registration time is utilized to create an environment for running

the handlers. Due to this semantics, the code for the handler has access to all the variables that exist in the context in which that handler is registered:

```
14    Value lastVal = new UnitVal();
15    List<Exp> handlers = event.handlers();
16    List<Env<Value>> handler_envs = event.handler_envs();
17    for(int handler_index=0; handler_index < handlers.size(); handler_index++) {
18      Env<Value> handler_env = handler_envs.get(handler_index);
19      for (int index = 0; index < actuals.size() ; index++)
20        handler_env = new ExtendEnv<>(handler_env, contexts.get(index), actuals
              .get(index));
21      lastVal = (Value) handlers.get(handler_index).accept(this, handler_env);
22    }
23    return lastVal ;
24 }
```

Finally, the handlers are invoked one by one, in the order in which they have been registered. For each handler invocation, a custom environment is created that extends the stored environment with context variables and their values. The value produced by the last event handler is the value of the event announcement.

This semantics of event announcement blocks the execution of the subject expressions until the event announcement is complete. Also, the handlers are run in the order in which they are registered and run sequentially. Some languages have explored an alternative design, in which the event announcement happens in parallel and event handlers are run in parallel.

12.5   Semantics of Handlers and the When Expression

Next, we discuss the semantics of event registration.

The listing here shows the semantics of the when expression. To evaluate the when expression when e do e′, first e is evaluated to an event value. Then, the expression e′ and the current environment are used to register with the event. The value of the when expression is a unit value. An alternative design could evaluate to the event value that is the value of e:

```
1 public Value visit (WhenExp e, Env<Value> env) throws ProgramError {
2    Exp event_exp = e.event();
3    Object result = event_exp.accept(this, env);
4    if (!( result instanceof Value.EventVal))
5      throw new ProgramError("Non–event value cannot be used in when
              expression " + ts.visit(e, null)) ;
6    EventVal event = (EventVal) result ;
7    Exp handler = e.body();
8    event.register(handler, env);
9    return new UnitVal();
10 }
```

Summary

In this chapter, we reviewed event-driven programming, which is an important programming pattern, as well as linguistic support for event-driven programming. Generally, three kinds of language features are supported: for declaring an event, for announcing an event, and for registering with an event to receive notifications. We designed and realized the programming language Eventlang, which provides mechanisms to declare anonymous events that act as first-class values, as well as the when expression to register with the event, and the announce expression to trigger these events. In Eventlang, registered expressions (handlers) run sequentially in the order in which they are registered, and handlers have access to variables that are in the lexical scope of registration, as well as context variables declared by the event.

Exercises

12.5.1. *[Count Down]* Write a Eventlang program that declares an event, `CountDown`, that accepts a single context variable, `n`. Register a handler with this event such that when the event is announced with the number `n` as the payload, the handler prints the number `n` and announces another event, `CountDown` with `n-1`, as the payload. This handler terminates the countdown when `n` is 0.

12.5.2. *[Vending Machine]* Write an Eventlang program that models a vending machine that dispenses four objects: milk, cookies, chocolate, and candy. The vending machine accepts an amount, dispenses the appropriate product, and gives change. Milk costs \$1, cookies cost \$0.75, chocolate costs \$0.50, and candy costs \$0.25.

The program works as follows:

- When the event `CoinInserted` is announced with amount inserted as the payload, the handlers for milk, cookies, chocolate, and candy are all run, as well as a handler to prompt for adding more money.
- If the amount inserted is greater than \$1, then the handler for milk announces the event `Dispense` with the string "milk." It also announces the event `Change`, with the remaining change as the payload.
- If the amount inserted is greater than \$0.75 and less than \$1, then the handler for cookies announces the event `Dispense` with the string "cookies." It also announces the event `Change`, with the remaining change as the payload.
- If the amount inserted is greater than \$0.5 and less than \$0.75, then the handler for chocolate announces the event `Dispense` with the string "chocolate." It also announces the event `Change`, with the remaining change as the payload.

- If the amount inserted is greater than \$0.25 and less than \$0.5, then the handler for candy announces the event `Dispense` with the string "candy." It also announces the event `Change`, with the remaining change as the payload.
- If the amount inserted is less than \$0.25, then the handler for adding more money prints "Add more money." It also announces the event `Change`, with the remaining inserted money that is less than \$0.25, is returned as the payload.
- The handler for the event `Change` prints the change to be given, and the handler for the event `Dispense` prints the product that is being dispensed.

12.5.3. *[Event-Driven Sorter]* Using Eventlang features, define an event-based sorting structure for positive and negative numbers. This structure will consist of four bins represented as global references (`posevenbin`, `posoddbin`, `negevenbin`, and `negoddbin`), each of which holds a list of numbers. Each bin is initially an empty list.

The sorting structure itself consists of seven events organized as a perfect binary tree. The handler for the first event, named `main`, checks the input number and announces `pos` or `neg`, based on whether the number is positive or negative. The handlers for the `pos` and `neg` events each announce `poseven` and `posodd`, and `negeven` and `negodd` events if the number received is even or odd, respectively.

The handler for the `poseven` event adds the number to the global reference `posevenbin`. The handlers for the events `posodd`, `negeven`, and `negodd` behave similarly; that is, once the `posodd` event is announced, the handler adds the received number to the global reference `posoddbin`, and the process continues.

12.5.4. *[Priority among handler]* The goal of this question is to learn about a variation of event-driven programming language features. A common variation of event support in languages and libraries allows programmers to specify a priority among observers, and the observers run according to the specified priority. A common usage of priority among observers is to prevent low-priority observers from blocking higher-priority observers, or to ensure that the higher-priority observers finish their task.

In the current semantics of Eventlang, the when expression registers observer expressions to run when an event is signaled. The current syntax of this expression does not allow priorities within observer expressions. Observer expressions are executed in the order in which they are registered at run time; that is, the observer expressions execution order is the same as its dynamic registration order.

Modify the syntax, AST, and semantics of the when expression to the following:

```
whenexp : '(' When exp Do exp (exp)? ')';
```

such that the last optional expression in the syntax must evaluate to a number between 0 and 10, which specifies the priority of the observer expression. In other words, the first expression `exp` evaluates to an `EventVal`, the second expression is the observer `body`, and the third expression evaluates to the observer priority, which is a number between 0 and 10.

When a priority is not given, it is assumed to be 5; that is, the when expression of the form `(when ev do (+ a b))` is the same as the when expression `(when ev do (+ a b) 5)`.

Modify the semantics of the event announcement (i.e., the semantics of the announce expression) such that it runs observer expressions in the order of their priority from `0-10`. All observers that have the same priority are run in the order in which they are registered.

Some examples illustrating this new semantics appear here:

```
$ (define ev (event (a b)))
$ (when ev do (+ a b) 0)
$ (when ev do (* a b) 1)
$ (announce ev (2 3))
6
$ (when ev do (/ b a) 1)
$ (announce ev (2 3))
1.5
$ (when ev do (- b a) 2)
$ (announce ev (2 3))
1
$ (when ev do (+ a a))
$ (announce ev (2 3))
4
```

12.5.5. *[Results from all observers]* The goal of this question is to learn about another variation of event-driven features by extending the semantics of the Eventlang language. We will learn about announce expressions that return results of all observers, which is different from the announce expressions that we have been seeing so far.

The current semantics of the Eventlang language provides the result of the last dynamically registered observer as the result of the announce expression. If no observer expressions are registered, then the result is a unit value. This is why you see only one value as the result of the announce expression, even though there can be zero or more registered observer expressions.

Modify the semantics of the announce expression such that its result is a list of the values of all the observers in the order in which they ran.

Some examples illustrating this new semantics appear here:

```
$ (define ev (event (a b)))
$ (when ev do (+ a b))
$ (when ev do ( * a b))
$ (announce ev ( 6 7))
(13 42)
$ (when ev do (+ a ( * a b)))
$ (announce ev ( 6 7))
(13 42 48)
```

Notice that whether you do this problem before or after question 12.5.4, the result should be the same because all observers are registered with priority 5, and so their result should appear in the order in which they are registered.

12.5.6. *[Unregister expression]* The goal of this question is to extend the Eventlang interpreter to add expressions for unregistering an observer expression. So far, we have only discussed registering an observer expression using the when expression, but once registered, the observer expression cannot be removed. Some programming languages also provide facilities for unregistering an observer expression.

Modify the semantics of the Eventlang language to provide facilities to unregister an observer expression. You can support this new expression by making two extensions. First, extend the semantics of the when expression to return a unique identifier that can be used to identify a registered observer expression. Then, implement the new unregister expression as given in this problem.

Some examples illustrating the new semantics of when expression appear here. A when expression returns a numeric value (an identifier) that can be used to unregister the observer expression:

```
$ (define ev (event (a b)))
$ (when ev do (+ a b))
5.001
$ (when ev do ( * a b))
5.002
```

Notice that the encoding for the identifier is not important, so long as it can uniquely identify the observer expression to be unregistered.

The new expression `unregister` takes two parameters, an event and the unique identifier corresponding to the observer expression to be unregistered, and removes that observer expression so that when that event is announced, the unregistered observer expression is no longer evaluated.

The syntax for this new expression appears here:

```
unregisterexp: '(' unregister exp exp ')';
```

In the syntax of the unregister expression, the first expression evaluates to an `EventVal` and the second expression evaluates to the unique identifier representing the observer expression. This expression unregisters the observer corresponding to the unique identifier:

```
$ (unregister ev 5.002)
#t
$ (unregister ev 5.001)
#t
$ (unregister ev 5.002)
#f
$ (announce ev (6 7))
```

The value produced by an unregister expression is true if unregistration was successful, and false otherwise.

Notice that in the current design of the unregister expression, it is possible to fool the interpreter by guessing the identifier of the registered observer expression. A more secure design is possible, but that task is outside the scope of this problem. Readers are encouraged to consider such designs on their own.

Appendix
ANTLR: A Brief Review

ANTLR (www.antlr.org/) is a tool for constructing programming language implementations, especially lexical analyzers and parsers. It follows the rich tradition of this type of tool, such as YACC for the C programming language. ANTLR started as a replacement for YACC for the Java programming language, but it has since evolved to support many other programming languages.

To define a grammar, you can write it in a file with the extension `.g` or `.g4`. This file is then processed by the ANTLR tool to generate the code for a lexical analyzer, a parser, and a few other supporting tools.

Grammar rules in ANTLR start with lowercase. A comment is written by prefixing it with "//":

```
// – this is a comment.
```

In ANTLR, a grammar can begin with the following declaration:

```
grammar ArithLang;        // Define a grammar called ArithLang
```

which says that we are defining a grammar and giving it the name `ArithLang`. There are other kinds of grammar that ANTLR supports, but that does not concern us at the moment.

The ANTLR tool generates source files in your target programming language, such as Java or Python, depending on the version of this textbook that you are using. To import code elements from other files, you could include them in the header of the grammar file. The contents of the header are inserted verbatim in the generated source files. For example, the header declaration here says to insert a Java import statement in the source files generated by the ANTLR tool ANTLR header declaration:

```
@header {
    import arithlang.parser;
    import static arithlang.AST.*
}
```

The following is an example of a production rule in simplified form:

```
program : exp ;
```

This rule says that the `program` nonterminal can be expanded into the `exp` nonterminal.

The rule in its full form is shown here, where actions enclosed in { } are used to construct abstract syntax tree (AST) nodes:

```
program returns [Program ast] :
    e=exp {$ast = AST.Program($e.ast); }
;
```

```
1    grammar ArithLang;

3    program : exp ;

5    exp :    numexp
6    | addexp
7    | subexp
8    | multexp
9    | divexp ;

11   numexp : Number ;

13   addexp : '(' '+' exp (exp)+ ')' ;

15   subexp : '(' '-' exp (exp)+ ')' ;

17   multexp : '(' '*' exp (exp)+ ')' ;

19   divexp  : '(' '/' exp (exp)+ ')' ;

21   Number :
22   DIGIT
23   | (DIGIT_NOT_ZERO DIGIT+);

25   DIGIT: ('0' .. '9') ;
26   DIGIT_NOT_ZERO: ('1'..'9');
```

Figure A.1
Grammar for the Arithlang language (without actions)

The syntax `returns [Program ast]` says that this rule produces an object of type `Program`, and other rules can access that produced object using the name `ast`. If that rule is the start rule, which is the case here, then `ast` is the object returned by parsing the program. In this rule, the syntax e=exp should be read as "let us call this nonterminal e." Furthermore, the statement within { } is an action that runs when the parser is successful in demonstrating that a string belonging to the language was the input. For instance, in this rule, when the parser is successful in demonstrating that it has parsed an expression, the action { *ast = AST.Program*(e.ast); } runs, which creates a new object `Program` using the object produced by the rule for nonterminal e.

The following is another example of a production rule in simplified form:

```
exp :
     numexp
     | addexp
     | subexp
     | multexp
     | divexp
```

This rule in its full form, where actions are enclosed in { }, is shown here:

```
exp returns [Exp ast]:
    n=numexp {$ast = $n.ast; }
    | a=addexp {$ast = $a.ast; }
    | s=subexp {$ast = $s.ast; }
    | m=multexp {$ast = $m.ast; }
    | d=divexp {$ast = $d.ast; }
    ;
```

Each statement of the form *ast*=n.ast; simply assigns the object generated by the child rule, such as numexp, to the rule generated by the parent rule, exp. It is possible for these actions to also modify the objects generated by the child rule. For instance, an interesting example might be to implement a simplification of simple arithmetic expressions like 1 + 1 and produce a number expression 2 instead. Such simplifications are typically not implemented in the parsing stage.

The following is another example of a production rule in simplified form:

```
numexp :
        Number
    | '–' Number
    | Number Dot Number
    | '–' Number Dot Number
    ;
```

This rule in its full form, where actions are enclosed in { }, is shown here:

```
numexp returns [NumExp ast]:
    n0=Number {$ast = AST.NumExp(int($n0.text)); }
    | '–' n0=Number {$ast = AST.NumExp(–int($n0.text)); }
    | n0=Number Dot n1=Number {$ast = AST.NumExp(float($n0.text+"."+$n1.
        text)); }
    | '–' n0=Number Dot n1=Number {$ast = AST.NumExp(float("–" + $n0.text
        +"."+$n1.text)); }
    ;
```

The variable access syntax $n0.text is ANTLR's syntax for obtaining the string that is parsed by the rule named n0. This rule encodes four possible forms of writing numbers that are supported by this language: a positive number without any decimal point, a negative number without any decimal point, a positive number with a decimal point, and a negative number with a decimal point. In the first case, the number text is parsed and converted to a positive integer and then converted to NumExp. In the second case, the number text is parsed and converted to a negative number and then converted to NumExp. In the third case, both the text before the decimal point and after the decimal point are converted to a float, which is then converted to NumExp. In the final case, both text before the decimal point and after the decimal point are converted to a negative float, which is then converted to NumExp. The following is another example of a production rule in simplified form:

```
addexp :
        '(' '+'
            exp
            ( exp )+
        ')'
        ;
```

This rule in its full form, where actions are enclosed in { }, is given here:

```
addexp returns [AddExp ast]
    locals [ list ]
    @init { $list  =  [] } :
    '(' '+'
    e=exp { $list .append($e.ast) }
    ( e=exp { $list .append($e.ast) } )+
    ')' {$ast = AST.AddExp($list)}
    ;
```

In this action, the `locals` clause declares variables that will be available throughout that production rule, and the `@init` clause indicates actions that will run before we start parsing this production rule. In summary, this rule creates a list before it parses any subexpressions of the add expression, inserts subexpressions in that list as it parses them, and finally creates an `AddExp` object using those collected expressions.

Bibliography

Aho, Alfred V., Monica S. Lam, Ravi Sethi, and Jeffrey D. Ullman. 2006. *Compilers: Principles, Techniques, and Tools*, 2nd ed. Addison Wesley.

Colmerauer, Alain, and Philippe Roussel. 1996. "History of Programming Languages—II." In *The Birth of Prolog*, edited by Thomas J. Bergin Jr. and Richard G. Gibson Jr. (pp. 331–367), ACM. doi:10.1145/234286.1057820.

Dahl, Ole-Johan, Bjørn Myhrhaug, and Kristen Nygaard. 1968. "Some Features of the SIMULA 67 Language." In *Proceedings of the Second Conference on Applications of Simulations* (pp. 29–31), Winter Simulation Conference.

Dijkstra, Edsger W. 1968. "Cooperating Sequential Processes." In *Programming Languages* (Academic Press).

Donovan, Alan A. A., and Brian W. Kernighan. 2015. *The Go Programming Language*. Addison-Wesley Professional.

Gamma, Erich, Richard Helm, Ralph Johnson, and John Vlissides. 1995. *Design Patterns: Elements of Reusable Object-Oriented Software*. Addison-Wesley Longman.

Goldberg, Adele. 1984. *SMALLTALK-80: The Interactive Programming Environment*. Addison-Wesley Longman.

Hansen, Per Brinch. 1973. *Operating System Principles*. Prentice-Hall.

Hansen, Per Brinch. 1975. "The Programming Language Concurrent Pascal." *IEEE Transactions on Software Engineering* SE-1 (2): 199–207.

Hansen, Per Brinch. 2002. "The Programming Language Concurrent Pascal." In *The Origin of Concurrent Programming: From Semaphores to Remote Procedure Calls* (pp. 297–318). Springer-Verlag.

Hoare, C. A. R. 1978. "Communicating Sequential Processes." *Communications of the ACM*, vol. 21, no. 8 (August): 666–677. https://doi.org/10.1145/359576.359585.

Hopper, G. M. 1952. "The Education of a Computer." *Proceedings of the ACM National Meeting*. Pittsburgh, PA.

Krishnamurthi, Shriram. 2008. "Teaching Programming Languages in a Post-Linnaean Age." *SIGPLAN Notices*, vol. 43, no. 11: 81–83. http://doi.acm.org/10.1145/1480828.1480846.

Leveson, Nancy G., and Clark S. Turner. "An Investigation of the Therac-25 Accidents," IEEE Computer, July 1993.

Lions, J. L. et al., "ARIANE 5: Flight 501 Failure, A Report by the Inquiry Board," July 1996. Excerpts: *The internal SRI* software exception was caused during execution of a data conversion from 64-bit floating point to 16-bit signed integer value. The floating point number which was converted had a value greater than what could be represented by a 16-bit signed integer.*

Long, Yuheng, Sean L. Mooney, Tyler Sondag, and Hridesh Rajan. 2010. "Implicit Invocation Meets Safe, Implicit Concurrency." In *GPCE '10: Ninth International Conference on Generative Programming and Component Engineering*. Eindhoven, Netherlands, October.

Odersky, Martin, Lex Spoon, and Bill Venners. 2011. *Programming in Scala: A Comprehensive Stepby-Step Guide*. 2nd ed. Artima Incorporation.

Parr, Terence. 2015. *The Definitive ANTLR 4 Reference*. The Pragmatic Bookshelf.

Pierce, Benjamin. 2002. *Types and Programming Languages*. MIT Press.

Rajan, Hridesh, and Gary T. Leavens. 2008. "Ptolemy: A Language with Quantified, Typed Events." In *ECOOP 08: 22nd European Conference on Object-Oriented Programming*. Paphos, Cyprus, July.

Reppy, John H. 1993. "Concurrent ML: Design, Application and Semantics." In *Functional Programming, Concurrency, Simulation and Automated Reasoning: International Lecture Series 1991–1992, McMaster University, Hamilton, Ontario, Canada* (pp. 165–198). Springer-Verlag.

Reynolds, J. C. 1983. "Types, Abstraction and Parametric Polymorphism." In *Information Processing 83, Proceedings of the IFIP 9th World Computer Congress* (pp. 513–523).

Sussman, Gerald Jay, and Hal Abelson. 1979. *Structure and Interpretation of Computer Programs*. 657. MIT Press.

Virding, Robert, Claes Wikström, Mike Williams, and Joe Armstrong. 1996. *Concurrent Programming in ERLANG*. 2nd ed. Prentice Hall International (UK).

Index

abstract superclass, 11
abstract syntax tree (AST), 46
actor, 170
AddExp, 40
always consistent memory model, 172
announce expression, 255
ANTLR, 47, 265
application programming interface
  (API), 6
Arithlang, 35
arrow type, 191
assignment expression, 152
AST design, 81
asynchronous message send, 244
atomic expressions, 194
automatic lock release, 178
automatic memory management, 148

base case, 15
base types, 191
behavioral specification, 211
binary trees, 19
binding, 90
blame assignment, 188
blocked task, 178
blocking, 172
blocking semantics, 175
blocking send, 244
boolean, 9
Boolean value, 139
BoolVal, 139
bound variable, 77
built-in functions, 108

call expression, 128
call-by-name evaluation, 134
call-by-name parameter passing, 134
call-by-need evaluation, 137
CallExp, 128
car, 109

cardinality, 239
cdr, 109
class declaration, 8
client of the procedure, 188
closure rule, 15
code formatter, 54
comparison expressions, 138
compiled language, 45
compiler, 44
conclusion, 8, 193
concurrency, 169
conditional expression, 138
cons, 109
constructor, 10
contract of the procedure, 188
core, 172
curried form, 124

data abstraction, 60
data race, 177
data type, 121
deadlock, 178
default specification, 212
define declaration, 95
defined language, xx, 44
Definelang, 97
defining language, xx, 44
deref, 157
deref and assignment only, 148
dereference expression, 152
derivation, 40
deserialization, 241
digit, 16
dining philosophers problem, 179
dispatch, 13
domain, 20
domain-specific language (DSL), 6
domain-specific programming
  language, 3
double-dispatch pattern, 56

dynamic error, 129
dynamic scoping, 76

empty environment, 85
empty list, 18, 108
EmptyEnv, 85
environment, 84
environment-based semantics, 84
event, 251
event announcement, 252
event expression, 255
event registration, 252
eventually consistent memory model, 173
experiential learning style, xix
explicit features for concurrency, 170
explicit reference, 148
explicitly typed language, 190
ExtendEnv, 85, 86
extending the front end, 82

fenv, 130
field declarations, 9
first-class feature, 126
first-class value, 256
First-In-First-Out (FIFO) strategy, 242
Forklang, 173
free, 159
free expression, 152
free variable, 77
fully mathematical specification, 189
Funclang, 106
function type, 201
functions, 7
FunVal, 127

garbage, 163
garbage collection, 163
garbage memory, 163
general-purpose computer programming
  language, 4
generating lexer and parser, 265
global variables, 96
grammar, 38
grammar actions, 265
grammar name, 265
grammar rules, 265

handler, 252
heap, 148, 154
higher-order function, 115
hole, 76

if expression, 138
ill-typed, 193

implicit concurrency, 231
implicit features for concurrency, 170
implicit invocation, 251
implicit reference, 148
implicitly typed languages, 190
inductive case, 15
inductive sets, 15
informal contract, 189
interfaces, 13
interpreted languages, 45
interpreter, xx, 45
invariants, 227

Java, 8
join semantics, 171

lambda abstraction, 106
lazy evaluation, 136
leaf node, 19
left subtree, 19
leftmost derivation, 42
legal values, 59
let expression, 73, 79
letexp, 79
lexical analysis, 46
lexical scoping, 75
lightweight specifications, 189
list, 18, 109
ListVal, 141
locals clause, 268
lock expression, 171
logical rules, 8, 61

manual memory management, 148
means of abstraction, 6, 71
means of combination, 6
means of computation, 6
membership test, 17–19
memoization, 137
memory consistency, 172
message buffer, 241
message cardinality, 239
message passing, 232
message processing, 242
method arguments, 9
method call, 12
method declaration, 9
method name, 9
method return value, 9
Msglang, 232

name dependence, 252
natural numbers, 17
nested holes, 77

nested scopes, 75
nonblocking, 172
nonblocking send, 244
nonterminals, 38
`Null`, 141
null pointer error, 161
`null?`, 109
`NumExp`, 40

object-oriented programs, 14
observer, 252
observer pattern, 251
out-of-memory error, 162
out-of-order delivery, 246
overriding method, 11

pair, 108
`PairVal`, 141
parallel array, 170
parameter-passing variation, 137
parameterization, 106
parse tree, 46
parsing, 46
postcondition, 211
precondition, 211
predicate function, 214
prefix, 35, 73
premise, 8, 193
process expression, 239, 243
processes, 232
processor, 172
production rule, 265
programming language features, 6
promise, 135
publish-subscribe systems, 251
pure expression, 220
pure functional programs, 147

range, 20
reachability, 163
read program, 79
Read-Eval-Print-Loop (REPL), 45
receive expression, 232, 239, 245
receiver, 12
recursion, 23
recursive function, 109
reentrant semantics, 172, 175
`ref`, 157
reference, 148
reference arithmetic, 148
reference expression, 151
Reflang, 151
`RefVal`, 153
REPL, 45, 79

request-response pattern, 236
right subtree, 19
rightmost derivation, 42
root node, 19
rule, 38

scope, 72, 73
scoping rule, 75
self-addressing, 236
self-expression, 236
semantics, 61
send expression, 232, 239, 243
sentential form, 41
Separation of Concerns, 53
serialization, 241
`setref`, 157
sets, 7
sharing semantics, 172, 174
side effects, 147
side-effect freedom, 220
side-effect visibility, 155
specifications, 189
static scoping, 75
stop expression, 237
subclass, 10
subject, 251
substitution-based semantics, 84
superclass, 10
survey-based learning style, xix
synchronous message send, 244
syntax analysis, 46
syntax derivations, 80

target language, 44
template metaprogramming, 102
terminals, 38
timeout, 173
tokens, 46
tree, 19
type environment, 196
type error, 193
type for a function, 200
type system, 193
typechecking, 193
typed heap, 148
Typelang, 187
types, 189, 190

ultra-lightweight specifications, 189
unary notation, 18
unified modeling language (UML), 49
`UnitVal`, 100
unlock expression, 171
untyped heap, 148

value environment, 196
value of a program, 60
`varexp`, 79
variable, 71, 105
variable definition, 73
Varlang, 72
visitor design pattern, 53, 81
visitor pattern, 56

well-typed, 193
when expression, 255